Revitalizing
Rural
America

Revitalizing Rural America

A Perspective on Collaboration and Community

To Richard,

with best wishes —

Michael

Michael Murray
University of Ulster at Jordanstown,
Northern Ireland

and

Larry Dunn
Colorado State University, USA

JOHN WILEY & SONS
Chichester • New York • Brisbane • Toronto • Singapore

Copyright © 1996 by John Wiley & Sons Ltd,
Baffins Lane, Chichester,
West Sussex PO19 1UD, England

National	01243 779777
International	(+44) 1243 779777

Other Wiley Editorial Offices

John Wiley & Sons, Inc., 605 Third Avenue,
New York, NY 10158-0012, USA

Jacaranda Wiley Ltd, 33 Park Road, Milton,
Queensland 4064, Australia

John Wiley & Sons (Canada) Ltd, 22 Worcester Road,
Rexdale, Ontario M9W 1L1, Canada

John Wiley & Sons (Asia) Pte Ltd, 2 Clementi Loop #02-01,
Jin Xing Distripark, Singapore 0512

British Library Cataloguing in Publication Data

A catalogue record for this book is available from the British Library

ISBN   0 471 96349 6 (hbk)
        0 471 96350 X (pbk)

Typeset in 11/12pt Palatino by Saxon Graphics, Derby
Printed and bound in Great Britain by Biddles Ltd, Guildford
This book is printed on acid-free paper responsibly manufactured from sustainable forestation,
for which at least two trees are planted for each one used for paper production.

Contents

The authors

Michael Murray teaches regional and local development in the School of Public Policy, Economics and Law at the University of Ulster, Northern Ireland. He holds a doctorate in town and country planning. His research interests include rural development in advanced capitalist economies and environmental management policy, on both of which he has published widely. He is the author of *The politics and pragmatism of urban containment* (1991) and is co-editor of and contributor to *Rural development in Ireland: a challenge for the 1990s* (1993).

Larry Dunn retired from Colorado State University in 1993 after 23 years' service in Faculty. He established the Center for Rural Assistance at the University in 1989 and was its first Director; he was also Director of the Colorado Rural Revitalization Project. His doctorate is in adult education and he continues to work in the leadership/development field under sponsorship from the W K Kellogg Foundation. During his career he has published a wide range of training materials related to community leadership/development for US and international audiences.

Preface

Rural development is being hailed throughout America and Europe as a new challenge for policy makers during the 1990s. It is widely accepted that a richer understanding of rural policy formulation and implementation fixed in one socio-economic, cultural, institutional and political context can be obtained from research carried out in other settings. In order to facilitate this process of shared learning, the authors received an offer of financial support from the British Council for an international exchange in early 1992. A McCrea Research Award from the University of Ulster allowed additional contact and fieldwork over a two year period. One outcome was the realization that the evolving framework for rural development in the United States, with its emphasis on collaboration, could provide a set of useful signposts for policy succession on the opposite side of the Atlantic. Within the United States there is also, at present, widespread recognition of the potential value of human capital approaches to rural development. The experience of one initiative in Colorado, linked to a wider program of foundation-funded action research could, therefore, prove equally valuable to all whose brief and interest lie in this sphere. Accordingly, a decision was taken to produce a book which could capture both these dimensions.

This book is not a comparative account of policy- and practice-related matters as between America and Europe; indeed the gap in the literature still remains to be filled! The focus is specifically on the United States and the aim, quite simply, is to make a contribution to the wider international debate about the shape of public policy for multi-level involvement in the rural development process. The discussion in the following chapters thus centers on an examination of the interplay between federal, state and local participants. The momentum over the period since the mid to late 1980s now places the rural development effort at a crucial crossroads in its history. The core argument advanced in this book is that the future well-being of rural America depends increasingly on acceptance of a paradigm based on collaboration between and within these levels, which goes beyond mere rhetoric.

Chapter 1 commences with a brief overview of the condition of rural America during the 1980s and into the 1990s and introduces important aspects of the institutional context for rural development. Key conceptual material relating to community, community development, capacity building and collaboration is set out in order to provide a context within which to locate the subsequent empirical discussion.

A recurrent theme in this book is how the relationship between community and governance works itself through in terms of rural development policy and practice. Accordingly, Chapter 2 is concerned with an institutional perspective on policy formulation and implementation. Over the period since the late 1980s a fresh inquiry into the rural revitalization challenge has been launched. This must be seen as but part of a wider debate about new governance in the United States. It extends from the New Federalism agenda initiated under the Reagan Administrations to the more recent Reinventing Government Program launched by Vice-President Al Gore. The chapter examines the ways in which the principles of subsidiarity and collaboration are informing rural development policy. New structures on the institutional landscape which seek to support rural development initiatives are critically reviewed.

In Chapter 3 the focus switches to the contribution of institutional and community linkage in rural revitalization. The discussion is located within the conceptual framework of capacity building and collaboration and concerns itself with an examination of the Rural America Program. This involved some 28 major rural development projects spread across the United States, partially funded by the W K Kellogg Foundation. The chapter reports on evaluations of the initiative completed during 1994.

Capacity building and collaboration are examined more closely by way of a case study in Chapter 4. This relates to the operation of the Colorado Rural Revitalization Project which was initiated in 1988 as a joint venture between Colorado State University, the University of Colorado and the State of Colorado Department of Local Affairs. It concluded in 1992 having worked with 47 rural communities. The chapter reports on the goals and activities of the Project, and reviews the findings obtained from an *ex post* evaluation. Multilevel collaboration-related issues emerging from the Project are identified.

Chapter 5 seeks to get deeper than an aggregate analysis of community-based rural development by telling the stories of six communities which participated in the Colorado Rural Revitalization Project. The unfolding of local efforts during the Project is identified and the short-term legacies are reviewed. In each instance attention is given to the extent to which the presence or absence of collaboration has assisted or frustrated these communities in achieving their development missions.

Finally, in Chapter 6 an attempt is made to synthesize the many threads of previous discussion through consideration of key issues which have local, institutional and national relevance. The book is premissed upon the value of capacity building and collaboration as important processes underpinning community-led rural revitalization; the empirical evidence endorses this position but also highlights the necessity of public policy support. Thus to assist further with shifting the rural development paradigm in a manner consistent with this argument, the chapter concludes by identifying a number of matters which deserve the attention of policy makers, educationalists and communities.

The authors owe a large debt of gratitude to many people whose time and assistance have made the completion of this book possible. At the outset it is appropriate to acknowledge the considerable financial support and help received from the WK Kellogg Foundation through the

good offices of Gary King, Thomas Thorburn and Susan
Jenkins. Mary Andrews and her staff at Michigan State
University were also most supportive. Their willingness to
encourage publication of the experiences of the Rural
America Cluster Evaluation Project, with which Larry
Dunn was associated, is deeply appreciated. We would
like to express our thanks to Margaret Holt at the
University of Georgia for her invaluable contribution, as
co-investigator of collaboration at four Rural America
Project sites. The results of this research are reported in
Chapter 3.

Within Washington DC, Bob Lovan from the National
Rural Development Partnership Office gave us the benefit
of his many insights into the emergence of current federal
initiatives and their possible future direction. Bonnie
Justice and her colleagues in the Rural Development
Administration, Susan Odell at Forest Service, Patricia
John from the Rural Information Center, Lorette Hanson
of Rural Coalition, Randy Williams in the United States
Department of Agriculture Extension Service, John
Simmons from the United States Department of Housing
and Urban Development and Danny Gibb at the United
States Small Business Administration also provided
opportunities for shared dialog on rural development
matters.

Within Colorado we are grateful for the opportunity to
visit with Colleen Murphy from the Center for the New
West, Florine Raitano from the Colorado Rural
Development Council, T Michael Smith from the Department of Local Affairs, Tim Katers from the Colorado
Community Development Technical Assistance Office and
David Herlinger from the Colorado Housing and Finance
Authority. During the course of our fieldwork we met
with over sixty residents and officials from the six case
study communities included in Chapter 5 of this book.
Our special thanks are warranted for the warmth of the
welcome extended and the openness with which local
development issues were discussed. Any criticisms
offered or implied in this book in no way detract from our
admiration of the energies being expended by everyone
we met on the rural development front. The shortcomings
of the chapters which follow remain totally our responsibility.

We would like to pay particular tribute to the hospitality of Sheila Knop in her capacity as Coordinator of the Center for Rural Assistance at Colorado State University. Every kindness was shown regarding the availability of a room and telephone, and access to the library resources of the Center.

At the University of Ulster we would like to acknowledge the support given by colleagues within the School of Public Policy, Economics and Law. For their efforts in grappling with our handwritten manuscript we are especially grateful to Beverly Coulter, Sharon McCullough, Jacqueline Ferguson and Pamela King. Killan McDaid brought his considerable flair to preparation of the illustrations.

At a personal level it is appropriate to record the open-house hospitality given by Michael, Linda, Rory and Ryan McGrenaghan. Many summers spent with them in Denver provided the initial opportunity for Michael Murray to pursue an interest in US rural development policy. Fondest appreciation goes to his wife, Sheelagh, for her unstinting support during frequent absences and even longer periods of necessary solitary confinement in Rathwarren.

Finally, we wish to thank John Owens at David Fulton Publishers for his initial interest in this book and Iain Stevenson at John Wiley and Sons Ltd for enthusiastically carrying forward its publication. Lindsay Jackson as Production Editor provided support in a most helpful and pleasant manner.

Acknowledgements

The following sources are gratefully acknowledged

Table 1   Farm and total population of the United States 1880–1990, has been adapted from Mayer, LV (1993) Agricultural change and rural America, in *Annals of the American Academy of Political and Social Science*, **529**, September, p83, and published by Sage Publications Inc., with permission.

Table 2   Non-metro jobs in 1990 by industry and regions in the United States, has been adapted from data in *Rural conditions and trends* (1993), **4(1)**, 27, and published by the United States Department of Agriculture Economic Research Service.

Table 3   Key economic indicators for the periods 1960–1980 and 1981–1988 in the United States, has been adapted from Nordhaus, WD (1991) The United States, in Llewellyn, J and Potter SJ (eds), *Economic policies for the 1990s*, p30, and published by Blackwell Publishers, Oxford.

Table 4   Federal programs serving rural America, 1983–1992, has been adapted from data presented in General Accounting Office (1994) *Rural development – patchwork of federal programs needs to be reappraised*, p14, and published by the United States General Accounting Office, Washington DC.

Table 5   Critical issues, clients and educational responses for rural America, is taken from Cooperative Extension System (1986) *Revitalizing rural America – a Cooperative Extension System response*, as prepared by the Priority Initiatives Taskforce, out of University of Wisconsin, Madison.

Table 6 Characteristics of new governance, is taken from Kettl, DF
(1993) The new governance and rural development, *New
Governance Discussion Paper Series*, **No 2**, and published by the
National Rural Economic Development Institute, University of
Wisconsin-Extension, Madison.

Table 7 National participants in the National Rural Development
Partnership, 1993, is taken from Shaffer, R (1994) State Rural
Development Councils and the National Partnership for Rural
Development, *New Governance Discussion Paper Series*, **No 7**, and
published by the National Rural Economic Development Institute,
University of Wisconsin-Extension, Madison.

Figure 1 Participants in the Rural America Program was prepared
under the Rural America Cluster Evaluation Project, out of
Michigan State University.

Figure 2 Selected county characteristics in Colorado, is adapted from
data in *Rural conditions and trends* (1993), **4(3)**, and published by the
United States Department of Agriculture Economic Research
Service.

Figure 3 Organization of the Colorado Rural Revitalization Project, is
taken from Kincaid, JM and Knop, EC (1992) *Insights and implications from the CRRP 1988–1991*, and published by Colorado State
University, Fort Collins.

Table 8 Classification of Colorado Rural Revitalization Project communities, is taken from Kincaid, JM and Knop EC (1992) *Insights
and implications from the CRRP 1988–1991*, and published by
Colorado State University, Fort Collins.

The content on page 222 relating to Community Visions, is taken from
the video tape, Barker, JA (1990) *The power of vision*, and published
by Charthouse Learning Corporation, Burnsville.

The content on page 234 relating to Team Building and Conflict
Management, is taken from Conflict and conflict in management,
in the *Handbook of industrial and organisational psychology*, prepared
by Kenneth Thomas.

The content on page 235 relating to Strategies, is taken from Fisher, R
and Ury, W (1983) *Getting to yes*, published by Penguin Books,
New York.

1 Unraveling rural America

A kaleidoscope of images

Images of rural America abound. Popular perceptions have been conditioned by a heady cocktail of literature, film and music and, of course, by the marketeers of the travel industry. Across time the variation in messages is enormous. It extends from the poverty and despair of the Oklahoma migrants in Steinbeck's *The grapes of wrath* (1939) to the adventure and freedom of spirit proclaimed in Kerouac's *On the road* (1955). Very often the emotions stirred are those of nostalgia, even sadness, about the passing of a way of life. A good example here is Osha Gray Davidson's *Broken heartland* (1990) which recounts the more recent demise of much family farming during the 1980s. Indeed, the inevitability of change had prompted the United States Department of Agriculture (USDA) to publish its 1976 Yearbook as a visual record of rural life at that time. The business of agriculture is well represented in this portfolio of photographs, but so also are rural people and the communities to which they belong. A meaningful insight into the very lifeblood of rural America is gained.

If the great outdoors, as captured in the songs of John Denver, is a recurrent theme in the contemporary imaging of rurality, its reciprocal must be the special affection for small town America as eulogized by John Mellencamp and Bruce Springsteen. Back in the 1930s the wholesomeness of small town life was portrayed in the film *Mr Deeds goes to town*. The current popularity of traveling between Chicago and Los Angeles on Route 66 can be interpreted as a quest for comparable virtue and quality of life. It is a search for a goal which may be ultimately elusive and even illusory but which leads Bill Bryson in his book *The lost continent* (1990) on a 14 000 mile trip across 38 states. His description of Amalgam, his ideal small town, does indeed offer a familiar set of images:

> In this timeless place Bing Crosby would be the priest, Jimmy Stewart the mayor, Fred MacMurray the high school principal, Henry Fonda a Quaker farmer. Walter Brennan would run the gas station, a boyish Mickey Rooney would deliver groceries, and somewhere at an open window Deanna Durbin would sing. And in the background, always, would be the kid on a bike and those two smartly striding men. (p. 39)

While small town America as a romantic concept is arguably but a subset of the Old West paradigm, the reality is that these places do contain communities whose struggle within a climate of economic change may often be for nothing more than mere survival. As noted by Luloff and Swanson (1990) small and rural communities can and do act. This book on revitalizing rural America celebrates the serious intent of such communities and offers encouragement to others who may wish to invest in their future.

The book explores some of the key realities of living in rural America during the latter part of the 1980s and through to the mid-1990s. The concern is not with agriculture, although farmers and ranchers are part of the story. Nor indeed does the book address any other specific sector of economic activity, though all sectors have a contribution to make to the well-being of rural society. The discussion is about places which people are happy to call "home" and about individuals who are committed to shedding an imagery of rugged independence in favor of a caring responsibility for communal betterment. The achievement of this development goal depends in no small measure on the leadership capacity of rural communities and the relationship which is nurtured with responsive external bodies. The central argument in this book is that multilevel interdependency among all whose interest and mission is rural development, expressed in its richest form as collaboration, is a necessary condition for sustainability of effort.

The condition of rural America

For the greater part of the country's history the rural population of the United States has been in the majority. Only in 1920 did it constitute a minority for the first time at 49 percent (Hyman, 1991). By 1990 the non-metro county population represented 22.7 percent of the total population of the United States (McGranahan and Salsgiver, 1993). This decline parallels a dramatic drop in the farm based population from 32.1 million in 1910 to 4.6 million in 1990 (Table 1). During the 1970s the rural population as a whole did record faster growth than the urban population but as Johnson (1993) comments, population gains in non-metro areas were due more to widespread and substantial net immigration than to natural increase. Between 1980 and 1990 rural population continued to grow, notwithstanding

Table 1   Farm and total population of the United States 1880–1990

Year	Population (millions)	
	Farm	Total
1990	4.6	248.7
1980	6.1	226.5
1970	9.7	203.2
1960	13.4	179.3
1950	23.0	151.3
1940	30.5	132.1
1930	30.5	123.2
1920	32.0	106.0
1910	32.1	92.2
1900	28.9	76.2
1890	24.8	63.0
1880	22.0	50.2

Source: adapted from Mayer (1993).

the severity of the farm crisis during that period. There was spatial variation, however, with increases recorded in the West and the South, as well as in the recreational, scenic landscape and retirement areas of the Great Lakes, New England and the Ozarks. In contrast, population decline was particularly evident in the Mississippi Delta and in the Corn Belt and Great Plains. An analysis by Albrecht (1993) of population loss in the non-metropolitan Great Plains is especially illuminating on this matter. He concludes that during the 1980s some 84 percent of 293 counties recorded population declines, a proportion higher than during any other decade since 1950 and giving rise to renewed problems of service availability and delivery, tax base loss and high levels of dependency. The Appalachian coal fields and the mining communities of the West have also been shedding population consistent with falling mineral and energy commodity prices, and an international oil glut which rendered many marginal domestic oil fields uneconomic (Glasmeier and Conroy, 1994).

These adjustments in the spatial distribution of the population base have been driven by macro shifts in the rural economy. As noted by Summers et al (1990) this has changed since the mid-1950s from a very heavy dependence on agriculture and other natural-resource-based industries to a greater diversity of economic activities. Data from the United States Department of Agriculture (Table 2) point to the relative significance in rural America of jobs outside primary-based activities. Indeed, only some 8 percent of non-metro jobs were in farming in 1990. Looked at from a regional perspective it is clear that there is little dramatic variation in the sectoral profiles across the United States except for farming and manufacturing. The significance of agriculture for the Plains, Southwest and Rocky Mountain regions is especially strong with manufacturing under-represented *vis-à-vis* the national level in the Rocky Mountain, Southwest and Far West regions.

While offering an interesting snapshot of one dimension of the rural economy, these data give little insight into key trends during previous years. A large and wide ranging literature has sought to capture the dynamics and outcomes of change. Deavers (1992) has suggested that since 1945 factors such as the consolidation and mechanization of farming, rural electrification, the modernization of transport and communications infrastructure and the spatial integration of the United States and world economies have joined forces to shape the sectoral composition of the rural economy. The difficulties of the farm sector, in particular, received considerable attention during the 1980s. The consequences of financial stress, foreclosure and displacement were graphically documented by Davidson (1990) and

Barlett (1993) with evidence from the US Department of Agriculture suggesting that between 200 000 and 300 000 people left the sector during the worst period (Mazie and Killian, 1991). However, as noted by Bonnen (1992) the flow of farmers from the land was but part of a wider outmigration from rural America by people searching for better economic opportunities. Bonnen has suggested that:

> the 1980s rural distress is only partially due to the loss of economic welfare among farmers. The globalization of international commodity markets and the resultant competition are now affecting the employment potential of many firms in rural America. For a decade US monetary policy and the slow economic growth of the nation have also had a serious impact on rural community employment. (p. 194)

Table 2 Non-metro jobs in 1990 by industry and regions in the United States

	US	New England	Mid-East	Great Lakes	Plains	South east	South west	Rocky Mount-ain	Far West
Total (millions)	26.360	1.229	1.824	4.406	4.005	9.088	2.473	1.415	1.919
Job type (%)									
Farming	7.7	2.0	3.9	7.3	13.3	6.6	9.8	8.1	6.7
Agricultural services	1.4	1.8	0.9	0.9	1.1	1.2	1.6	1.8	4.2
Mining	1.6	0.1	1.1	1.1	0.9	1.4	4.8	2.9	1.0
Construction	5.3	7.8	5.5	4.7	4.5	5.5	5.4	5.7	5.5
Manufacturing	17.4	15.5	17.6	21.0	13.0	22.7	9.7	8.4	10.7
Transportation	4.2	3.6	4.4	4.4	4.3	3.9	7.4	4.8	4.2
Wholesale	3.2	3.0	2.9	3.2	4.2	3.0	3.0	3.0	2.7
Retail	16.5	17.8	17.7	17.0	16.0	16.0	16.1	17.5	16.9
Finance	4.8	6.0	4.7	4.9	4.9	4.2	4.8	5.5	5.4
Services	20.9	27.6	24.3	21.1	20.9	18.5	20.1	23.5	23.4
Government	16.9	14.8	16.9	14.5	16.8	16.9	19.7	18.7	19.4

Source: adapted from USDA (1993a) *Rural Conditions and Trends,* 4(1), 27.

Thus the USDA has, for example, shown that some 632 000 people moved out of non-metro areas between 1985 and 1986, greater than the average of either the 1950s or 1960s, and a reversal of the 1970s when non-metro areas netted over 350 000 persons per year (USDA, 1988).

Nordhaus (1991) points to clear supporting evidence that the economic performance of the United States deteriorated dramatically during this period. Compared with the years 1960–80, dominated by a Keynesian style management of the economy, the 1980s witnessed a shift to the preferred orthodoxy of supply side economics in which the market was presented with a mandate to achieve growth. But as illustrated in Table 3 such expectations were disappointed:the national and personal savings rates declined; government debt increased; the trade balance moved into a deficit; unemployment rose; productivity dropped; and average hourly earnings remained static.

Table 3   Key economic indicators for the periods 1960–80 and 1981–88 in the United States

Indicators	Performance 1960–80	Performance 1981–88
Inflation rate (% per year)	5.1	4.7
National savings rate (% of NNP)	8.1	5.5
Personal savings rate (% of income)	7.3	5.2
Government debt to GNP (% at end of period)	21.0	37.0
Trade balance ($ billion)	2	− 86
Unemployment rate (%)	5.6	7.5
Labour productivity growth (% per year)	1.9	1.5
Growth in real average hourly earnings (% per year)	0.7	0.0

Source: adapted from Nordhaus (1991).

The distress of much of rural America is deeply rooted and wide ranging. While some rural areas have managed to thrive on their popularity for tourism and recreation, or retirement, the wealth-creating capacity of many rural communities has been eroded. The 1980s recession in manufacturing, downsizing of manufacturing plant, a changing occupational mix favoring white collar metropolitan area employment and shifting patterns in the location of industry, whereby new opportunities have largely been urban opportunities for people with relatively high levels of education, have adversely affected rural communities (Deavers, 1988; McGranahan, 1991). During this time rural manufacturing experienced substantial labor shedding with employment, for example, falling by almost 400 000 between 1979 and 1986 (Hady and Ross, 1990). Furthermore, the point has been made (Brown and Deavers, 1988) that rural manufacturing employment is heavily concentrated in low wage industries, for example textiles, wood products, leather goods. Job losses in these essentially blue collar occupations have thus had a disproportionately greater impact on non-metro areas. These losses combined with declining sales among agribusiness firms and main street businesses have threatened the very survival of many communities (Leistritz et al, 1989).

The net result is nothing short of a litany of multiple rural disadvantage across many parts of the United States, a situation given added poignancy by the rediscovery of persistent poverty in the contemporary literature (Tickameyer and Duncan, 1990; Rural Sociological Society Task Force on Persistent Rural Poverty, 1993). A common perception that poverty is an urban issue has been challenged by the assertion that poverty rates in non-metro areas are actually higher. Lyson (1989), in a scholarly analysis of the economic condition of the southern Sunbelt region, highlights the growing divergence between its cities and rural communities which "have been and remain mired in the economic backwaters of the country". Summers (1991) puts emphasis on a number of performance indicators such as increasing rural unemployment, increasing rural part-time employment, lower earnings among rural workers and the widespread existence of a working rural poor to demonstrate the deteriorating social and economic state of rural society. Recent evidence confirms the persistence of higher poverty rates in rural areas over the period since 1959. Notwithstanding a narrowing of the gap during the 1960s and 1970s, the rate of rural poverty at 16.1 percent remains higher than the urban poverty rate at 13.7 percent (USDA, 1993a).

Detailed research by Fitchin (1991) succeeded in getting beneath this aggregate picture and revealed the prevalence of a number of varied settings for the rural poor. In a deeply insightful analysis of New York State rural counties, concentrations of poor rural people are differentiated thus:

- pockets of long-term, intergenerational poverty in the open countryside;
- rapidly growing trailer parks and informal trailer clusters as a response to a desperate demand for inexpensive and readily available accommodation;
- poverty in small towns and villages comprising groupings of people living in rental apartments.

Clearly this pathology of disadvantage goes beyond any simplistic association of rural poverty with merely agriculture restructuring. Indeed many of those affected have not had any connection at all with the land yet, as suggested by Fitchin, they share an "impoverization in place". Under these circumstances it is axiomatic that small communities should become the crucible for rural revitalization. Deepening poverty is profoundly debilitating and can make communities less able to meet the needs of all their residents. As illustrated in the following chapters a combination of institutional capacity and local initiative is essential if an effective attack is to be made on these problems.

The institutional context for rural development

Policy making and delivery for rural America have long been dominated by agricultural interests. Institutional innovation in the nineteenth and early twentieth centuries, which established the United States Department of Agriculture, the land-grant universities and the Cooperative Extension System, has been complemented by an evolving raft of legislation and programs (see, for example, Lapping et al, 1989). Collectively these have shared a largely agrarian perspective which is still present today. Thus, for example, the New Deal agenda of the 1930s championed farm modernization as a response to rural poverty. But in so doing it introduced a new level of government involvement in and bureaucratic control over farm production, contributed to the displacement of small tenant farmers and secured greater benefits for large landowners. Federal financial transfers, encouragement of technological investment and scientific advancement have created an enduring legacy (Harrington, 1986; Barlett, 1993). At a broader level the New Deal programs established a role for federal government as a provider of a social safety net in times of adversity (Freshwater, 1991). This agenda continues to form an element of rural policy although the main developments over time have been to improve infrastructure and widen the availability of finance through a combination of loans and grants.

As noted by the General Accounting Office (1994), the federal government has focused historically on farms and the needs of the farm population in its rural development efforts. However, the range of federal assistance to rural areas is currently much broader and comprises a spectrum of programs that aid a variety of rural interests. Between 1983 and 1992 no fewer than 689 programs assisted rural development, representing a total commitment of $667.1 billion. Some 35 schemes targeted economic development (Table 4) and channeled $15.5 billion to rural areas through seven different bodies comprising the US Departments of Agriculture, Housing and Urban Development, Commerce, Defense, and Health and Human Services together with the Small Business Administration and the Appalachian Regional Commission. Moneys were used, inter alia, to construct industrial floorspace, help start small businesses, and assist with the preparation and implementation of local economic development plans. A further 109 agriculture/natural resources-related programs administered by the US Departments of Agriculture, Labor, Commerce, Interior, Energy and Transportation as well as the Small Business Administration allocated $288 billion to rural areas. Expenditure related to commodity price support, environmental protection and energy efficiency. Some 461 human resource programs provided $119.8 billion to rural areas from at least 17 different federal sources. The assistance here included job training, rural health care and housing benefit. Finally, some 84 infrastructure programs, administered through 13 different sources, provided some $243.8 billion to rural areas. Key items of expenditure comprised airport development, road planning and construction, public transportation and waste water treatment.

Table 4 Federal programs serving rural America, 1983–1992

Type of program	Number of programs	Expenditure ($ billion)
Economic development	35	15.5
Agriculture/national resources	109	288.0
Human resources	461	119.8
Infrastructure	84	243.8
Total	689	667.1

Source: General Accounting Office (1994), p.14.
Note: Table excludes 139 programs which supported individual well-being in rural America with an expenditure of $1138.7 billion.

This proliferation of federal programs has generated criticism that it is both time consuming and costly for rural officials to identify and apply for assistance and also to comply with the accompanying regulations. The General Accounting Office has outlined four major problems:

1. Identifying the sources of federal assistance. For example, some rural areas may find it too costly to subscribe to information sources on existing and new federal programs or may lack expert staff to access computerized information networks.
2. Learning the intricacies of different application procedures. This may require rural areas to engage expensive consultancy expertise in order to complete the necessary proforma and to administer the grant funds.
3. Understanding the various program rules about factors such as eligibility, funding availability and the type of projects allowed. Regulations are often ambiguous, subject to different interpretations and may change frequently.
4. Resolving inconsistencies between the programs, including differences in environmental impact statements and timing schedules for loan and grant applications. A large number of programs, each with particular objectives and regulations, can contribute to inconsistency.

The complex process of stitching together a patchwork of contributions from different sources for a single goal can be unquestionably a daunting challenge. Thus, for example, in regard to water and sewerage projects, rural areas can consider assistance from no fewer than 11 different programs offered by 6 federal agencies. Problems such as these occur, it is suggested by the General Accounting Office, because the federal government substitutes a large number of narrowly focused programs to address specific needs for a single policy that would support an integrated set of economic development programs in rural areas.

The absence of a coherent rural development policy in the United States is perhaps a reflection of the imperative within individual agencies to protect annual appropriations. In addition, there would not seem to be a sustained high level political commitment to the achievement of adequate agency responsibility to and authority for rural America. Compared with the 1970s, which saw the passage of the 1972 Rural Development Act, a new impetus for rural development within the USDA to be coordinated by its Secretary, the expansion of rural business finance and a policy statement in 1979 on rural development from the Carter Administration, the 1980s evidenced an alarming indifference to the problems of rural society. A note of promise was sounded by the 1980 Rural Development Policy Act which required the identification and reporting of explicit rural development measures. But subsequently concern by Congress was muted and, in accordance with the political orthodoxy of New Federalism, rural program support actually declined. As observed by Freshwater (1991), federal budget outlays for economic and regional development fell by 56 percent between 1980 and 1990 and the budgets of the USDA rural development programs dropped by 52 percent. New Federalism also supported the doctrine of subsidiarity with state and local government being mandated to become more closely involved in rural policy formulation and implementation. However, these increased responsibilities were not matched by additional resources.

Only in the late 1980s did rural development emerge once again as an issue of political significance, albeit a minor one. As suggested by Swanson (1991) the old axiom that farm well-being and by inference farm programs determine rural well-being was no longer useful; while some rural economies did depend on farming, this was the exception rather than the rule. The timing of this realization corresponds neatly with much of the empirical content of this book which is concerned with a number of community-based revitalization initiatives which by then were just commencing. Moreover, some fresh concern about rural development did facilitate the introduction of a suite of measures into the policy landscape of the 1990s. The extent to which this more recent progress represents a real opportunity for rural revitalization will be an important line of inquiry in Chapter 2.

A second dimension to the institutional apparatus for rural development in the United States is the work of the land-grant universities and colleges in vocational education, research and outreach. By tradition a core mission has been to assist the agriculture sector, with research, for example, progressing over time from a concern with farm production, to sustaining agribusiness industry and, more recently, to analyzing the impact of agricultural restructuring on farm families and communities in agricultural areas. Responding to the broader rural economic development challenge has generated tensions. Cantlon (1989) has observed that some commodity groups and individual farmers prefer university expertise to be confined to traditional areas of endeavor and that their recruitment strategies often seek out experts with even narrower sub-disciplinary specialities than those of retiring Faculty. Furthermore, the point is made that project proposals and budget requests which address broad economic development strategies are more difficult to win support for compared with narrowly targeted, technology-specific or basic research projects.

A significant strength of the land-grant universities in responding to the needs of rural society is Cooperative Extension, yet here also there are issues of focus. Byrne (1989) points to the fact that many extension offices still concentrate on agriculture, home economics and youth which results in their allocating most of their resources to these program areas. However, some progress with Foundation financial support is being made on this front, albeit at the margins. This is consistent with the assertion of Pulver and Somersan (1989):

> Perhaps the single most important initiative that could be under-taken to improve the economic well-being of America, especially its rural areas, is the expansion of education and technical assistance in community economic development policy provided to units of local government, business people and other local leaders. (p. 25)

Leadership training is central to this challenge and as a substantive area of involvement by the Cooperative Extension System it is interesting to note its prominence within the 1986 policy statement on critical issues, client groups and educational responses for rural America published by the System (Table 5). Notwithstanding the breadth of this manifesto, resource allocation has remained problematic and efforts directed at community development have been pulled back (Swanson, 1991). At one stage even the four Regional Rural Development Centers (at Oregon State University, Pennsylvania State University, Iowa State University and Mississippi State University) were under threat of having their Extension Service funding withdrawn. A national review carried out in 1991 endorsed their research and development work linked to five main and related goals: to improve economic competitiveness and diversification; to support management and strategic planning for economic investment; to create capacity through leadership; to assist in family and community adjustments to stress and change; and to promote constructive use of the environment. These goals have been cited at length because they demonstrate the breadth of the rural development challenge and its legitimacy. A key argument in this book is that it is assistance in precisely these areas which can bring major benefit to rural society and economy. As land-grant universities, the Cooperative Extension System, governments and local communities seek to forge new alliances related to rural development, the community-based case study content included in this book offers a contribution to the wider debate about the preferred shape of this collaboration.

The rural community perspective

The theory and practice of rural development increasingly place emphasis upon community as the basic building block for turning policy into action. This principle has relevance in countries other than the United States.

In developing countries the limitations of comprehensive top-down development have generated support for small scale initiatives which are rooted in localities through mechanisms of community participation and self-help. Indeed Integrated Rural Development (IRD) as a term has

Table 5 Critical issues, clients and educational responses for rural America

Issues	Clients				
	Families	Producers, agribusinesses and organizations	Youth	Business and communities	Natural resource managers and interest groups
The economic competitiveness of rural areas is diminishing	• Employee fitness programs • Public policy education for community economic development and support for family needs • Family business management assistance	• Systems management for agricultural firms • Farm and ranch management and marketing • Global marketing • Strengthen cooperatives • Global trade opportunities	• Youth entrepreneurship	• Business management • Global marketing • Retention and expansion programs • Education on sources of capital and structuring finances	• Improving efficiency of natural resource-based industries • Increasing rural income through natural resource development • Sea Grant Program
Rural communities are dependent on too few sources of income	• Home-based business development • New employment opportunities • Consumer cooperatives and business	• Alternatives for agricultural resources and new enterprises	• Off-farm jobs • Non-agricultural career assistance	• Community economic analysis • Downtown revitalization • Institution building – industrial development corporations, etc. • Business development • Economic development finance • Grant and aid sources	• Recreation and wildlife development • Alternatives for fishers, private forest landowners • New forest products development and marketing • Sea Grant Program
Service demands on local governments and community organizations are growing while attendant resources are diminishing	• Volunteer management • Organizational skill and knowledge for volunteers	• Strengthen cooperatives • Organizational skill and knowledge for volunteers/leaders	• Youth citizenship • Organizational skill and knowledge development for volunteers	• Public policy education for local officials • Local government operational management assistance • Community planning • Growth impacts analysis	• Organizational skill and knowledge development for volunteers • Water and waste management

Table 5 *contd.*

	Clients				
Issues	Families	Producers, agribusinesses and organizations	Youth	Business and communities	Natural resource managers and interest groups
Rural families and communities are experiencing difficulty adjusting to the impact of economic, social and political change on rural life	• Community services to support families • Dependent care • Family support network and training • Family resource management • Stress management • Health education	• Financial management • Global understanding	• Stress management • Self-esteem • Global understanding	• New institutional arrangements to support transition needs • Global understanding • Home-based business	• Value added processing of natural resources • Marketing
Rural revitalization is dependent on skilled community leadership	• Personal leadership skills and knowledge • Family Community Leadership (FCL)	• Agricultural Rural Leadership Program • Personal leadership skills and knowledge	• Personal leadership skills and knowledge • Youth and community pride	• Comprehensive Rural Leadership Program • Personal leadership skills and knowledge development • Community pride	• Comprehensive Rural Leadership Program • Personal leadership skills and knowledge development
The quality of the natural resource base is critical to revitalizing rural communities	• Public policy education • Coalition development	• Public policy education • Coalition development	• Public policy education • Natural resource management for conservation and profit	• Public policy education • Land use planning • Coalition development • Risk management	• Public policy education • Land use planning • Public policy development • Organizing for political action

Source: Cooperative Extension System (1986).

its origin in Third World countries (Greer, 1984) and encapsulates a broader set of policies than merely agricultural reform. These were designed to address problems of unemployment and under-employment, lack of productivity in the agricultural sector, high rates of rural to urban migration, a constricted internal market, high population growth rates, large foreign deficits and shortages of staple foodstuffs (Grindle, 1981). The literature points to the association of IRD with a plethora of characteristics and objectives (see, for example, Khan, 1977; Leupolt, 1977; Dawson, 1978; Wulf, 1978; Basler, 1979; Ruthenberg, 1981):

1. A multisectoral approach to development. While improvements in agricultural performance and structures are crucial elements in addressing the problems of disadvantaged rural communities, measures to promote other sectors of the economy to supplement or to provide alternatives to incomes from farming are fundamental to the process of improving the standards of living in such areas.
2. Economic measures to be paralleled by initiatives in education, training and investment in physical infrastructure.
3. An attempt to concentrate effort on aiding poor areas and more specifically poor people living in such areas. As a corollary, development inputs must be matched with the specific needs and aspirations of the target groups to which IRD programs are addressed.
4. A requirement that local people become actively involved, not only in identifying needs and opportunities for development, but also in the implementation of projects located within the guiding framework of an action program.
5. A preference for institutional reform, expressed mainly as the devolution of some powers and responsibilities from the national to regional and local levels of administration.

These considerations offer a major challenge to an orthodoxy of top-down, single sector strategies for economic change. Moreover they place heavy emphasis upon the potential contribution of rural communities to working out a better future for themselves.

Contemporary rural development theory and practice in Europe have been greatly influenced by these ideas. Thus the adoption of the term "integrated development" into the vocabulary of the European Commission may be traced to the late 1970s and has been attributed by Van Der Plas (1985) to the influence of expatriate experts returning from working on development projects in the Third World. The imperative of agricultural restructuring under the European Union Common Agricultural Policy in the late 1980s, linked with the domestic politics of enlargement and the international agenda of the General Agreement on Tariffs and Trade, has collectively allowed rural development to become a priority policy area (Murray and Greer, 1992). Central to this paradigm shift is the relationship between government and community. While the geographical spread of experience is wide, common trends are towards rural diversification, bottom-up approaches relying on local initiatives, and sustainable development (Clout, 1993).

In Ireland, for example, analysis of the background and effectiveness of approaches to community-led rural development has generated a substantial scholarship (see, for example, Bohan, 1979; Regan and Breathnach 1981; Commins, 1983; Varley, 1988, 1991; Bryden and Scott, 1990; Murray and Greer, 1993). Key findings in this literature include the following:

1. With deepening recession and rising unemployment during the 1980s the social role of community participation has increasingly been overshadowed by an economic development agenda in which the tendency has been to stress financial returns from local and external markets which are comparable to the private sector.
2. Community-based rural development is looking to take up tasks passed over by government and private enterprise. However, there remains a dependence on public funding and in working out the preferred balance of support it would seem important not to surrender too much self-direction and thereby increase this dependency relationship.
3. It is frequently the case that community groups have to fit their ideas for action into an inappropriate and unfriendly system of public policy support. Accordingly, there is a need for appropriate institutional structures which are sympathetic to local development efforts.

4. The management style of individual community groups is important. They may lack the hands on control and business sensitivity of the entrepreneur and suffer from weakly developed organizational skills and a precarious financial structure. Community development processes must underpin the product-related goals of rural groups.

5. The community-based approach to rural development requires multilevel networking if it is to be sustained. Shared learning, group strategies and resource lobbying need acceptable representation outside government.

These insights from Third World and European experiences have a profound relevance for the adoption of a community perspective on rural development in the United States. Notwithstanding challenges to the value of community which include the denial of the functional and social relevance of local territory, the substitution of community as locality by the nation as a whole, its often perceived anti-urban bias and an allegation of class elitism underpinning the community concept, defense of community is extensive. Wilkinson (1991a) is most persuasive in confronting these issues with his assertions that the community is not the locality but the locality is its base; that mobility creates choices which may feed through to changes in the local community but not necessarily a decline in the extent of community in the locality; and that conflict tensions in a community can exert a positive developmental dynamic. Community, it is argued (Wilkinson, 1991b), requires three things:

1. A locality or place where people achieve their daily needs together
2. A more or less complete local society
3. The opportunity for the local residents to express mutual locality-orientated interests in collective actions.

Community, according to Wilkinson, is thus an interactional structure comprising people and place. Its maintenance requires overcoming the adverse economic and social conditions described above, which in turn provides an essential rationale for community development. If the future of rural America is inextricably linked to the health of its communities, then Wilkinson's advocacy, based upon careful understanding, allows community development to rest comfortably within the remit of the rural development challenge. The selective context-setting review in this section of the chapter confirms the universality of these concerns and underlines the contribution of this book to the wider international debate on community–state relationships in rural revitalization.

Community development in rural America

Community development is concerned with both process and product. In other words, the emphasis is on building local identity and participatory structures which can facilitate collective action towards achieving agreed goals. Global and national conditions provide a context within which positive change may be extremely difficult to accomplish. This does not mean that communities should abandon efforts to improve lifestyle and livelihood, but rather that realistic expectations of what can be achieved should inform their missions. It is easy to criticize community development as promising more than can be delivered, particularly owing to its ideological association with more radical notions of empowerment and local democracy. Funding is the oxygen for sustained action and the contribution that communities can make to local revitalization is circumscribed ultimately by its availability. With resources allocated increasingly on a competitive basis, the onus must be on communities to demonstrate a keen sense of readiness. Community development processes are central to reaching that condition.

Revitalizing rural America is inextricably linked to community development. Etzioni (1993) observes that an important way to build community is to insure that there are numerous opportunities for the active participation of the members in its governance. The commitment and expertise which this generates can in turn greatly influence community responses to the changing conditions described earlier in this chapter.

While revitalization covers issues of social, cultural and economic concern, there exists a special relationship between community development and economic development. The latter has become a principal policy issue facing most local governments in rural areas in the 1990s (Green et al, 1993). Not surprisingly, self-development projects have a high profile. Yet any success in the pursuit of such an agenda remains predicated upon a keen appreciation of the value of community development. This has been succinctly highlighted by Wilkinson (1986) in a submission to a Congress Joint Economic Committee:

> Community development refers to the process of increasing the capacity of a local population to pursue its own interests through effective collective actions. This should not be confused with developments in the community which do not develop the community as such. Economic development without community development, for example, tends to be exploitive and divisive; but, when pursued as a strategy of community development, local economic development can enhance social wellbeing. (pp. 343–344)

The beneficial impact of these processes of interaction has been usefully investigated by Flora and Flora (1990). Their work, which draws upon analysis of farming-dependent communities in the Great Plains that have displayed initiative, suggests the need for a set of entrepreneurial characteristics to inform good practice:

1. Acceptance of controversy as normal, with the weekly newspaper, for example, providing information and debate for informed public decision making.
2. Replacement of the politics of personalities by a focus on issues and policies.
3. A long-term emphasis on academic achievement rather than solely sporting excellence in schools.
4. Enough surplus resources to allow for collective risk taking.
5. A willingness to invest that surplus in local projects for community betterment.
6. A willingness to raise capital through local taxation in order to help maintain rural infrastructure.
7. An ability to accept a broad spatial definition of the community.
8. An ability to network widely with government agencies and other rural communities.
9. A reflective, wide ranging community leadership which involves newcomers.

While Flora and Flora argue that communities which share these characteristics represent a distinct minority, the contribution of community development in helping to forge these entrepreneurial conditions is underscored. Critical to this process is the role of the community development practitioner who, as noted by Pulver (1989), can serve as a catalyst in bringing together diverse interests to agree goals and strategy, can act as a bridge between outside interests and local people, can initiate community training and technical assistance based on identified community concerns and can complement local effort from community volunteers in implementing action plans. At a time when rural development policy in America (and in Europe) is changing to reflect the importance of local initiative and involvement in successful economic development (Unruh, 1991), community development expertise remains an essential component in helping community capacity to mature. Accordingly, it is appropriate at this stage to consider the concept of capacity building as a stage-setting contribution to a development process which in the final analysis must occur within each community itself.

Capacity building

An essential component of community-led rural development is the ability of local people to solve problems. Capacity building seeks to bring about this organizational expertise by forging new skills within rural communities related to leadership, mediation and conflict resolution, group processes, understanding the business of government, and the articulation and achievement of a shared vision. In simple terms, capacity building can be defined as increasing the ability of people and institutions to do what is required of them (Newlands, 1981). The goal is to secure the empowerment of those living in rural areas to better manage their own affairs, thus reducing dependency on state intervention. The concept looks to positive attitudes and constructive approaches for the promotion of change.

There are constraints, however, which must be faced in working through the process of effective capacity building. Hustedde (1991) has identified three special challenges for rural communities:

1. Rural development groups must frequently draw upon a small population base with the result that there may be fewer participants available.
2. Smaller sized rural development groups and communities may be unable to recruit specialist assistance and thus depend more on volunteers who may lack the technical or organizational skills necessary to deal with the complex challenges of leadership.
3. Many rural communities are geographically remote from educational institutions whose brief may well be to bring knowledge and skill-based resources to rural areas; limited manpower and finance may further curtail this involvement.

Nevertheless, for those communities which move into capacity building there are major benefits to be gained. These have been succinctly summarized by Luther and Wall (1989) as follows:

1. Evidence of strategic thinking by community leaders, which draws upon historical strengths and an appreciation of new opportunities.
2. The presence of an entrepreneurial spirit, which is prepared to be creative in community problem solving.
3. An orientation towards positive attitudes and action, based on a confidence that local people can make a better future for themselves.
4. Evidence of a planned program for community improvement, which may include responding to the challenge of economic development through organized action.
5. A thoughtful approach to the future which is concerned with wider quality of life issues in the local economy.

Arriving at these outcomes requires time and commitment by a range of participants. Outside involvement by community facilitators, whose brief is wider than group formation, would, as noted in the previous section of this chapter, seem a necessary prerequisite. Their mission should be to reinforce learning by doing, for example, by assisting rural communities with the formation of a common vision, developing community audit skills, demonstrating the importance of setting and prioritizing realistic objectives consistent with local values, facilitating a strategic plan and phased operational measures, and encouraging the monitoring and evaluation of progress.

Across rural America a host of local self-development strategies has been initiated, many as a result of the depressed rural economy during the 1980s. A prime emphasis has been job creation and in this respect the evidence suggests a reasonable degree of success (Green et al, 1990; McGuire et al, 1994). But considerable effort has also been directed at helping rural communities prepare for economic development through initiatives drawing upon a partnership of university, government and corporation investment. In Illinois, for example, a program has been developed which emphasizes education, local leadership and community development rather than quick fix remedies. Training modules have been designed which run the gamut from identifying and recruiting leaders, through strategic planning for community and economic development, to maintaining interest in and support for development groups. The goal of the project is community actualization as expressed by six shared indicators among residents: a perception of collective identity; consciousness of collective belonging by residents; a sense of community solidarity; shared pride in the community; a sense of achievement among community residents; and finally a feeling of fulfillment (Robinson and Silvis, 1993). In Nebraska a self-help approach that uses various media to present information to local leaders, facilitators and participants has served over 40 communities, while a tool kit for Alternative Economic Development produced by the University of Missouri Department of Community Development has been used by some 200 communities across 35 states (Reed and Blair, 1993). In each instance the concern of capacity building is to lessen dependency on outside experts and institutionalize a condition of readiness into a rural community's structure. A crucial component of this competency is being able to work collaboratively.

The collaboration theme

Collaboration is a word which trips easily off the tongues of politicians, officials and academics. It promises to be one of the guiding canons for public policy during the 1990s, a principle for behavior which is easy to identify with and be supportive of, but which in practice is open to a host of interpretations. If collaboration is to avoid becoming a fad, whose currency is diminished by simplistic overexposure, then the building of a common vocabulary of understanding and application is crucial. The danger is that without these deeper roots, an ongoing process of searching, adoption and discarding could turn the concept into nothing more than a pious platitude. This could make it as redolent as advocacy today of the blueprint planning approach belonging to the 1950s or dogmatic attachment to rational comprehensive planning from the following decade. Collaboration deserves a better fate.

Within the sphere of rural development, the pursuit of modernization through agency-led agriculture intensification and industrial recruitment has failed to secure a much vaunted rural renaissance. The contribution of community-based approaches to economic and social regeneration has sought to offer an alternative paradigm. The picture emerging is frequently one of enormous citizen imagination and commitment linked to an unremitting struggle for resources. This effort has often made little impact on the critical rural problems of poverty, population loss, services rundown and infrastructure obsolescence. The adoption of Integrated Rural Development, as described in a previous section of this chapter, posits a fresh perspective on theory and practice, which combines the best of top-down and bottom-up conventions into a new multilevel, multisectoral operational framework. Collaboration is an implicit component of IRD through its quest for strategic unity of purpose between local people and agency personnel, for economic measures to be paralleled by initiatives in education and training, and for development inputs to be matched with the specific needs and aspirations of target groups. The purpose of the discussion below is to define collaboration in terms which are more explicit and to identify a set of benchmarks against which the empirical analysis in the following chapters can be located.

The attractiveness of collaboration in the tool kit of public policy can be illustrated at the outset by comments from the President's Council on Rural America in its 1992 report *Revitalizing rural America through collaboration*. The Council states the following:

It is our conviction that federal, state and local government, private enterprise, and local communities must all work collaboratively; that it must be a unified process with necessary disciplines. (p. 1)

The key to success is to create a system of effective collaboration among federal, state and intergovernmental entities which builds to include local and tribal government, as well as the private sector. (p. 4)

The vision we offer calls for . . . people committed to collaboration and cooperative partnerships in rural America. Among individuals, communities, levels of government and between the public and private sectors, collaboration is an essential way of doing business that builds upon empowered people and caring communities. (p. 5)

What is needed to meet the demands of the 21st Century is a new response to changing needs, and a new standard for government action. That standard must begin with an understanding that the fundamental goal is to empower rural communities to develop themselves. It must foster an ethic of collaboration among governments at all levels and with private organizations. (p. 11)

Government should encourage and support multicommunity collaboration. By working on a pooled regional basis, rural communities can share solutions and resources. (p. 14)

These excerpts identify collaboration as a unified process, a system of governance, a vision based on cooperative partnerships, an ethic of community empowerment and a methodology for multicommunity action. Notwithstanding the rhetoric, it is difficult to disagree with these ideas which at the very least offer common-sense invocations; indeed few people would represent themselves as advocates for the contrary. But herewith is one of the challenges facing the collaboration concept: the retention of integrity by a popular slogan. More rigorous circumscription is, therefore, appropriate.

In a much cited definition Gray (1989) has specified collaboration as:

a process through which parties who see different aspects of a problem can constructively explore their differences and search for solutions that go beyond their own limited vision of what is possible. Those parties with an interest in the problem are termed stakeholders. Stakeholders include all individuals, groups, or organizations that are directly influenced by actions others take to solve the problem. The objective of collaboration is to create a richer, more comprehensive appreciation of the problem among stakeholders than anyone could construct alone. (p. 5)

Accordingly, collaboration is essentially a relationship-based approach to problem solving and action which recognizes that people working independently cannot deal most effectively with the complexity of issues facing individuals, communities and institutions. Mattessich and Monsey (1992) explicate some of the subtleties of such a situation in their definitive review of the research literature on factors influencing successful collaboration. Elements of commitment which are advanced include: mutual relationships and goals; a jointly developed structure and shared responsibility; mutual authority and accountability for success; and the sharing of resources and rewards. Thus, an invitation to collaborate calls for collective mobilization into teams which can visualize a shared future, determine joint goals, and agree a way by which individual diversity and strength can be harnessed for the common good. Collaboration is built upon respect for diversity and does not seek to homogenize individual identity. One of the strengths of any collaborative venture is that effectiveness can be enhanced by a richness of organizational and personal attributes. The fundamental tasks are to create a sense of oneness among the members of a team and to motivate working together on the basis of trust.

The catalyst for collaboration must be leadership and here capacity building processes for the enhancement of institutional and community abilities, as discussed in the section above, are vital. Bryson and Crosby (1992) underscore this essential connection with their assertion that quality leadership can build teams, empower other members of groups or organizations to be leaders themselves, and encourage collaboration. The additional indirect benefits are increased creativity, experimentation and innovation.

The pursuit of collaboration, in terms of resource requirements, need not be financially expensive. Indeed a key feature of its current attractiveness is the potential to reduce operational and capital costs and avoid duplication. Thus rural tourism ventures, for example, can benefit significantly from the establishment of collaborative structures which can mobilize resources not available to any single individual. Community structures can internalize many of the risks and uncertainties which an individual would find daunting to take on board. The opportunities for achieving economies of scale become even more pronounced when this collaborative effort is extended to embrace a multicommunity dimension. Wider strategic planning, joint marketing and shared product development become interesting possibilities. Collaboration can be a mechanism not only for greater efficiency in a climate of diminishing and competitive resource allocation, but also for greater effectiveness in securing change at a local level.

Collaboration tends to reverse agency and community value systems which traditionally are based on independence and competition. Baker (1993) has pointed out that effective collaboration may lead to new networks, the natural integration of policies and programs, and new forms of working together. But it is at this stage that progress on the collaboration front can fall victim to no small amount of misinterpretation. There are, in short, ambiguities regarding practical use of the term which can include frequent interchange with cooperation and coordination. Mattessich and Monsey (1992) offer guidance on this matter. Cooperation is defined as comprising informal relationships that exist without any commonly defined mission, structure or planning effort; information is shared as needed and authority is retained by each organization; there is little risk and both resources and rewards are particular to each participant in the process. Coordination is typified by more formal relationships and common understanding of comparable missions; there is some joint planning, the division of roles and the establishment of communication channels; authority still rests within individual organizations, but there is increased risk to all participants; resources are available to participants and rewards are mutually acknowledged. Finally, collaboration is identified as a more durable and pervasive relationship; it brings previously separate organizations into a new structure with full commitment to a common mission; the sustainability of these relationships is dependent upon planning and well-defined and reliable communication channels operating on many levels; authority is determined by the collaborative structures and risk is much greater because each participant contributes reputation and owned resources; the latter are pooled or jointly secured for a longer term effort that is managed by the collaborative structure; product outcomes are shared and more is accomplished jointly than could have been individually.

The location of collaboration, therefore, is at the high end of any partnership continuum. While partnership itself is frequently used as a synonym for many of the above actions, it is perhaps more appropriate to reserve this term for any system of working together ranging from informal arrangements to legally binding contracts (Huillet and Van Dijk, 1990). In short, partnership can operate at different levels of responsibility and commitment. Institutional relationships can be horizontal as between federal agencies, or can be vertical as between local, state and federal governance. Rural development, with its involvement of representative community personnel, university expertise and a diversity of economic and social interests (public, private and voluntary) creates more complex multidimensional configurations. It is collaboration which can provide the fullest expression of conceptual guidance for nurturing and maintaining these relationships.

To sum up, the collaboration theme provides a useful analytical tool for unraveling rural America in terms of policy formulation and performance. At the cutting edge of community revitalization it offers valuable guidance for the examination of the collective effort between individuals, and between organized groups and support institutions. The chapters which follow seek to address these matters by examining attempts to increase joint capacity to tackle common problems. Borich (1994) has captured the essence of the collaborative theme as being concerned with the following processes:

1. Interdependent stakeholders dealing constructively with differences.
2. Interdependent stakeholders having joint ownership of the decision involved.
3. Interdependent stakeholders assuming collective responsibility for future joint action.
4. Interdependent stakeholders creating alternative power systems which complement rather than promote the termination of existing organizations.

The empirical and prescriptive content of this book revolves around these key ideas.

Rural development and institutional capacity

Introduction

Chapter 1 has identified a close theoretical relationship between the need for and scope of rural development policy and the institutional apparatus of governance. The characteristics of Integrated Rural Development, in particular, have major relevance. Included in this agenda for the reshaping of policy is a preference for institutional reform, expressed mainly as the devolution of some powers and responsibilities from national to regional and local levels of administration. This seeks to promote better sensitivity to local conditions, enhanced citizen participation and greater effectiveness of development measures. As an innovative way of doing business in rural areas this set of ideas echoes closely the contemporary emphasis in the United States on new arrangements for public administration. Much of the rural development challenge revolves around the relationship between top-down and bottom-up processes. While ideas and solutions can originate at either level, a notable tendency in the 1990s has been the movement towards a more collaborative, multilevel and inclusive approach to governance. This chapter picks up on these themes. The discussion, at the outset, can be located usefully within the

wider arena of governance restructuring over the period
since the early 1980s.

Restructuring governance

During the past 15 years there has been substantial effort
by the governments of many advanced economies to
secure institutional reform in order to respond better to
changes in the environment of late-twentieth-century capi-
talism. Roselle (1992) claims that governments such as
those in the United Kingdom, Canada, New Zealand,
Sweden, Singapore and the United States have shared a
common concern of responding to the social and technological changes associated with the emergence of a global
information society. With an ever increasing range of connections, more information, shrinkage of time and space
and more uncertainty, government has had to adopt a different set of working practices. As noted by Self (1993) the
goals of political leaders have been to slim bureaucracy, to
revamp the machinery of administration, to change patterns of service delivery, and to introduce a new managerial philosophy of resource efficiency and expenditure
control.

Within the United States the approach of the Reagan
Administrations, marked by a commitment to New
Federalism, may be regarded as a useful baseline for examination of these adjustments. Key features of President
Reagan's federalism reform included a desire to reduce the
role of federal government, to reduce federal grants and to
widen the policy remit of state governments. Reagan's
period in the White House was characterized by an ideological commitment to increased reliance upon market
forces and to much greater control by individuals over
their own economic fortunes. Large tax cuts, it was
assumed, would fuel economic growth and private enterprise, released from government restraints, would flourish
through its own initiative. One legacy of the Reagan
Presidency on this front has thus been the deregulation of
major businesses comprising airlines, telecommunications,
trucking, banking and natural gas which as suggested by
Finkelstein (1992) was largely successful for consumers as
well as improving the performance of the industries
involved. However, it remains questionable whether all

rural areas have benefited to a comparable degree since notoriously they can be subjected to conditions of service withdrawal or lack of investment, a simple acknowledgement of the reality that market failure and public policy oversight can compound disadvantage.

New federalism policies also began an era of reduction or withdrawal of federal funding for many grant aid programs, block grant programs, and general revenue sharing (Brown and Deavers, 1988). During Reagan's terms federal aid to states and localities was reduced by 25 percent (Conlan, 1988). Not only did the 1980s mark a period of retrenchment for federal urban policy (Rich, 1991) but they also evidenced a deterioration of federal aid flows to rural government (Sokolow, 1986). In an analysis of financial transfers to 13 states in the West, Clark and Clark (1992) conclude that the small and rural local governments in the region lost from the Reagan revolution; in addition to a substantial drop in federal aid during the 1980s, cities in the West lost much of their previous advantage in the system of federal aid flows.

The 1980s, finally, witnessed the shifting of responsibility for key areas of program delivery from federal sources to state government. The Reagan Presidency had sought to give each state a larger role in governing the United States. However, in many instances Congress appropriated little or no additional money and frequently imposed unfunded mandates which involved passing laws for states and localities to follow. By December 1992 there were at least 172 separate pieces of federal legislation in force (National Performance Review, 1993). For officials in rural areas these unfunded mandates affect economic development because they may divert existing resources away from current or proposed local initiatives. As a consequence of the reduction in federal aid many states increased taxes, while cuts in services aimed at the more disadvantaged members of society were not uncommon (King, 1992). Fiscal stress continues to dominate the state political agenda in the 1990s as governments search for new ways to deliver services and balance their budgets through a combination of tax increases and cutbacks (Bowman and Pagano, 1992).

Accordingly, the restructuring of governance during the Reagan Administrations did produce major modifications to the federal system and certainly in so far as local–state–federal relationships are concerned. State gov-

ernments have acquired a new managerial status.
Notwithstanding this adjustment, significant challenges
remain at the federal level. The view that the federal government, with its large financial and staff resources, should
take the lead in solving national problems has increasingly
been replaced by concern about the size of the federal
bureaucracy and its perceived ineptitude. Related to this is
the criticism that federal policy responses demonstrate little appreciation of the uniqueness of circumstances and
the subtleties of problems being addressed. A fresh agenda
related to the restructuring of governance has gathered
momentum with the stirring of public consciousness
assisted in no small measure by Osborne and Gaebler in
*Reinventing government: how the entrepreneurial spirit is trans-
forming the public sector* (1992).

Reinventing government has established itself as a
national bestseller and has dominated the current debate
surrounding more effective government management.
Both President Clinton and Vice-President Gore have
become confirmed disciples of this governance doctrine
and in their pre-election manifesto *Putting people first* (1992)
were keen to argue that:

> We can no longer afford to pay for more – and get less from – our
> government. The answer for every problem cannot always be
> another program or more money. It is time to radically change the
> way the government operates – to shift from top down bureau-
> cracy to entrepreneurial government that empowers citizens and
> communities to change our country from the bottom up. We must
> reward the people and ideas that work and get rid of those that
> don't. (pp. 23–24)

These comments echo the message of Osborne and
Gaebler who have searched widely among state and local
governments in the United States for illustrations of successful entrepreneurial government. The empirical evidence allows for the identification of 10 principles which
taken together represent, they claim, a new paradigm for
making government work better and thus address directly
a public crisis of confidence in a stagnant bureaucracy. The
messianic tone of the book is well captured in the following paragraph:

> Today's environment demands institutions that are extremely
> flexible and equitable. It demands institutions that deliver high

quality goods and services, squeezing ever more bang out of every buck. It demands institutions that are responsible to their customers, offering choices of nonstandardized services; that lead by persuasion and incentives rather than commands; that give their employees a sense of meaning and control, even ownership. It demands institutions that empower citizens rather than simply serving them. (p. 15)

While the analysis and prescription of Osborne and Gaebler have drawn criticism about the absence of information both on data collection methods and on the conditions under which the delivery systems examined do operate, a more fundamental objection cited (Rhodes, 1994) is that the source of the innovations which they extol is the bureaucracy which they excoriate. As a bestseller, however, it has captured the *Zeitgeist* by asserting that government should seek to become more catalytic, community owned, competitive, mission driven, results oriented, customer driven, enterprising, anticipating, decentralized, and market orientated.

Kettl (1993) observes that support for this vision of new governance (Table 6) crosses the Democratic and Republican political divide with supporters of the New Left and New Right having more in common with each other on this matter than with the traditionalists in either party. Ultimate success depends, however, on tough decisions being taken to make the processes of governance work in ways that promote the identification and pursuit of rewards. This in turn, argues Kettl, will require strong and aggressive leadership by top officials to create a bureaucratic culture that rewards managing for results. However, the boundaries among government programs and the agencies that manage them constitute a core problem in this quest and the related mission of serving the customer. Kettl suggests that, all too often, the results tend to be defined by the narrow goals of each program instead of citizens' needs. Government managers should, therefore, be boundary spanners who seek to insure that citizens' relations with government are seamless and that problems are solved quickly and with a minimum of difficulty for citizens themselves. Such concerns fit well, for example, with the rationale for and operational practices of new State Rural Development Councils as discussed later in this chapter.

The currency of these sentiments in regard to national renewal can be illustrated with reference to the publication in 1993 of two reports which seek to reinvent government. The National Governors' Association was first off the starting blocks with *An action agenda to redesign state government.* Key concerns include performance-based governance, human services consolidation and coordination, privatization of government services and assets, and reform of management systems. Wider interest has been given, however, to the Report of the National Performance Review (1993) *From red tape to results: creating a government that works better and costs less.* Its chapter headings which refer to cutting red tape, putting customers first, empowering employees to get rewards and cutting back to basics firmly place this report also within the entrepreneurial management paradigm. With over 800 recommendations aimed at producing savings of some $108 billion over five years the proposals represent in many ways a major step towards the completion of the unfinished business left over from the Reagan Administrations.

Table 6 Characteristics of new governance

	New	Old
Contact with citizens	Engage, enable	Direct, announce
Goals	Mission, value driven	Program driven
How problems are defined	Proactive, create opportunities	Reactive, solve individual problems
Behavior	Decentralized, flexible, entrepreneurial	Centralized, hierarchical
Citizens	Customers; government is customer centered	Clients; government is special interest centered
Measuring success	Results achieved	Inputs spent
Spending	Long-term benefits	Short-term payoff
Organizational linkages	Horizontal alliances; collaboration with stakeholders	Hierarchical; one size fits all

Source: Kettl (1993).

President Reagan was committed to curbing the size of the federal establishment. A major recommendation of the National Performance Review is to downsize the executive branch by 252 000 over a five-year period, a figure corresponding to some 12 percent of the total workforce. But the political ramifications of this review run deeper. It seeks to challenge the traditionally strong management role of Congress, melt the boundaries between organizations and give federal workers greater decision-making authority. When related to the focus of this book on revitalizing rural America, it is interesting to note that the acclaimed precedent for restructuring the organizational chart is the Rural Development Council initiative, under the direction of the USDA; this involves partnership between several federal departments as well as states and localities to improve delivery of rural aid programs. The report simply makes the point: "We should bring the same approach to other parts of government." (p. 49)

Notwithstanding fundamental criticism that the management of the executive branch is not like the management of General Electric or Ritz Carlton Hotels (Moe, 1994), in other words that there are limitations to a business-based paradigm derived from public accountability and public service imperatives, the debate on governance restructuring has moved a considerable distance. Compared with previous failed efforts in the United States to make government work better, there is some optimism that this exercise could produce change. Peters and Savoie (1994) suggest that the report has eschewed the simplistic notions offered by Osborne and Gaebler in favor of a more complex and realistic view of the problems of government and the means available to correct them; that it has the clear support of the highest levels of government; that it has successfully co-opted civil service officials; and that its authors have addressed the difficulties of implementation.

Many of the reforms now being called for by the Clinton Administration seek to place the responsibility for change at state and local levels in accordance with the principle of subsidiarity: that decision making should occur at the lowest possible level. Individuals and communities are central, therefore, to this renewal process. The future well-being of rural America depends upon the capacity of governance to respond to the challenges of this new management paradigm. It is against this backcloth that the next section of this chapter can now move on to trace the unfolding discourse in regard to institutional arrangements for rural development in the United States.

Towards a new institutional capacity for rural development

As outlined in Chapter 1, the 1980s were a difficult period for the economy of much of rural America. The financial stress in agriculture and its related industries combined with slow employment growth or decline in natural resource-based industries and manufacturing were major impediments to rural prosperity. Federal funding for rural development activities decreased steadily throughout the decade and, as noted by Unruh (1991), the Community Development Block Grant, Farmers' Home Administration grant and loan programs and Environmental Protection Agency wastewater treatment funds were all reduced. This had the effect of greatly limiting the options available to rural communities for financing new or improved infrastructure or for assisting new or expanding businesses.

The need for a policy stance on rural America which responded to this complexity of circumstances was finally recognized in 1987 with the publication by the USDA of Information Bulletin 533 *Rural economic development in the 1980s*. An analysis of rural conditions and economic forces at work provided for the identification of a suite of alternatives for future rural policy. There was scathing criticism of subsidy-led intervention and strong endorsement of a reduced federal role in capital funding in line with the political orthodoxy of the period. Regional rural approaches involving the states and local rural communities represented the preferred position. This indication of a change of direction for public policy set in motion a lengthy debate between multiple interests regarding the most appropriate institutional framework for rural development. The subsequent high profile involvement of the President, Congress, federal departments, and the National Governors' Association would suggest that the debate was as much about ownership as about the shape of policy initiatives.

The National Governors' Association was the first key interest to advance its vision for rural America as a result of the 1987 USDA alternatives paper. In 1988 the deliberations of its Task Force on Rural Development were presented under the title *New alliances for rural America*, the timing designed to lobby the support of incoming President George Bush. No fewer than 12 recommendations were advanced which sought to give the states a leadership role in rural revitalization. In summary these were:

1. To provide reliable, individually tailored expertise and information to rural communities to help them prepare and implement their own development strategies.
2. To encourage individual communities and counties to pool their resources and build sub-state regional mechanisms for cooperation.
3. To hire special staff, create offices of rural affairs, or create written guidelines to insure that rural areas had adequate access to state resources and decisions.
4. To help traditional rural industries develop new products and seek new markets.
5. To provide local governments with the resources and authority to manage growth and support regional and state-wide efforts for growth management.
6. To increase the flexibility of state requirements and procedures and support local efforts to restructure health care systems.
7. To encourage rural school districts to develop distinctive ways of restructuring, including closer integration of schools with other community activities, active participation by schools in community development, sharing services among districts and distance learning.
8. To relate highway investment decisions to economic opportunities and adopt more flexible standards and formulas.
9. To orient economic development activities towards existing and new businesses.
10. To modernize industrial recruitment activities.
11. To help make available a broad range of technical information and expertise to rural businesses and broaden the kinds of financing easily available in rural areas.
12. To invest in upgrading the skills of workers in rural areas.

A further three recommendations addressed the federal agenda for rural America:

1. The mix of federal spending should be adjusted to encourage adaptation to changing economic conditions in rural America by making a greater investment in human skills with less emphasis on income redistribution.
2. The incoming President should work with Congress, the states and local government to build a new federal–state–local alliance that consolidated and increased the flexibility of programs that serve rural America.
3. Federal policies in the areas of health, transportation, international trade and economic growth must be attuned more closely to rural needs.

These aspirations have been cited at length to demonstrate the multiple concerns of a comprehensive policy initiative in rural development which sought to reach out to individual and community needs. Indeed the agenda being pursued fits well with the conceptual thrust of Integrated Rural Development as identified in Chapter 1. As a lobbying instrument with investment priorities the report is quickly transparent. More interesting, however, are the process-related concerns which deal with leadership, partnership, community initiative and entrepreneurship in the redefined mission of federal, state and local governance. The conviction rhetoric and strong rationale of *New alliances for rural America* give seminal status to this contribution to the rural development debate in the United States. (It is worth noting that this was also a time when the European Commission had published a report of equivalent importance for the subsequent direction of rural development policy in the European Union called *The future of rural society*).

The search for a more definitive expression of appropriate institutional arrangements continued with the publication in 1989 by the USDA of *A hard look at USDA's rural development programs: the Report of the Rural Revitalization Task Force to the Secretary of Agriculture*. There is a refreshingly critical flavor to this analysis as illustrated, for example, by the assertion:

> Throughout the governmental system, rural development programs operate without clearly stated and understood goals. As a result, rural policy at all levels of government consists of a collection of programs that, however useful individually, do not add up to a coherent and consistent strategy to achieve any well understood goals. (p. 3)

The commentary then deals specifically with the role of the USDA and the legislative mandate for policy provided by the Rural Development Act of 1972. Rural development, it is suggested, is defined in terms of programs rather than the intended outcomes of the rural development process. There are no measurable goals, nor any attempt to address policy questions concerning the relative emphasis between short- and long-term issues or whether action initiatives should target worst cases or those with better chances of success. The USDA programs, it is claimed, are operated individually with little attention given to how they can mutually support local development efforts. More damning, when set against the previous NGA report on new alliances for rural America, is the charge that programs often take their focus from a federal agency perspective and thus are more likely to reflect federal rather than state or local priorities. The analysis mirrors many of the characteristics of new governance as discussed earlier in this chapter, with the emergent influence of the preferred style of public management coming through under the call for organizational linkages based on coordination. Administrative changes at both Washington and state levels are needed, it is claimed, to create effective coordination structures. It is recommended that state level Food and Agriculture Councils should: (i) be restructured to embrace more fully farm and non-farm interests; (ii) be placed under the jurisdiction of the Under Secretary for Small Community and Rural Development; and (iii) be renamed to include the USDA's rural development mission. Suggested titles include Rural Coordinating Council or State Coordinating Council. Relegated to an appendix are the recommendations from a Work Group created to advise the Revitalization Task Force. One proposal, significantly, calls for the creation of State Rural Development Councils, with full-time professional staff support, under the direction of State Coordinating Councils.

The report by the USDA Task Force thus made an important contribution to the rural development debate by beginning to move in the direction of enhancing institutional capacity for effecting action. However, while the limitations of past and contemporary practice were clearly identified, the prescription was almost totally confined within the territorial boundaries of the USDA. Only passing mention was made of the potential contribution to be made by other federal, state and local agencies. The politics of turf protection and the forthcoming agenda of the 1990 Farm Bill undoubtedly conditioned a response which fell short of the promising analysis.

With both the NGA and the USDA having, as it were, made their preliminary bids, the timing could not have been more opportune for the involvement of the White House in seeking to push forward the rural development cause. With a possible eye on his re-election strategy (Radin, 1992) President Bush grasped the rural development nettle.

The President's Initiative on Rural America

Early in 1990 President Bush announced a six point initiative on rural America. Its formal origins can be traced back to March 1989 when the President's Economic Policy Council formed a Working Group on Rural Development. Key officials from a wide range of federal departments, executive agencies and the White House came together to explore five major areas of rural development:education and training, economic development, infrastructure, housing and health care. The findings of the Working Group were published in January 1990 and among its recommendations for change were improved coordination of all federal, state and local government rural development efforts and improved support and training of local community leaders in the development process (a key role here for community colleges and land-grant institutions). A plan of action detailed what subsequently was launched on 22 January 1990 as the Presidential Initiative on Rural Development. The following action steps were called for:

1. The establishment of the Economic Policy Council Working Group on Rural Development as a permanent Cabinet level policy body with responsibility for implementing the President's Rural Initiative.
2. The creation of a President's Council on Rural America to recommend strategies for rural development.
3. The creation of State Rural Development Councils comprising *federal* officials to conduct comprehensive federal/state rural development programs. A pilot scheme involving the establishment of eight councils was initiated.

4. The improved targeting of federal rural development resources by allocating funds from programs with discretionary accounts to those activities where the pay-off is greater.
5. The organizing of a rural development demonstration program to identify regional rural development needs, implement a plan of action and evaluate the process and outcomes for possible wider application.
6. The expanding of rural development information availability through the Rural Information Center.

Essentially this initiative was conceived as a way of doing the work of government differently and interestingly predated the new governance ideas of Osborne and Gaebler. As suggested by Shaffer (1993) the package represented the culmination of at least two years of internal discussion within the Bush Administration and built on discussions started in the closing days of the Reagan Presidency.

While the establishment of a Cabinet level policy body and a White House Council can be interpreted as attempts to satisfy the need for vigorous action, there is little doubt that President Bush was mindful of his difficult relationship with Congress. It has been said that no arm of American government enjoys complete or exclusive control over any policy matter (Denenberg, 1992), and with Congress debating the provisions of the 1990 Farm Bill, containing rural development measures, the Presidential Initiative can be interpreted as a bid to secure the political high ground. Radin (1992) has commented, for example, that this focus on rural issues by President Bush provided a way to give attention to rural states without major expenditures and to emphasize the importance of rural constituencies for the 1992 election. Efforts had, therefore, to be visible, developed quickly and shaped by the White House rather than Congress.

Finally, the Presidential Initiative placed great weight upon federal leadership in State Rural Development Councils. The statement issued by the White House Press Secretary specifically nominated the state representatives of all federal departments administering rural development programs locally. They would be joined by representatives from the Office of the Governor in each state. However, the involvement of personnel from state government agencies, local governments and the private sector was designed to be through "organizational linkage". Full membership of the Rural Development Council is not readily apparent for these additional interests, a clear shortcoming in this initial interpretation of state level collaboration. Further efforts to build institutional capacity were set to continue on a number of fronts.

The 1990 Farm Bill and the Rural Development Administration

The Presidential Initiative was not alone in promoting actions related to rural development. Congress and individual departments and agencies were also involved in bringing forward related legislation. Thus, for example, the Aviation Safety and Capacity Expansion Act of 1990 required large public use airports levying a passenger facility charge to relinquish a portion of their entitlement funds in order to benefit small commercial and general aviation airports which usually serve rural areas. The Rural Small Business Enhancement Act of 1990 established an Office of Rural Affairs within the Small Business Administration to encourage a fair distribution of financial assistance to rural areas, compile information on government and private programs of assistance to rural areas, and assist with rural tourism development. Also significant was the Food, Agriculture, Conservation and Trade Act of 1990, otherwise known as the Farm Bill, which introduced a number of measures related to rural development.

These emerged from a series of compromises between House and Senate proposals for the Farm Bill. As recorded by Freshwater (1991) the Senate Bill followed a traditional strategy of proposing new ways to fund infrastructure and business development together with some provisions to improve planning and invest in human capital; some $300 million of new funding per year was authorized. In contrast, the House version assumed no significant increase in funding and provided for the improved coordination and efficiency of existing programs. Mediation during the last stages of the Farm Bill debate laid the foundation for a rural development title in the new legislation which provided for the following:

1. The creation of a new Rural Development Administration to be made up of several agencies within the Department of Agriculture under the management of the Under Secretary for Small Community and Rural Development.
2. Investment of the Department of Agriculture with new authority in several program areas, including water and sewerage, small business development, assistance for natural resource impacted communities, capital formation and strategic planning.
3. The establishment of two 5 year pilot projects to test new models for improving rural development program delivery. The first comprised the setting up of State Rural Economic Development Review Panels in up to five states to obtain state and local input in planning, prioritizing and evaluating business and community programs. The second included the formation of a Rural Business Investment Fund, again in up to five states, to help finance rural business development projects under the auspices of Rural Partnership Investment Boards. These bodies would be eligible to apply for federal capital to maintain a revolving loan fund.
4. Investment of the Rural Electrification Administration with new authority to fund rural business incubators, distance learning and medical link telecommunication facilities.
5. The expansion of the responsibility of Extension Service for education and training in support of rural development programs.
6. Authorization of the Forest Service to give technical assistance to rural communities in or near national forests and offer loans to economically disadvantaged rural communities in forest-impacted areas.

Coordination, efficiency and enhanced state and local involvement would appear to be the major guiding principles underpinning these measures and, in particular, the creation of the Rural Development Administration (RDA). The intended brief of this new agency was specifically to handle certain financial provisions previously assigned to the Farmers' Home Administration (FmHA). That had been established in the 1940s with a mission to provide temporary, supervised credit to farmers who had a reasonable chance of success but who could not obtain loans from

commercial sources at reasonable rates. Later it began making housing loans to low and moderate income rural residents and then moved on to giving loans to communities
for waste and water projects and guaranteeing loans for
businesses in rural communities to promote job creation.
With an increasing number of programs administered by
the FmHA providing assistance to rural America, the official view emerged of the need to place community and
business programs under a separate administration.

The new agency became operational on 31 December
1991 with a spatial structure organized on the basis of
seven regions. Below this was a proposed network of some
125 area offices. However, from the outset the activities of
the RDA have been the subject of some controversy. One
difficulty has been its relationship with Congress, where
responsibility for rural development is divided among
numerous committees and subcommittees. During the
hearings for the 1994 appropriations, for example, questions were raised about the need for an additional layer of
bureaucracy in the form of regional offices, higher than
anticipated staffing levels, working relationships with
FmHA, and the future role of the RDA within a reorga-
nized Department of Agriculture. The tone of some of the
cross-examination suggested a high level of skepticism
regarding its claimed value. The announcement in
September 1993 by Agriculture Secretary, Mike Espy, of a
proposed restructuring of the Department with the goal of
reinventing government, provided justification for that
concern. The RDA was targeted for dismantling. In
October 1993 Congress mandated the closing of the seven
regional offices by 1 April 1994.

Rural development is still, however, viewed as a priority
through the recommended establishment of three new
organizations reporting to the Under Secretary for Rural
Economic and Community Development. The Rural
Utilities Service will combine the telephone and electricity
programs of the Rural Electrification Administration (REA)
with the water and sewerage programs of the RDA. The
Rural Housing and Community Development Service will
include FmHA rural housing programs as well as REA and
RDA Rural Community loan programs. Finally the Rural
Business and Cooperative Development Service will
include the RDA and REA business development programs
in its portfolio.

At the headquarters level, the number of separate USDA agencies and offices will be reduced from 43 to 30 and the field operations structure reduced from 3700 to 2485 offices. With the restructuring of the USDA designed to realize $1.3 billion in savings and a rural staff reduction of 7500 employees over five years, the winding up of the RDA can be seen as fitting well with the new governance agenda. The difficult political context of the 1990 Farm Bill within which it emerged, an uncertainty over its function and value, and the accepted need to meet rural challenges with improved program design and delivery have dogged its short existence. Its pragmatic creation belied the need for more radical measures. Should the proposed restructuring of the USDA come about as planned, and here Congressional support will be vital, one lesson learnt from the RDA experience must be that building institutional capacity is not a tension-free process.

Agency adaptation – the Forest Service

Throughout the 1980s the forest area within the United States remained essentially stable and comprised some 728 million acres (32 percent of the land area). Of this, approximately 66 percent comprised timberland; just over one-quarter of the commercial forest was in public ownership (Sedjo, 1991). Management of this estate on the basis of multiple use and sustained yield is long established, but recent years have evidenced increasing environmental concern about the impact of timber harvesting on biodiversity and amenity. This has resulted in the withdrawal of areas of forest from the timber base, primarily the federal forest estate. Moreover, as part of a national plan to reduce the federal budget deficit, the Forest Service, the relevant federal agency, has proposed the phasing out of unprofitable sales of public timber to private companies across America. On both counts, there can be major economic consequences for timber-dependent communities. In Colorado, for example, where the Forest Service lost some $14.8 million on logging operations in 1992, the policy change would have eliminated commercial timber production in all 11 of the state's national forests within four years. The annual loss in timber payments by the Forest Service to local governments has been calculated at $1.5

million (*Denver Post*, 20 June 1993). It was against concerns such as these that the Forest Service embarked in 1989 upon a review of its rural development efforts by establishing a National Rural Development Task Force.

In June 1990 the publication of *A strategic plan for the 90s: working together for rural America* (USDA, Forest Service, 1990) confirmed the agency's position as an active rural development participant with significant human, technical, financial and natural resources to assist local communities. A new policy on rural development was stated as follows:

> The Forest Service will provide leadership in working with rural people and communities on developing natural resource based opportunities and enterprises that contribute to the economic and social vitality of rural communities. The Forest Service can make lasting improvements in rural America by helping people solve their local problems in ways that enhance the quality of the environment in accordance with our existing authorities. (p. 5)

This statement was explicated by reference to six implementation goals:

1. To communicate to both Forest Service employees and the public that rural development is a key part of the Forest Service's mission.
2. To include rural development in agency resource decisions in order to achieve long-term economic development and improved quality of life.
3. To participate actively in community rural development efforts.
4. To understand and integrate the needs of diverse communities in Forest Service activities.
5. To strengthen participation in cooperative USDA efforts at the local level.
6. To provide timely and current research and resource information on rural development opportunities.

A commitment to locally driven collaborative work with other interests across rural America has thus emerged as a central theme informing the mission of the Forest Service. The timing of this adaptation could not have been more opportune. As noted in earlier sections of this chapter, a sweeping review of rural development programs had been undertaken by the USDA, and in January 1990 President

Bush had announced a six point initiative on rural America. But it was the passage of the 1990 Farm Bill which galvanized the broader development remit espoused by the Forest Service. The appropriate authority is set out under the Rural Development Title (XXIII) and more specifically in Subtitle G (Rural Revitalization through Forestry). The following purposes are cited:

1. To provide assistance to rural communities that are located in or near national forests and that are economically dependent upon forest resources or are likely to be economically disadvantaged by federal or private sector land management practices.
2. To aid in diversifying such communities' economic bases.
3. To improve the economic, social and environmental well-being of rural America.

Under this measure assistance is provided by way of an economic recovery fund to enable communities to create local action teams, prepare local action plans and implement projects contained within them. As reported by McWilliams et al (1993) Forest Service field units in fiscal year 1992 organized 171 local action teams which generated 127 local action plans. A total of 185 counties or communities obtained financial assistance for 102 individual projects. Economic recovery funds in fiscal year 1993 amounted to $5 million.

There is little doubt that this proactive approach to community-based rural development, as adopted by the Forest Service, is viewed with some envy by other agencies with a comparable mission. The adaptation as a whole is seen as focused, well resourced and able to take advantage at an operational level of a national policy statement with unambiguous goals. Perhaps this high profile outreach approach can be no better illustrated than by a note carried on the front page of the regular Forest Service news release, *Working Together*, from August 1993:

MAKE US A PROPOSAL . . .
We're looking for a huge variety of ways to help. Our policy is to count you in, not out. And there are several themes we're looking for in proposals that help guide our efforts to work with you.
    We are interested in the whole community, not just the business sector. We're looking for proposals that are community based

and community led. The proposal should be part of a comprehensive approach, emphasizing working cooperatively with other local, State and Federal groups by making them your partners. The proposal should be driven by local needs, from the bottom up. The long term is more important than the quick fix. Flexibility is key to addressing diverse problems, and the proposal should be accomplished through partnerships.

We are looking for opportunities for the Forest Service to help you capitalize on your natural resource based potential and assets, and an opportunity to strengthen the community's capacity to diversify its economy. Proposals that also address the desired quality of life in a community are more likely to be chosen. Proposals that are sustainable over time will have priority. Finally, broad based **local** planning should be an important prerequisite. (p. 1)

Developing the collaboration-based approach

Collaboration is fast emerging as the overarching concept for rural development practice in the 1990s. It is a hallmark of the President's Initiative on Rural America and provides the operational rationale for the State Rural Development Councils. This topicality can be illustrated with reference to two reports published during 1992.

The National Governors' Association (1992) issued its contribution under the title *State–federal collaboration on rural development*. This is based on an examination of eight rural initiatives each of which involved cooperative planning and program implementation by state and federal officials with private sector participation in some instances. Obstacles to intergovernmental collaboration are identified as bureaucratic inertia, inflexible regulation, changes in federal or state administrations and shifting policy priorities, delays between policy innovation and implementation, and personality clashes. On the other hand, the elements for successful partnerships are listed as including commitment by top level leadership, flexibility and sensitivity to local diversity, mutual support for agency objectives which are shaped by policy makers and program managers to be consistent with the overall rural development goal, creating a sense of ownership by all the partners and achieving early tangible successes.

The tone of these sentiments remains strongly managerialist and, arguably, loses sight of the direct involvement of the rural constituency as a key part of the collaboration process. This limitation, however, is confidently addressed by the President's Council on Rural America (1992) in its report to President Bush *Revitalizing rural America through collaboration*. Its recommendations are built around two principles for action: creating a more responsive government and supporting the central role of communities. Rural development, it is asserted, demands much more than an increase in the level of local economic activity. The following passage explicates this point:

> Rural development is and must be, fundamentally, development of the whole community, and not merely its business sector. Community development is not an act but a process, by which the community's level of wellbeing is increased. That process must be a bottom up process. It begins with expansion of the community's ability to act effectively on its own behalf and to develop creative and effective partnerships with the private sector. It depends heavily on the ability of local leadership to guide the community to a clearly understood vision and a plan for achieving it. It depends equally on the capacity of local citizens and local institutions to carry the load of creating their own futures, which is why we use the words "rural community development". (pp. 12–13)

This advocacy lies close to the spirit and purpose of this book and provides a powerful endorsement for the community perspective in rural development advanced in Chapter 1. Subsequent chapters will expand on this theme. When related to the currency of the collaborative approach, the clear message is that rural communities should be at the center of efforts by policy makers and program managers. As the report states:

> Governments must be prepared to cooperatively direct their investments, in response to locally driven actions, toward those areas – including education – that will prepare rural America to confront the 21st century head on. (p. 13)

The experiment in establishing eight pilot State Rural Development Councils (SRDCs) is applauded as a significant way by which this challenge can be met and its extension to all states as a means for promoting collaboration between federal and state governments, local governments and local communities is called for.

State Rural Development Councils

As outlined above, President Bush announced a six point initiative in January 1990 which was designed to

strengthen the delivery of federal support for rural development. The establishment of state level Rural
Development Councils was a key element. By the end of
1990 Rural Development Councils had been established on
a pilot basis in eight states comprising Kansas, Maine,
Mississippi, Oregon, South Carolina, South Dakota, Texas
and Washington. Each was encouraged at the outset to
develop its own approach to the issues being faced at individual state level, but in general each council has been concerned with:

- inviting key players and involving them in the State
  Rural Development Council;
- developing an effective organization based on a shared
  sense of purpose and goals, and mutual contributions
  to the State Rural Development Council work;
- assessing the broad range of needs and opportunities
  in rural areas and setting priorities;
- identifying the full scope of natural, human and economic resources (including current public and private
  sector programs) available within the state;
- creating a strategy for a future in which rural communities can thrive;
- promoting the implementation of that strategy by giving special attention to the identification and elimina-
  tion of administrative barriers to rural development.

In short, the overall goal is to create a working partnership among all who have a stake in rural development
within each state. Radin (1991) suggests that a number of
aspects of the measure are unique compared with earlier
intergovernmental change projects. Firstly, it is organized
at the state level, rather than in Washington or at the federal regional level. Secondly, it involves a range of federal
and state officials, drawn from many different federal
departments, who are not often brought to the same table.
Thirdly, the eventual resolution to allow equal representation of federal and state officials in a state level organization is not typical. Finally, the federal participation
operates through procedural guidance rather than substantive direction.

An evaluation of the pilot scheme after one year of experience (Radin, 1992) has identified less than expected private sector involvement in agenda development, difficulties

in defining "rural", and the expending of more time than anticipated in securing collaborative relationships and shared goals. On the other hand, greater all-round understanding of the nature of policy issues facing the revitalization challenge has been gained, together with greater familiarity with existing federal and state programs, and deeper appreciation by participants of the problems of rural people. Enthusiasm for the process has remained strong.

The State Rural Development Councils have also been active at a project-specific level and a wide range of accomplishments has been reported in newsletters.

1. Kansas Rural Development Council was associated with a reservoir construction project which involved four local agencies, two state agencies, two federal departments and two private companies. The council was able to bring all parties to the negotiating table and agree a strategy to accelerate the construction of the dam to benefit industrial and domestic users.
2. In Mississippi there were problems for small business borrowers in obtaining poultry loans. The State Rural Development Council successfully mediated with private sector banking, two federal agencies and the State of Mississippi. The cooperation of all parties has allowed for some 100 poultry-related loans to be made since February 1992 amounting to over $33 million.
3. Again in Kansas seven federal and state agencies have developed a single small business loan application form.
4. The Texas Rural Development Council brought five funding sources together to provide the necessary capital for building a processing facility for a sunflower seed company which previously had to sell its seed out-of-state.
5. In Oregon, state and federal interests collaborated through the Rural Development Council to fund a restoration plan for a coastal estuary. The plan, developed by local communities, contained agreements between industrial and environmental interests.

Towards the end of 1991 President Bush announced that the State Rural Development Council initiative would be extended. By April 1993 some 47 states had expressed a desire to participate and Memoranda of Understanding, which represent a commitment on the part of both federal and state governments to establish an intergovernmental partnership for rural development, had been signed by the Secretary of Agriculture with the governors of 36 states. This increased to 39 in August 1994 with a target for something like 53 Councils in participating states and territories over the following 12 months. From the limited experience to date of the operation of State Rural Development Councils, it would seem that the partnership process has the potential to fundamentally change the way that government at all levels does business. There is much optimism that the collaboration-focused work of the Councils will show that government can be effective and responsive to the needs of those it seeks to serve; that consistent with the reinventing government agenda it can be entrepreneurial and results oriented; and that it can be caring and empowering instead of dictatorial and self-serving. This popular consensus for new governance can, perhaps, be no better illustrated than by the mission statement of the New Mexico Rural Development Response Council which was formally established in July 1992 as a partnership of federal, state, tribal and local governments, the private sector and public/private non-profit organizations.

> The New Mexico Rural Development Response Council believes that our future depends on the vitality of our small communities. We are concerned about the preservation and enhancement of the state's rural quality of life, scenic beauty, diverse cultural heritage, and economic opportunities. Our mission is to assist rural communities throughout New Mexico in implementing their own **locally determined** development objectives – objectives that are consistent with local values. Our job is to build working relationships among public, private and tribal groups and to develop "resource networks" that address rural concerns. We strive to eliminate barriers that may hinder effective rural development efforts. Our objective is to improve the flexibility and responsiveness of government programs and maximize the use of resources, thus encouraging innovative solutions to problems in small communities. We can provide the framework for public and private sectors to move beyond piece-meal delivery of services, towards a more comprehensive and strategic approach to addressing rural needs.

Pulling it all together: National Rural Development Partnership

What started out in 1990 as a Presidential Initiative for Rural America, changed title in 1992 to the National Initiative on Rural America and has, since 1993, become the

National Rural Development Partnership (NRDP). Regarding the latter change the consensus among members was that this new name better communicated the missions, principles and roles of the Washington-based organizations and of the entire national effort in rural development.

Expressed briefly, the goal of the NRDP is to promote public/private collaborative partnerships within an entrepreneurial environment for identifying and implementing innovative approaches to the social and economic problems of rural areas. These collaborative arrangements extend across federal, state, local and tribal governments, private profit and non-profit organizations, and community-based organizations within each state. Consistent with the theme of new governance an important objective is to address intergovernmental and interagency impediments, bureaucratic red tape, turf issues, language problems and other barriers that hinder effective rural development efforts. The Partnership comprises five key elements: the National Rural Development Council, the National Partnership Office, the National Rural Development Council Steering Committee, State Rural Development Councils and the National Rural Economic Development Institute. Each may be considered briefly.

The National Rural Development Council (NRDC)

This was formerly known as the Monday Management Group (MMG) and comprised staff level senior program managers operating under the authority of a Cabinet level interdepartmental decision-making body, the Policy Coordinating Group's Working Group on Rural Development. The MMG acquired its title for no less a reason than the fact that its meetings were usually convened on a Monday! By April 1992 the MMG membership represented some 31 departmental agencies and two White House bodies. It has operated primarily through 12 project Task Forces running the gamut from preparing public information materials in support of the Presidential Initiative, defining the role and organizational structure of State Rural Development Councils, moving the pilot

Council phase towards national implementation, to developing an annual report to Congress.

The sheer scale of the rural development challenge is demonstrated by the expansion of the MMG through to NRDC; in the autumn of 1993 it comprised 70 members from a range of federal agencies, the National Governors' Association and several public interest groups (Table 7). Under the terms of reference of the NRDP, the NRDC sees itself as a responsive initiator for the promotion of change, reduction of barriers and sharing of information. Its activities are not seen as being top-down and directive, but rather collaborative, multilevel and inclusive. Ennis and Hage (1993) have expressed this new approach quite succinctly:

> The [NRDC] as responsive initiator takes the ideas and/or problems brought to it and mixes them with individual and collective knowledge and experience; establishes and nurtures the dialog on issues, problems, etc; feeds back information on known alternatives to the SRDCs; explores and develops possible alternatives that can be shared with SRDCs and others; and develops initiatives where appropriate. While we leave our "agency hats" at the door as far as participating solely for the benefit of our organization's interest, we bring to the group our organization's experience and knowledge of what has worked successfully. This offers the opportunity to make the whole greater than the sum of its parts. (p. 13)

The National Partnership Office (NPO)

This comprises a small cadre of Washington-based staff whose mission is to "focus, support and energize collaborative partnerships in support of the NRDP". It is very much a think tank operation searching for new ways of approaching governance, disseminating ideas and helping to build the capacity of the national partnership family through a focus on operational and educational needs.

National Rural Development Council Steering Committee

This represents the NRDC as a full partner with the NPO in managing the NRDP and acts as a secretariat for the NRDC. It comprises five members drawn from the NRDC.

Table 7 National participants in the National Rural Development
Partnership, 1993

Federal government participants	Appalachian Regional Commission
	Congressional Relations
	General Accounting Office
	National Endowment for the Arts Outreach Office
	Office of Management and Budget
	Tennessee Valley Authority
	Community Resource Development
	US Department of Agriculture
	Agricultural Marketing Service
	Cooperative State Research Service
	Economic Research Service
	Extension Service
	Farmers Home Administration
	Forest Service
	National Agricultural Library
	Rural Development Administration
	Rural Electrification Administration
	Soil Conservation Service
	US Department of Commerce
	Economic Development Administration
	Minority Business Development
	Office of Legislative and Intergovernmental Affairs
	US Travel and Tourism Administration
	US Department of Defense
	Office of Economic Adjustment
	US Army Corps of Engineers
	US Department of Education
	Office of Vocational Education
	US Department of Health and Human Services
	Office of the Secretary/Intergovernmental Affairs
	Office of Rural Health Policy
	US Department of Housing and Urban Development
	Office of Block Grant Assistance
	US Department of the Interior
	Office of Program Analysis
	Bureau of Indian Affairs
	US Department of Labor
	Employment and Training Administration
	US Department of Transportation
	Office of the Secretary
	Federal Highway Administration
	US Department of the Treasury
	Office of Economic Policy
	Financial Management Services
	US Department of Veterans Affairs
	Intergovernmental Affairs
	US Environmental Protection Agency
	Water Policy Office
	Office of Administrator/State and Local Relations
	US Small Business Administration
	Office of Business Development
	Office of Rural Affairs
	Office of Advocacy
	Development Company Branch
State and local government participants	National Association of Counties
	National Association of Development Organizations
	National Association of Regional Councils
	National Association of Towns and Townships
	National Governors' Association
	National League of Cities
Private sector participants	American Bankers Association
	Independent Bankers Association of America
	Rural Coalition

Source: Shaffer (1994).

State Rural Development Councils (SRDCs)

As discussed in the previous section of this chapter, these are collaborative ventures which seek to develop strategic responses to a state's rural needs; they do not function as a new service delivery mechanism nor as a channel for federal funds, but seek to build inter- and intragovernmental relationships, make better use of existing resources, intervene in a problem-solving role and address regulatory and administrative impediments.

National Rural Economic Development Institute

The Institute, based at Madison, Wisconsin, works closely with the NPO staff by providing educational support, organizational development assistance and strategic planning guidance to SRDCs, particularly during their formation period. Much of the work is carried out within the conceptual framework of new governance, discussed earlier in this chapter. It seeks to build support among participants for the idea of doing the business of government differently and within each Council much emphasis is placed on the creation of a learning through action environment. This is especially important over the initial 12 to 18 months as members seek to establish a sense of unity from a background of diversity. Facilitators from the Institute help to build the agendas for preliminary meetings, promote the sharing of experiences and information and inspire team commitment. As noted by Shaffer (1994) the Institute represents an external intervention to help each State Rural Development Council make progress on its agenda, not to determine the content or goals of that agenda.

The operation of the National Rural Development Partnership allows a number of observations to be made on the relationship between rural development and institutional capacity. On the positive side, there is firstly an apparent broadening of concern beyond the traditional remit of the USDA consistent with the wide ranging nature of the rural development challenge. The perceived power of the USDA in dominating the work of the Partnership has had to be carefully dealt with. Thus, for example, it was widely believed at one stage that the creation of the

SRDCs was but part of an empire building strategy by the Rural Development Administration. However, each state representative from that latter agency is only one voice at any SRDC forum, notwithstanding the almost similar job descriptions of the State Rural Development Administration Coordinator and the Executive Director of each State Rural Development Council. Moreover, within the NRDC it has been important to reduce the visibility of the USDA and elevate the impact of other participants, thus widening the scope of the effort and building internal support from non-USDA agencies for the concept of collaboration. Even the location of the National Partnership Office in different premises from the USDA is strongly symbolic of this position.

A second positive aspect of the current initiative as a whole is the absence of a hierarchical blueprint for the design and operation of the Partnership. There are goals related to improved intergovernmental and public–private–community working practices but here the emphasis is on the accompanying processes rather than on the structures in themselves. Key qualities being pursued comprise: (i) flexibility, as evidenced by the absence of a "one size fits all" perspective; thus rural development approaches at state level are encouraged to respond to local circumstances and not to Washington-oriented controls; (ii) diversity, as facilitated by the removal of impediments to access and the bringing to the table of as many interest groups and perspectives as possible to share their experience of problems and possible solutions; this participation process, which values inclusion more than equality, does not seek to alter power relationships; (iii) collaboration, as marked by the promotion of an attitude favorable to collective working with a sense of oneness and an appreciation of shared gains or losses as decisions are made and work completed.

A third dimension to the Partnership is its consistency with the longstanding federal preference for not depending totally on fund-driven, product-related programs for rural development action. The Partnership is not about a new source of moneys and indeed the overall costs of the initiative, borne by some 18 departments, are remarkably low. In 1994 its budget stood at around $4 million and if fully funded, consistent with maximum operational targets, it would possibly require little more than double this amount.

There is, however, a fundamental limitation to the over-all effort. As discussed earlier in this chapter, the Presidential Initiative on Rural America called for the establishment of the Economic Policy Council Working Group on Rural Development as a permanent Cabinet level policy body. Initially, the working group, chaired by the Secretary of Agriculture, did meet on a regular basis and was responsible for the establishment of the Monday Management Group (now the National Rural Development Council) as its action arm. Towards the end of the Bush Administration period the Working Group became somewhat uninterested in its brief, it was not reconstituted by the Clinton Administration and by sum-mer 1994 had not met for about two years. While the NRDC continues to meet regularly at full and subcommit-tee levels, it can do no more than foster discussions among its membership; it is impotent because it has no authority to make program decisions. This serious administrative shortfall has been investigated by the General Accounting Office. In a report (General Accounting Office, 1994) to congressional requesters, the following observation is made:

> ... without the involvement of the Working Group or another high level executive committee, it is difficult to make interdepart-mental policy decisions at the federal level on how to improve or change programs to better assist rural America. For example, one of the principal concerns of local and regional officials we spoke with was that the large number of narrowly focused programs in multiple federal agencies made participation difficult and costly. While the NRDC has sought to stimulate better coordination among these programs, it has not been successful in fostering the development of more fundamental solutions to the problems, such as the problem of inconsistent, unclear and costly program rules and regulations. Similarly, the NRDC has asked the SRDCs to identify potential impediments to rural development activities and submit those they cannot resolve to the NRDC. The SRDCs have done so, but the NRDC has not had the authority to take action, and has done little to evaluate or otherwise address their concerns. According to many NRDC members, these and other problems have not been addressed because the NRDC has not had the support of high-level policy makers that it needs in order to have leverage with executive agencies. (p. 36)

In Chapter 1 consideration was given to the inefficiency problems associated with federal assistance for rural areas. When these are added to the absence of decision-taking muscle suffered by the NRDC, it is interesting to note the suggestion by the General Accounting Office to Congress regarding the adoption of a two part strategy to improve the federal approach to rural development. The first step would involve making short-term changes in the way that federal aid is delivered to rural areas. The second step would be to develop and implement a more comprehensive and cohesive national strategy for rural America that would over the longer term substantially alter the current fragmented approach. In order to drive forward these proposals, Congress is invited by the General Accounting Office to consider the establishment of a permanent inter-agency executive committee (similar to the Economic Policy Council Working Group on Rural Development) "to oversee and provide better delivery mechanisms for federal programs and services to rural communities". It is suggested that the committee would be jointly chaired by officials from the USDA (the traditional focal point of federal rural development activities) and from the Office of Management and Budget (the agency with overall fiscal authority for federal programs affecting rural development). The support role of the NRDC for this executive committee is endorsed. The General Accounting Office defends its advocacy by acknowledging that similar calls made in the past for more multiagency, cross-departmental collaboration have suffered from a lack of follow through by federal government. It suggests that the inclusion of an official from the Office of Management and Budget as the co-chair of a new interagency committee and the involvement of Congress in direct oversight of this committee may provide the impetus finally to initiate action.

Perhaps it is not surprising that the report has been warmly endorsed by the NRDC. The USDA is less full in its praise, but acknowledges that the General Accounting Office has helped to lay the foundation for formulating new policies for rural America. The USDA in its response has called for a fresh linkage between responsibility and authority by the creation of a new Department of Rural Development. This would be headed at Secretary level and be given a remit to consolidate the relevant rural development functions spread throughout currently a large number of federal departments and agencies. The creation of strong rural development committees within the House and Senate of Congress is also urged by the USDA, possibly with the agriculture committees having oversight of all rural development matters.

Bureaucratic and political turf protection will inevitably intervene in any mediation process designed to bring about change. The probable overstating of USDA ambitions *vis-à-vis* the more pragmatic approach of the General Accounting Office provides, at the very least, some parameters for debate. When these matters are considered alongside the prospective entry of the White House into the rural development arena by way of President Clinton leading a first ever national rural conference billed for December 1994, and a forthcoming Farm Bill in 1995, then it is easy to conjecture a neat return to the almost similar events of 1990. Notwithstanding the fact that the policy process has moved some distance during the interim, this totality of involvement, urgency and uncertainty will influence greatly whether and how rural development is itself reinvented.

Conclusion

This chapter has reviewed the recent evolution of searches for a more complete rural development policy in the United States. The progression of the debate can be firmly rooted in the broader concerns of new governance which have sought to reshape the prevailing orthodoxies of institutional behavior, responsibility and performance. Collaboration has emerged as a central theme for contemporary public policy in this sphere, both as to where structures and missions are currently positioned, and also as to future directions. Without doubt rural development in America is at a crossroads. Policy commitment and delivery have not yet reached the high point of achievement which expectation and promise would seem to promote. If collaboration is to become a guiding paradigm for change, wider and stronger support is required.

Collaboration is not, however, an end in itself. As a feature of government action it has to be designed to insure that disadvantaged rural communities can prosper. This perspective leads on to the important contribution made by community development as part of the economic development process. Indeed, it is accepted that the former must precede and then overlap with the latter. Infrastructure investment, so much a characteristic of rural development program assistance, is an insufficient condition. Local empowerment related to leadership enhancement and the creation of locally controlled arrangements for decision making and investment is crucial. Accordingly, it is appropriate that the next three chapters in this book should examine the contribution of community capacity building and collaboration as complementary components of the quest for greater institutional responsiveness in the revitalizing of rural America.

The Rural America
Program

3

Background to the initiative

The Rural America Program dates from the mid-1980s and comprises a set of 28 projects (Figure 1) funded, in part, by the W K Kellogg Foundation. This Foundation was established in 1930 and since its inception has expended more than $2.1 billion on assisting the meeting of societal goals within and beyond the United States (Annual Report, 1993). Attention has traditionally centered on individual and group initiatives. However, consistent with a wider interpretation of rural development and the need to support measures which could not only cut across issues and sectors but also strengthen institutional and organizational capacities to address rural needs, the Kellogg Foundation approved financial support for an innovative suite of projects in 1986. Originally 21 projects were funded up to 1989 with a total of some $14.5 million from Kellogg. A further seven projects were added thus allowing the Rural America Program to run through to the early 1990s.

The project portfolio was designed around four broad themes: leadership development, training of local government officials, coordinated delivery of human services and policy development for rural revitalization. Some

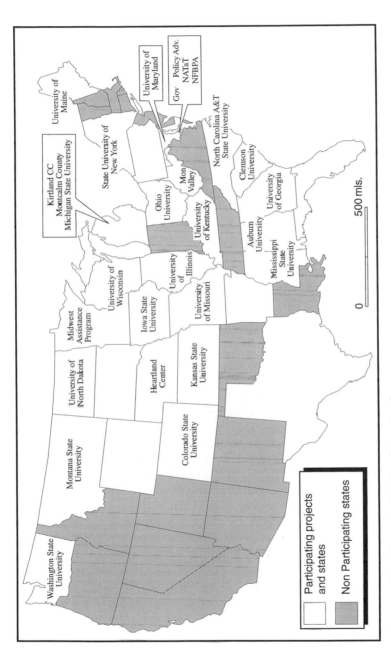

Figure 1 Participants in the Rural America Program

projects addressed more than one of these themes. Thus 18 leadership development projects were concerned with responding to community needs by bringing new people into leadership roles, by broadening the base of civic participation and by enhancing the capacity of local residents to serve their communities. Nine projects placed emphasis on improving the effectiveness and responsiveness of local government by training officers in information resources, technological applications, networking and peer support. Four projects were multidimensional in character and were aimed at improving the delivery of human services and developing innovative responses to important local concerns; community needs assessment and planning work were significant here. Finally, one project dealt solely with policy development. This involved the formation of state task groups to utilize the best available research, information and expertise for the shaping of policies which could respond more adequately to rural needs. Most of the projects drew upon university faculty or university cooperative extension support. The degree of partnership with other institutions or agencies varied between coordination, cooperation and collaboration, but the majority of projects did report a large number of external contacts; over 500 units were involved in service delivery. Furthermore, some 75 percent of the projects employed members of the target audiences in the decision-making process. This contribution to project administration included representation on policy boards, advisory boards and planning committees.

A synopsis of each project is included as Appendix 1. The purpose of this chapter is to present the findings which have emerged from a four year evaluation of the Rural America Program, completed in 1994.[1] A review of the aims and methodology of this research is presented first. This is followed by discussion of project achievements under the headings of leadership development, community change, institutional capacity and public policy. Finally, the results of a mini study on collaboration within four projects are set out. A more detailed account of one of these, the Colorado Rural Revitalization Project, is the subject of Chapter 4.

The Rural America Cluster Evaluation Project

In the late 1980s the Kellogg Foundation set about revising its program evaluation procedures across all its operations.

A new emphasis was placed on enhancing the specificity of requirements for internal project level evaluation and on creating a cluster approach which grouped sets of projects with similar strategies or target populations. The Rural America Program fitted well with this direction as illustrated by comments from the Foundation program director:

> this diverse group of grantees, doing different things in different settings yet directed at achieving similar long term goals – improving the quality of life for citizens in rural areas . . . forms the cluster of projects. (cited in Andrews et al, 1994)

This cluster-wide evaluation process was designed to increase project networking and to identify lessons learnt that crossed individual project boundaries. It was anticipated that Foundation programs would be strengthened through the collection of information about the context, implementation and outcomes of the cluster elements.

Accordingly, the Rural America Cluster Evaluation Project (RACEP) was launched in 1990 with a mission to summarize information on the 28 projects partially funded by the Kellogg Foundation. Academic staff from Michigan State University with skills in rural and community development, adult education and program evaluation acted as the core research team. They were assisted by two advisory committees, one internal to Michigan State University and the other external, for conceptual and operational guidance and support. The design and execution of the work schedule was steered by three overall objectives:

1. To describe the scope and diversity of project contexts and implementation approaches.
2. To estimate the collective impacts of the projects.
3. To investigate issues and hypotheses of interest to rural development.

The study methods included site visits, networking meetings with project staff, and the gathering of data from each project archive, for example, annual reports, training curricula and activity schedules. A set of specific investigations was also undertaken during 1993 and 1994. Three mini studies explicitly focused on analysis of the common outcomes of projects and their potential impact on individuals, communities and institutions. In these, the experiences of leadership development training, the training of local government officials and community action were examined. A second suite of three mini studies focused on broader developmental issues with themes related to collaboration, institutional change and sustainability of effort, and project sensitivity to diverse target populations.

The findings from RACEP provide significant insights into what works well and is valued within the sphere of rural development. Notwithstanding differences in project expectations, in support from sponsoring institutions, in training content and length and in target population size, the cluster evaluation approach offers a basis for shared learning and mutual support. The remainder of this chapter sets out some key results from this research.

Leadership development

As noted above, 18 of the 28 projects in the cluster identified leadership development as a major goal. While training styles, curricula and the recruitment of participants did vary, significant positive outcomes were achieved. Leadership capacity was increased across the board, connectedness to others was enhanced and awareness of the political and economic forces affecting communities was raised.

The enthusiasm for leadership development is captured well in anecdotal evidence from a former project director. At the outset of the project, some four years previously, there was a measure of indifference to this capacity building work by participants. Comments such as: "Do we have to attend the training sessions?" and "Look we are ranchers and farmers, we have real work to do and we can't be wasting our time on silly meetings", were not uncommon. However, these same people were asking for additional training material after the first year.

The cluster evaluation research confirms that the Rural America Program did impact on individuals, professionals and elected officials working in rural community development and economic revitalization. A wide range of new information was gained on technical matters, principles of governance and public policy, individual and community change, team member differences, how to address issues and the value of networking. Again, testimonies gathered by the research staff confirm the contribution made by this collective effort. In regard to the potential for community improvement an interviewee expressed the following opinion:

> This program has really given the **hope** for the changes that will make our community a better place in years to come: for I have not only been equipped with skills, but also exposed to the many resources available in effecting that change.

A related observation drawn from a review of individual project reports is the existence of an attitude shift among participants. This adjustment is from a view "Why don't they do something for our community?" to one which is more self-assertive: "Change cannot come from outsiders: it has to start in my living room". It is this transformation of dependency relationships which emerges as one of the most striking benefits of the capacity building work related to leadership development. The research evidence points to the following conclusions:

1. The training programs were valued.
2. A high level of application of ideas and information occurred as a result of training.
3. Leadership capacities were improved.
4. Participants did impact on organizations, communities and local governance.
5. Much of this enhanced capacity has endured and continues to benefit the quality of life in rural America.

Community change

The projects associated with the Kellogg Foundation Program involved a total of 727 rural communities. A common mission was to draw in community members to stimulate collective action. The cluster evaluation research identified a number of ways in which community change was promoted.

First, each project strengthened community involvement and commitment. A survey by the cluster evaluation team confirmed that more than 73 percent of all participants were associated with community or organizational change. For the most part this participation related to training activities, which had the effect of people not only coming together to learn but also becoming more aware of community needs. This, in turn, prompted deeper interest in contributing to practical opportunities for community betterment. When the evaluation team questioned a sample group about the scale of the impact that this involvement had in promoting community change, the average response rating was 6 on a 10 point scale; when asked to comment on the sustainability of this involvement, scores averaged 7.24 on a 10 point scale. Thus it would appear that the participants believed that the Rural America projects made a significant contribution to the initiation and sustainability of local improvement efforts.

Second, the participating communities were able to identify many practical achievements which were a direct result of project activities. The list is long and includes new businesses, tourism centers, industrial parks, resource directories, bike paths and recreation trails, town beautification and environmental conservation. The Rural America Program, in short, strengthened a range of economic development, service and educational efforts. While this external perception of real accomplishment is important, those who were very close to the work of individual projects have emphasized that these tangible outcomes must be regarded as only one aspect of a much greater impact; an exposure to development processes was complementary to product success.

Third, community representatives placed much weight on the value of individual networking, and indeed for many participants in the program as a whole these networking opportunities represent the most significant outcome. Illustrations were cited during the evaluation research about how town folk began to communicate with country folk and about how people from diverse backgrounds began to build relationships of trust based on a shared vision. In some instances the quality of this interaction was sufficient to begin changing the social fabric of entire communities. People began to trust each other and to tolerate differences that had previously divided them. A comment in one project report captures this spirit: "We came as strangers and left as family."

Fourth, the research team found that the projects helped to instill a new sense of pride and identity in rural communities. This confidence helped people to identify more with their local areas and thus become active community supporters.

Fifth, the communities confirmed that their involvement in the Rural America Program introduced them to a plethora of new resource opportunities. Community leaders were able to tap into assistance offered by universities and government bodies and as a result were able to recruit new enterprises, secure public and private grants for improvement schemes, and participate in national and state development initiatives.

Finally, the communities indicated that the combination of training and project experience allowed more effective systems for work completion to be established. These included the acquisition of time management skills and information technology proficiency for dealing with the complex and multidimensional issues facing small community, township or county government.

Institutional capacity

A third aspect of the Rural America Program concerns the strengthening of institutional capacity for sustainable development. Most of the projects had expectations of creating changes in the host institutions that would last beyond the initial funding cycle. For many there was a hope of continuing financial support and for some this expectation was met. Notwithstanding this variation a number of significant institutional changes did come about.

In the first instance the expertise, credibility and visibility of the host institutions were strengthened. The Midwest Assistance Program, for example, added solid waste to its service assistance portfolio, and the National Association of Towns and Townships offered help to small communities dealing with changes in local government. Many projects nudged their sponsoring institutions to become more committed to working on rural community issues. Thus, at present, a large number of the land-grant universities, which had supported project activities, are now continuing with this work. A number of institutions changed their arrangements for service delivery as a result of their involvement in the Kellogg Program. Three university centers were established comprising a Local Government Center at Montana State University, a Center for Rural Assistance at Colorado State University and a Rural Innovation Institute at the University of Missouri.

Universities in Ohio, Washington and Missouri developed delivery systems based on satellite tele-conferencing. Finally, the involvement of faculty staff and volunteers in community-led rural development was expanded. In Georgia, for example, faculty and staff from seven administrative units assisted 12 rural counties in their revitalization efforts while Kansas State University introduced students to rural communities through their community service program. Overall, project managers reported to the research team that approximately one-quarter of 2500 resource personnel utilized in the Rural America Program were new to rural community development.

In terms of enhanced institutional capacity it was also the case that project work facilitated the creation of new networks and associations. In total, more than 500 partnership relationships were developed, including a consortium of 100 organizations in the Mon Valley which helped rural communities bring forward new leaders and devise strategies for dealing with economic decline. In Washington DC three professional associations are working together as a result of a project-sponsored work effort. In Colorado, the two universities and the State Department of Local Affairs agreed to form a partnership, which, as discussed in Chapter 4, has enjoyed some continuance following completion of that project. In short, many of the institutional participants in the program were able to foster innovative working relationships. Universities began to work differently with other universities and with units of government, while within universities new work practices were forged with cooperative extension departments.

Finally, many institutions produced a wide range of educational and training materials to assist rural development efforts. Projects based in Alabama, Colorado, Illinois, Iowa, Kentucky, Maryland, Missouri, Montana, the Mon Valley, North and South Carolina, the Dakotas, Ohio, New York and Wisconsin devised, tested and refined support resources which are still in use and distributed throughout the United States. The quality of this material and the contribution to helping rural communities prepare for economic development are exemplified by the Rural Partners Project based at the University of Illinois which received the Innovative Program Award from the Community Development Society at its 1992 international meeting. A full listing of resource materials arising from the Rural America Program is included as Appendix 2 in this book.

Public policy

While only one of the cluster projects dealt specifically with public policy, it is the case that collectively the 28 projects have had an impact on national and state policy debates. In Iowa, when the Tomorrow's Leaders Today Project commenced, the state was not working actively with failing rural communities; but when this project demonstrated how small communities could work regionally on an economic development plan, yet protect their individual identity and lifestyle, the state reversed its policy position and is now fully supporting this effort. In North Dakota, the Midwest Assistance Project is credited with providing an awareness campaign which quickened the passage of a Bill designed to support a regional plan for solid waste management. The project in Kentucky sponsored a measure called Public Talk which provided an arena for citizens to discuss controversial issues facing their communities. In Washington, the project trained representatives of public and private organizations in the process of non-confrontational conflict resolution. This training was reported to the research team as having a very positive impact on policy discussions and decisions. But, perhaps, one of the most significant outcomes from the Rural America Program is the entry into local and state politics by many citizens for whom the initial stimulus can be traced back to a community development or training related experience. Their contribution, not documented in individual project evaluation reports, may prove to be a major factor in devising improved policies for the revitalization of rural America.

Collaboration

Collaboration, whereby people and agencies made an effort to cross their institutional boundaries, was a significant feature of many of the projects associated with the Rural America Program. As noted in Chapter 1, collaboration can provide the potential for achieving greater effectiveness and efficiency. Nevertheless, important empirical questions do arise as to how well collaboration is performing, what constraints are in evidence and how best collaborative ventures might be structured in the future. The cluster evaluation research provided an opportunity to revisit a sample of four of the rural community projects by way of a mini study, in order to examine issues of collaboration breadth and intensity among the project's major stakeholders. Two of the projects (Colorado and Georgia) directly identified collaboration as a goal in their initial proposals for funding. In the other two projects (Illinois and Mon Valley) there appears to be significant evidence of collaboration having taken place on the basis of content in interim and final reports; collaboration is identified in these as a secondary project goal. This section of the chapter reports the findings from this additional evaluation research.

The methodology adopted for the mini study comprised semi-structured interviews with some 52 individuals at the four project sites. Informal discussions were convened with a further seven project representatives. The main aims guiding the qualitative investigation included: (i) to identify evidence of ongoing communication, cooperation and collaboration; (ii) to assess learning by project stakeholders; (iii) to determine if communities have continued to move forward with rural development activities; and (iv) to explore the extent to which collaboration is more likely to occur in projects where it is expressed as a start-up goal as opposed to other projects where it is not mandated. Discussion of the research findings can follow this sequence of aims.

Ongoing communication, cooperation and collaboration

Almost unanimously, individuals identified both tangible and intangible examples of collaboration. Evidence of the former was cited as comprising the preparation of strategic plans, multi-institutional curriculum development, joint community needs assessment, a watershed plan and some enterprise creativity. With regard to the more intangible aspects of collaboration, interviewees mentioned the formation of coalitions among groups which previously did not work together, the involvement of new people in community development activities, conversations transcending the traditional academic/practitioner dichotomy, public/private sector mergers, and a spirit of "region" which moved people beyond prior held notions of single, autonomous communities. A few of the more dramatic statements to surface were the following:

Individuals are really the collaborators, not the institutions. As a result of this project, an overall mission of a greater region has occurred. We had virtually no relationship with these agencies prior to the project.

It's obvious to me that collaboration takes a lot of time.

I can see now that people are starting to look at a big regional basis – rather than every community looking out for itself.

The majority of respondents indicated that their organizations would not have been able to accomplish what they had without collaboration. Several noted that the regional perspective on issues was a direct result of collaboration. In some cases partners counteracted conflict by bringing a neutral or detached point of view to community challenges. Others were more tentative, suggesting that what was to be accomplished was not clarified at the outset of their projects. A number said that there would have been accomplishments without collaboration but they would have been quite different and perhaps not as successful:

The project was defined as a collaborative effort, so it took on the shape that it did. The direction and the dogma with a single unit would have been more rigid. In collaboration we have decentralized the decision-making process. It's been almost a democratic effort.

We would not be as involved with the partners in two other states as we now are if we had not had this project funded and developed. We would have lost the regionalism of it.

A few individuals seemed to reach the conclusion that in some circumstances collaboration makes sense; in others it does not. This conclusion was articulated in a University of Georgia report regarding collaboration among its own units:

The general missions of the units are traditionally unique and distinct, and their union in this project may reflect both the positive and negative aspects of any **arranged marriage**.

Similarly, one individual from Colorado observed:

We must be careful what we pick to collaborate on – the outcome must be worth the effort. We should not collaborate on everything because of the time it takes.

A majority of respondents said that prior involvement with many of the partners in this project did help to facilitate collaboration, although the prior relationships were often quite different in design and implementation. Many defined the new partnerships as more fully developed and expansive in scope. Some also noted elements of risk in collaboration: "Collaboration is a risky thing – because you have to be prepared to lose." Some respondents commented that they knew their partners prior to the project, but they had not actually worked with them. People moved from being mere acquaintances to being professional colleagues. Most reported that they seldom or never worked with the same clientele as their partners prior to their projects, although there were a few indications of some prior competitive relationships. Interestingly, most felt that the type of clientele they typically served did facilitate collaboration. When asked if they thought that they had worked with *appropriate partners* during the projects, most said yes. One observed that some partners wanted to work with a particular segment of the rural constituency, but they were encouraged to go back and work with people who are not traditionally represented. "Our office and staff forced the issue of inclusiveness." Probing on this question identified that groups and areas under-represented in some of the projects were youth, the elderly, political officials, small communities, remote rural areas, community colleges, higher education administrators, the media and the disenfranchised.

Learning by project stakeholders

Most of the interviewees commented that the project goals had either stayed the same or changed only slightly from the beginning to the end of these projects. Three individuals indicated that they thought the goals had changed dramatically from the beginning. In several instances there were reports of people not realizing initially how "evolving" and "experimental" these projects were. One very lively description of this early misunderstanding is reported below:

> I thought at first that Kellogg had singled us out at the beginning – that we were fortunate and lucky. This was my early feeling. Then at the seminar it became clear that the world was a lot bigger, and I'd been living in an egg. It was suggested that this was a pilot and we were guinea pigs. Then I said this wasn't what I

thought. Gee I was naive. My first reaction was anger – our advantage is lost. I looked at it as our advantage against the world. But now I conclude that our opportunity is that we will know it first. There are some attitudinal changes that have occurred. Some think the goals didn't change. This is not a new concept. We are going along where they want us to be. It took some a while to understand what the program was really about.

Several who said that the goals had changed slightly mentioned only modest changes in emphasis. In a few cases, people suggested that their projects became less academic and more practitioner oriented as they evolved. One interviewee observed:

I'm not sure I know what they [the goals] were when we started. There was initially a divergence of opinion of what the principal goal or mission was. Was it leadership or economic development? That conflict has remained from the beginning – and I think it is good that it has. We have consequently entertained both economic development and leadership development. The tension has been productive. You talk about building a bicycle, but eventually you've got to build the bicycle.

Probably the most pertinent questions in the survey were those that asked individuals to identify the most rewarding and frustrating aspects of collaboration, and if they had suggestions to offer future project directors. A fairly typical response was:

A better understanding of the community, of the different resources, groups, political groups, and every aspect of the community were brought together to reach a common goal. We learned more about the availability of services, we discovered things about our community that we did not know. We developed a familiarity with the leaders within the community on a more professional level. Now we have a greater appreciation of what each other does in our jobs. We found resources in our community that we were unaware of before this collaboration.

People in the private sector talked about working for the first time with people in the public sector and vice versa. They were now much more tied to the rural communities; they were in the field more and their roles had shifted. People in the communities talked about the pleasures of finding universities and agency representatives taking an interest in them, and helping them with special challenges. People were proud, for example, to see 10 colleges working together, racial boundaries transcended, and people in a "two bank" town finding ways to unite through these projects. Some reported it rewarding to get out of what they typically did day to day and work on something very different. Some of the rewards were in teaching others and some in learning from others.

There was no difficulty identifying frustrations, although some suggested that they were inevitable in projects such as these. Specifically on the concept of collaboration, one person said that there was never a shared definition which was agreed upon from top to bottom in the organization. Institutional differences, turf battles in small communities, political agendas, negative attitudes and nay sayers colored and conditioned by prior negative experiences were frequently cited as difficulties.

Time was the most frequently expressed frustration – time to achieve commitment, to build trust, to get rolling, to maintain resources. One respondent said: "Three years isn't enough to capitalize on the bridges that were beginning to be built." Another observed that the project took time away from work when some of the training was not pertinent. Some acknowledged that simply trying to build collaboration was frustrating, especially for task-oriented people. It takes years; budgets get cut; people move. Others felt that they had been overambitious. In one project it was suggested that 12 counties were too many in the early stages; 6 would have been better after materials were more fully developed; trying to get all these counties rolling and materials developed simultaneously was overwhelming. Several interviewees noted that they had tried to do too much – tried to do everything.

Another often repeated frustration related to a classic tension between academics and practitioners. This frustration surfaced throughout the interviews in different forms:

> There has been a bitterness towards the academic end in the developing of the curriculum. More like running a graduate course as opposed to an adult business and training course. They have a tendency to lecture too much and to hear themselves talking.

> It is driven by a University paradigm of education that learning occurs over a time. It does not deal with the real world of learning. We could get this course down to a weekend intensive seminar. We can have projects that are more realistic to build leaders.

> We were challenged to meet the expectations as though we were academics. We had to let them know we could not go on this way.

> Farmers have two month busy seasons in spring and fall. Things

tend to be scheduled for University people. Farmers' jobs are weather related. There was a lack of consideration for the different calendars of farmers and academics.

Other quiet desperations involved being democratic upfront, confessing that the project was experimental and that the work was going to be extensive, consuming, and require very serious commitment. People repeatedly mentioned not having sufficient orientation or explanation of what was ahead of them. Upfront clarification was lacking. Regarding this same issue, it was noted that people at the community level do need to be immediately drawn into early planning and should not have to wait for the process to be explained in the later phases.

In all but two of the interviews there were lengthy recommendations for future project directors. Particularly in the two projects where a greater overall sense of frustration with collaboration had been felt, there were comments about identifying people with the right mindset for collaboration and about the project director having more authority in the project generally. One observation that rang true with the overall findings was that collaboration at the institutional level is not a tension-free process:

> I don't feel we have good data on how it is done at the institutional level; new innovative ways need to be explored and shared. We need better tools for this endeavor. I think we all needed an indepth training on how to collaborate at the institutional level. Institutions don't change in 3 to 5 years. It may take a decade or more to bring about institutional change.

The extent to which communities have moved forward with rural development activities

Many specific activities were identified during the interviews. These included a community consortium for community development, Board of Community Betterment, a community fair, business retention/expansion programs, promotional video tape on one county, council of economic development, financial management training, downtown renovations, courthouse renovation, new drugstore, new hotel, leadership training, quarter horse show, riverfront design, mathematics/technology classroom, applications for grants, journal writing, multi-state tourism projects, retirement village, funding of community development personnel, conferences, and strategic plans for community and economic development.

Only one person noted that he would not continue any type of relationship with the partners after the project (but he was moving to a new position). A few thought that their relationship would be mostly communicative (providing or requesting reports and/or information about project work). Most indicated that they expected their relationships would be either cooperative (giving assistance via identification of resources for entering and working on projects, although these are not joint efforts) or collaborative (engaging in joint efforts on projects). One observed that the relationships would be collaborative if there were project maintenance activities along the way to keep them alive. The vast majority (all but three) said they would stay active in these efforts following the termination of the project. They were readily able to list specific work which they would be doing. As one interviewee put it: "I think there are irons in the fire. A group of people have come together who believe in the future. We are not finished creating."

Collaboration as a start-up goal

Only one respondent mentioned that collaboration was not a goal for a project. Many people believed, however, that the expectations regarding collaboration should have been clarified from the outset, both at the community and institutional levels. Although a slightly smaller number believed that it was mandated compared with those who perceived collaboration to be voluntary, comments did point to a measure of uncertainty around this obligatory/discretionary issue. One person, for example, stated: "It was more of a necessity. We had to collaborate in order to accomplish. We had no choice. We were surprisingly successful at collaboration." Another very provocative response was: "You should learn to collaborate rather than being mandated to collaborate."

The sensitivity of the collaboration agenda was again underlined by a spread of views on how staff and major stakeholders in the projects were believed to have accepted this goal. Comments varied from expressions of willing delight to confirmation of resistance by some extension service staff. But almost everyone agreed that collaboration was a reasonable expectation for their projects. In practice these had been remarkably effective in providing opportunities and situations which encouraged interactions between partners. The comments of one interviewee are especially pertinent here:

> Whether or not people take advantage of the opportunities – I'm not sure. There are people at the various sites who talk to each other regularly. They meet outside the normal academic setting. There is a little network out there. The project will pay lasting dividends. Things will happen that we never know about.

Conclusion

The cluster evaluation research related to the Rural America Program has provided firm evidence of the benefits which can arise from institutional and community linkage. Firstly, the training activities sponsored by the projects were highly valued. Leadership capacities were improved among community representatives and local government officials. Participants did make considerable impacts on organizations, communities and local governance; a high level of application of ideas and information occurred as a direct result of training. It is significant that ongoing capacities have been developed which will continue to benefit the quality of life in rural communities.

Secondly, community action activities were identified by the research as constituting important components of training. Those who had participated in an organizational or community improvement activity were more likely to perceive that their expectations were met, were more likely to continue to maintain contact with others, and were more likely to sustain their involvement in community change initiatives than peers who did not participate in such activities. These activities provided public visibility and enhanced community awareness. They offered significant product changes as well as reinforcing the process changes which can give people a deeper sense of community, commitment and ownership.

Thirdly, the Rural America Projects were aware of and sensitive to diversity issues and successfully attracted a variety of populations for participation. Indeed over half the projects adapted materials or promotion methods in order to attract this mix. Six projects had explicit goals to work with minority or limited resource audiences and almost all reported efforts aimed to achieve diversity among those involved in project activities.

Fourthly, the pursuit of collaboration was an active force in many projects and effort was expended in trying to build collaborative relationships within the host institutions and administrative bodies. Again, the research has identified some accompanying realities. It is the case that collaboration may be exaggerated, romanticized or simply confused with communication and coordination. If new collaborative partnerships are to work and endure they must have meaning and make sense to respective stakeholders. Thus conversations which span community and institutional participants require sensitivity, patience and, occasionally, translators. Stretching the boundaries of communities to encompass larger regions does not come naturally or easily. Certainly a capacity for collaboration results from an evolutionary process involving several developmental stages based on a common sense of purpose and shared expectations. Participants need, therefore, to be more realistic about the time needed and the type of investment required in order to build these collaborative relationships. The research has underlined the need for creative and inclusive leadership in bringing together process-oriented and task-oriented people in mutually beneficial enterprises.

Finally, the cluster evaluation yielded a variety of insights into the design and management of complex projects. The three year project cycle was unrealistic in many instances; project phases often took longer than expected with the result that a number of the planned development models were unable to be fully tested. These difficulties have been compounded by the accompanying limitations of project sustainability beyond an initial funding period; indeed during the late 1980s and early 1990s when these projects were operational, many universities (and their financial support bases) were being downsized. On the positive side, it is clear that the use of advisory or planning committees by the projects was of benefit to policy formation and implementation. And for the project staff, there is evidence that the time spent in networking, training and building partnerships has produced a cadre of professionals with a potential to be utilized effectively in future rural revitalization projects.

The following summary statement from the *Rural America cluster evaluation – final report* (Andrews et al, 1994) provides an appropriate conclusion to this program review:

> These projects verify that the social infrastructure of communities can be strengthened through training, technical assistance, and networking that creates capacities among citizens, local officials, and practitioners working in community and rural development. Enhanced human capacities make a difference in organizations, communities, institutions and ultimately, in rural America. Enhancing civic infrastructures creates the momentum needed for systematic change and long term sustainable development.

At this stage it is appropriate to move from an aggregate analysis of the Rural America Program to a review of a constituent element. Chapter 4 deals with the Colorado Rural Revitalization Project and considers more deeply the fusion of process and product concerns within an operational framework premissed on collaboration.

Note

1. The content of this chapter draws upon Andrews, M et al (1994) *Rural America cluster evaluation – final report*. Additional studies accompanying this report are:

    Andrews, M (1994) *Results of project managers' survey*. Michigan State University, East Lansing.

    Andrews, M, Favero, P and Brown, H (1994) *Training of local government officials: project manager, participant and collaborator follow-up surveys*. Michigan State University, East Lansing.

    Ashcraft, N (1994) *Sensitivity to diversity in the rural America projects*. Michigan State University, East Lansing.

    Dunn, L, Holt, M and Ashcraft, N (1994) *An impact evaluation of collaboration at four rural America project sites*. Michigan State University, East Lansing.

    Peak, C, Preston, J, Maes, S and Ashcraft, N (1994) *Institutionalization/sustainability of rural America projects*. Michigan State University, East Lansing.

Tanner, M C, Lambur, M, Young, D and Ashcraft, N (1994) *An impact study of leadership development projects in the rural America cluster evaluation project.* Michigan State University, East Lansing.

Wells, B, Sieverdes, C and Ashcraft, N (1994) *An impact evaluation of community action/problem solving in three rural America projects.* Michigan State University, East Lansing.

The Colorado Rural Revitalization Project

4

Introduction

The mid-1980s found Colorado's rural communities echoing many of the same problems and transitions found across much of rural America at that time. Its economy was shifting from a heavy dependence on agriculture and mining to one that was more grounded in creative business ventures. Between 1981 and 1990 farm employment declined from 44 650 jobs to 43 600 jobs, while mining employment declined from 50 000 to 26 500 jobs. During that same period total employment, in a 1990 census population of 3.3 million, increased from 1.7 million jobs to just over 2 million jobs. Some 80 percent of Colorado's population lives in the largely metropolitan front range corridor (Figure 2) along the eastern side of the Rocky Mountains stretching from Fort Collins in the north, through Denver, to Colorado Springs and Pueblo in the south. In a landscape of mountain to the west and high plains to the east lies a spread of rural communities whose population in 1990 of almost 600 000 represents only 17.5 percent of the state total. With local economies tied directly to agriculture or to the declining mining and lumber sectors, it has been inevitable that many small towns and unincorporated villages have been losing population; on the other hand some areas have been experi-

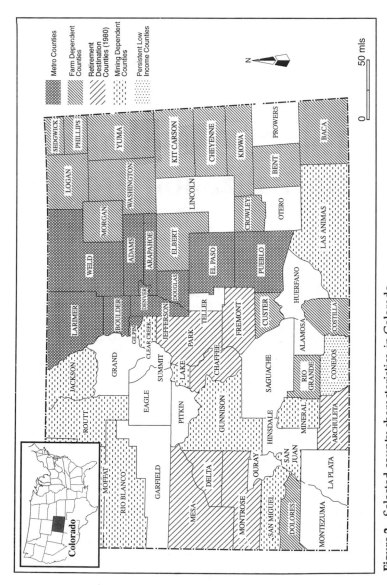

Figure 2 Selected county characteristics in Colorado

Source: Adapted from USDA (1993c) Rural conditions and trends, 4(3).

encing problems of growth management because of their popularity for retirement, recreation and tourism.

While the economic shifts which have prompted job losses and population decline have posed a major challenge to the maintenance of community vitality, a related and serious impact has been the draining of local leadership pools and the placing of ever greater civic responsibilities on fewer people. This has left many rural communities with a diminished capacity to plan and implement development strategies. One response to these problems was the initiation of a multiagency planning effort under the direction of the governor. The Rural Development Task Force reported in 1987 on opportunities to assist local economic development in rural Colorado. This essentially top-down approach to regional development was complemented by the drafting of a major proposal for community-led regeneration by a small group of academics and practitioners. An application for funding was submitted to the Kellogg Foundation and its approval facilitated the launching of the Colorado Rural Revitalization Project (CRRP) in 1988.

The discussion in this chapter seeks to review the aims and operational practices of the CRRP. Particular emphasis is placed on the administrative organization of the initiative, community selection, and development methodology involving training, technical assistance and implementation. The results of an *ex post* evaluation of the CRRP are reported and collaboration-related issues emerging from the Project are examined by way of conclusion.

In Chapter 1 it was stated that this book is aimed at making a contribution to the wider international debate on community–state relationships in rural development. The experience of the CRRP deserves close scrutiny by educationalists, policy makers and community leaders within and outside the United States. It provides a useful illustration of multidimensional collaboration in action and confirms the value of a human capital approach to rural development, not in isolation but as an accompaniment to physical investment.

The proposal

The proposal was originally submitted by the University of Colorado (UC). This first draft stressed technical assistance and was cast as a joint effort between staff and students

from the university, and personnel from the State of
Colorado Department of Local Affairs (DOLA). The
Kellogg Foundation reviewed the proposal in early 1986
and while the response was positive it was suggested that
Colorado State University (CSU), the state's land-grant
institution, should also be involved. Subsequent consultations with administrators, extension faculty and departmental staff at CSU resulted in a rewriting of the proposal
to include leadership training and the innovative collaboration of two universities and a government agency. This
training dimension was especially important and followed
on from the involvement of CSU in a recently concluded
state-wide leadership program. The emphasis in it had
been to help increase individual leadership capacity and
foster wider participation in the public policy decision-
making process. Much of the curriculum could, therefore,
be incorporated into the Kellogg proposal including segments on the strengthening of leadership roles, learning to
work together and resolving conflict. Mention was also
made of training components related to economic development, strategic planning, implementation and evaluation.
The use of problem-solving sessions was signaled in the
proposal as a way of addressing regional issues.

Accordingly, the Project goals listed in the revised joint
application documentation were as follows:

1. To focus attention on the problems of rural communi-
    ties in Colorado, and to increase the delivery of existing
    university and other state leadership training and tech-
    nical assistance resources to the people of rural
    Colorado.
2. To strengthen the role of institutions of higher educa-
    tion in supporting the economic improvement of rural
    Colorado by:
    (a) providing a programmatic framework for an effi-
         cient and effective delivery of research and educa-
         tional resources to the rural areas of Colorado;
    (b) encouraging greater involvement of university
         faculty, staff, and students in rural problem solv-
         ing;
    (c) providing leadership training to present and
         future rural residents;
    (d) integrating training with community technical
         assistance;
    (e) strengthening the support of existing rural assis-
         tance programs.

In May 1988 the Kellogg Foundation wrote to the President of Colorado State University to inform him that a commitment of $990 000 had been approved for the Project. This was designed to run through to April 1991. The drawing down of additional matching resources from each of the partners by way of in-kind contributions was an important part of the funding package. Applications from communities interested in participating in the CRRP were invited in June 1988. An experimental initiative for the demonstration of inter-institutional collaborative support to selected rural communities had commenced.

Project organization

As illustrated in Figure 3, the organization of the CRRP comprised a complex interaction of functional relationships and communication patterns among a suite of elements at different levels. In many ways this complexity was due to the participation of three sponsoring institutions and a preference among staff members for arriving at decisions through consensus. The sheer number of personnel involved generated large information flows. These factors conspired to demand an enormous time commitment. Personnel changes during the three year Project life further complicated the consensus model that participants were striving to maintain. Five key components related to Project organization can be identified: a policy board, the Project office, the core staff committee, the site managers and the community committees. Brief mention may be made of each.

The policy board comprised three members: the Provost and Vice-President for Academic Affairs at CSU; the Vice-President for Academic Affairs and Research at UC; and the Executive Director of DOLA. During the first year the board met frequently to establish guiding policies for the initiation of Project operations. In later years its role focused more on reviewing decisions on Project administration and operations in liaison with the core staff programming committee.

The Project office was located at Colorado State University and was headed by a CSU extension specialist as Project Director. As the work schedule evolved additional staff resources were employed including students, part-time computer assistants, contract help and, in the

final year, a program coordinator. The operational responsibilities of the Project office staff comprised in the main:

- program design, procedural directives, the training
  curriculum and community surveys;
- financial management and coordination;
- overall Project communication across the many institutional and community components;
- Project documentation and reporting;
- scheduling, coordinating and leading Project orientation and leadership training workshops;
- coordinating data for community selection;
- recruiting site managers;
- maintaining relationships with the Kellogg Foundation
  and establishing links with other programs or projects
  relevant to community-led rural development.

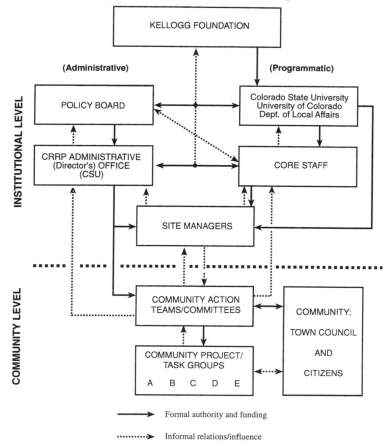

Figure 3   Organization of the Colorado Rural Revitalization Project
(From Kincaid and Knop, 1992)

The core staff committee comprised two representatives from each of the three partnering institutions. At an operational level it concerned itself with inter-institutional communication and program decision making. The monthly meeting agendas invariably contained topics related to changes in the community selection process, changes in the leadership training curriculum, and changes in site manager institutional representation.

The site manager element of the CRRP was designed to provide each participating community with an institutional level contact person. The job description involved meeting regularly with the community committee and assisting it in its revitalization activities by, for example, helping with the design and execution of a community needs assessment, an involvement in planned activities or events and facilitating the articulation of a community vision to guide future development. Some 32 volunteer site managers were recruited from the three partnering institutions during the course of the Project.

The community committees provided local level representation in the Project. Teams of volunteer citizens and local officials formed to provide the leadership and human resources needed for a variety of tasks:

1. To participate in orientation meetings and leadership training activities.
2. To identify the community's needs and desires regarding revitalization.
3. To communicate these findings back to the community as a whole.
4. To develop, communicate and obtain broad community support for the acceptance of a guiding vision for future revitalization efforts.
5. To plan and implement specific projects or events for the enhancement of the community, consistent with previously identified needs.

At an operational level each of the three institutions brought a different approach to community service with them during the course of their involvement with the CRRP. CSU, especially through cooperative extension, has served rural Colorado for many years. Through its area and county extension offices, it has delivered educational programs to farms and other business organizations, families and other social organizations, and the youth of rural Colorado. Within the CRRP, Colorado State University assumed a lead role, with assistance from the University of Colorado and the Department of Local Affairs for leadership training and skills building among community participants. The University of Colorado has, for a number of years, also provided a development service to local communities. Key activities have related to the preparation and undertaking of community needs assessments and design assistance for main street renovation, public parks and buildings. Within the CRRP the University of Colorado assumed lead responsibility for the delivery of this technical aid to the communities; Colorado State University and the Department of Local Affairs provided support. The mission of the Colorado State Department of Local Affairs involves assisting local governance to conduct its business more effectively. Small rural communities with limited economic resources are a key concern and much emphasis is placed on trying to maintain population and enhance quality of life through investment in physical and economic infrastructure. In short, the three institutional partners brought different approaches, resources and administrative structures to the CRRP. The challenge for the Project was to harness a common concern for the welfare of small rural communities and to blend the contribution of each into a collaborative partnership of service without losing the individuality of each organization. The discussion below considers how well this goal was achieved.

Community selection and working procedures

The opportunity for communities to become involved in a year-long program of learning and action drew widespread interest. This was due partly to the large grant from the Kellogg Foundation and also to the publicity generated by each of the institutions associated with the CRRP. An initial challenge was, therefore, the formulation of selection criteria to exclude those communities that did not really require help or would not be able to ready themselves to respond to the Project's rigorous demands. Recruitment for Year 1 of the CRRP was based on the following guidelines:

- that communities had a population size under 5000;
- that they demonstrated a need for assistance;
- that a community contact person was identified;
- that some 10 to 15 citizens (including 2 locally elected officials) volunteered to participate actively on a revitalization committee;
- that a local council resolution was obtained in support of this initiative.

During Year 2, these criteria were refined slightly to include a $500 application fee that would be given to the revitalization committee for use at its discretion. Committee membership rules were also modified to ensure a diversity of age, ethnicity, gender and profession and the inclusion of two young adults with leadership potential.

In Year 3 the selection procedure gave preference to those communities which were working with a Year 1 or Year 2 committee as a mentor. An example here is Empire, a small mining town (population 400) located on the eastern slope of the Rocky Mountains. This Year 3 community had followed with interest the progress made by neighboring Idaho Springs (a Year 1 community) and determined that it too wanted to be involved. Idaho Springs agreed to sponsor an application from Empire and following recruitment to the CRRP, its committee members maintained constant contact with the newly formed revitalization group in Empire. This process allowed advice to be given and confidence to be built in order to achieve a successful development experience.

The number of participating communities was also adjusted during the course of the Project. The commitment billed at the outset was for a one year learning/action process, but inevitably there were always overlapping requests for assistance that continued into the following year. With 20 communities participating in Year 1 and a further 17 in Year 2, these additional demands on limited resources prompted a decision to reduce the number of Year 3 communities to 10. Project staff needed time to catch up with their workloads.

A final change in the selection process allowed some neighboring communities to come in to the Project, either on a county-wide basis (for example Custer County – see case study in Chapter 5), or on the joint basis of two communities working together (for example Yuma and Wray). While this accommodation was well intentioned, the benefit of hindsight would suggest that greater returns could have been gained by working initially with these communities on an individual basis and then gradually encouraging collaboration based on joint participation and sharing.

Scattered throughout Colorado, the 47 CRRP communities represent 34 of the state's 63 counties (Figure 4). As illustrated in Table 8, the majority are well removed from the influence of metropolitan areas along the front range corridor and are located in the mountainous west and eastern plains. Most communities involved with the Project had 1990 census populations below 2000 persons; one municipality had a population as low as 148 persons. Just under half had lost more than 5 percent of their population over the period 1980 to 1990; only 11 communities recorded gains of more than 5 percent over the intercensus period. Again, consistent with the commentary at the outset of this chapter, the participating communities varied in their predominant economic base. Some are agricultural or mining towns and some, especially those located near mountain resorts and public lands, rely heavily on tourism. A few in metropolitan and adjacent counties are bedroom communities. Several were gearing up at the time of their selection for major developments (for example gambling enterprises or federal/state prison projects). The case studies chosen for Chapter 5 reflect this diversity of geographical circumstances.

Within each community the CRRP followed a series of procedures, which when refined in the second year, came to be called "the five step process". These steps included the following measures:

1. A community was selected to participate in the revitalization project and a community site manager was appointed;
2. A revitalization committee was formed to develop a clear picture of the community through surveys, analysis and other information-gathering methods. This information was used to prepare an action plan.
3. Leadership training was provided for the revitalization committee and other community members.
4. Resources were mobilized to broaden the base of the revitalization committee by involving local people and organizations and utilizing available external technical

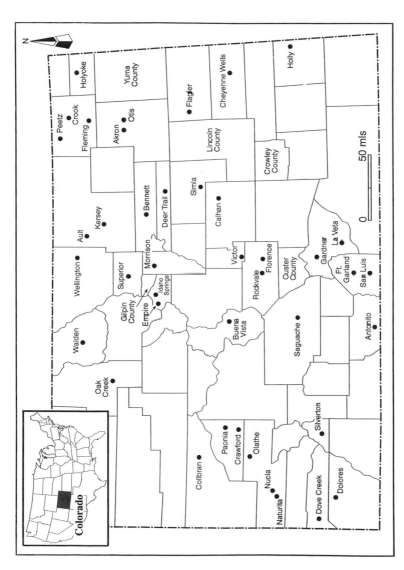

Figure 4 Participants in the Colorado Rural Revitalization Project

organizations and utilizing available external technical expertise.
5. The community action plan was coordinated among stakeholders and short-term projects were implemented. The entire local program was then evaluated, community projects were reprioritized and future plans were made. Accomplishments were celebrated and success stories written for the local media.

Table 8 Classification of Colorado Rural Revitalization Project communities

	(1988–89) Year 1	(1989–90) Year 2	(1990–91) Year 3	Totals
Number of participating communities	20	17	10	47
Geographic locations				
a. Eastern Plains	4	5	4	13
b. Metro Adjacent	6	5	2	13
c. Mountain/ Intermountain	10	7	4	21
Size of community (per 1990 census)				
a. 500 or less	2	7	4	13
b. 501 to 1000	6	6	3	15
c. 1001 to 2000	6	4	2	12
d. 2001 to 5000	6	0	1	7
Institution of site manager				
a. Colorado State University	1	6	7	14
b. University of Colorado	12	3	1	16
c. Department of Local Affairs	7	8	2	17

Source: Kincaid and Knop (1992), p.15.

The training component and technical assistance were crucial elements to the working procedures and these are dealt with in more detail in the following sections of this chapter.

A focus on training

The principal purpose of the training component of the CRRP was to develop the ability of existing and emerging leaders within rural communities to make sound decisions, to deal effectively with community problems and to look into the future to determine community potential. The linking of leadership development with strategic planning was thus a cornerstone of the Project and, as part of the learning/action process, was accomplished over a series of working sessions with the volunteer committee.

The initial orientation meeting between the Project facilitators and the community participants had a dual function. Firstly, it was designed to give the group (which had already been selected) an understanding of the purpose of the CRRP. The Project goals were defined, expectations were described and documentation regarding the achievements of other communities was shared. When possible the illustrations used were from neighboring communities. The staff provided adequate time for questions and the opportunity was given to the committee or individuals to opt out if any apprehension was felt about involvement. The need for strong commitment and hard work was emphasized and the message was reinforced by asking two questions. The first question was "Do you see this project working in your community and are you willing to support the effort?" The second question was "Do you have all of the people we need on the committee to make this happen?" The need for diversity and inclusion of a coalition of community voices was stressed. A frequent outcome from this exercise was the preparation of a list of three or four people to be added to the committee. A contact person was nominated and a time and venue agreed for a follow-up meeting.

The second element of this initial orientation involved a discussion of housekeeping duties, such as who would serve as temporary chair of the committee and how the committee would handle the $500 cash contribution provided by the Project for expenses. The meeting also dealt with preparations for undertaking a community survey. Those members of the group willing to work with the Project staff on the design, distribution and collection of a questionnaire were identified. Finally, a short evaluation procedure was used at the conclusion of the meeting to determine the extent to which those attending believed that the format and process were working satisfactorily.

The finalizing of the survey procedure by the assigned action committees usually required several further meetings. The length of time taken and the working of the process did, however, provide Project staff with a preliminary indication of how other planned activities would proceed. Important clues were also given regarding the most appropriate content of the leadership training phase. Following collection of the completed questionnaires, a staff member from one of the universities analyzed the data and reported back to the group.

The leadership curriculum was usually attended to over a two day session. The style was very informal and the discussions were documented on flip charts to allow for review of contributions and decisions, and the sharing of this information with others. The training topics included community visions, team building, refining the vision statement and action planning. Each may be briefly considered.

Community visioning

The purpose of this element was to get the participants to reach out into the future and to consider the possibilities. To prepare for discussion, the staff presented some general background facts on the changes that were taking place in rural America. This mini lecture drew upon census data, regional economic trends, and data from the community survey that had only recently been compiled. The exercise involved stimulating the participants to reach out in their minds and describe what they saw happening in rural communities in the next 10 to 20 years. The exercise then became more spatially focused and participants were asked to write down the vision they had of their *own* community 20 years into the future. These individual visions were shared and compared and a community vision drafted, utilizing as many individual views as possible. The exercise was guided by telling the participants that community visions were more than dreams and that they should be: leader-initiated; shared and supported; comprehensive and detailed; positive and inspiring. The draft of the vision statement was put aside until the conclusion of the session when it would be revised. An exercise on community images was then undertaken in an attempt to compare this committee-generated community vision with the perceived images currently held by other people. Community images were discussed from the perspectives of neighbors, newcomers and visitors. This, in essence, provided a reality check for the vision statement.

Team building

In order to broaden the participants' view of who they could work with, this part of the training program commenced with a mini lecture titled "Celebrating Differences", during which individual differences were described using the type preference approach from the Myers Briggs Type Indicator (MBTI). This is primarily concerned with identifying the valuable differences in people that result from where they like to focus their attention, the way they like to take in information, and their preferences and styles of action. The MBTI is useful in demonstrating the importance of each group member's contribution. Knowledge of members' strengths allows individuals to be called upon to assume leadership roles in those areas where they feel most comfortable. Since individuals had completed a MBTI form prior to the session, the type characteristics of each group could be discussed. This critique proved extremely useful in helping the committees to understand the internal adjustments which they might need to make so as to develop into effective teams.

A group discussion then focused directly on team building. Participants were asked to define what a team is, to identify what the elements of a good team are, and to give examples of good teams which they had known. Since many were familiar with sports teams, these examples usually involved specific baseball, football and basketball teams. In exploring how community members could work together, some time was taken to consider aspects of effective communication and conflict resolution. Material prepared by the Harvard Negotiation Team, titled "Getting to Yes", was utilized to pursue the subtle theme that successful collaborative action depends on being able to get beyond individual interests and desires. The experiences of group members were applied to this theoretical foundation by asking them to identify conflict situations which had emerged within their community. An effort was always made to demonstrate the application of techniques to alleviate some of the bitterness and hurt often associated with these tensions.

At this stage the agenda moved on to deal directly with leadership development and how new leaders should be recruited, trained and assisted. The simple message here was that effective teams have effective leaders. The group exercises asked the participants to describe effective leaders that they had known and to prepare a list of attributes that they felt were essential for such a person.

The last element in this team-building session was designed to explore what makes an effective team meeting. At this point each group developed its individual meeting template including matters related to date, time, location, purpose, agenda, recording minutes and evaluation methodology. Documentation associated with all these exercises is included as Appendix 3 in this book.

Refining the vision statement

With a wealth of new ideas and enthusiasm, the group was then asked to refine and rewrite its draft vision statement. This task did take time to complete because of the need to be concise, yet comprehensive and detailed. When the revision had been completed and agreed upon, a group brainstorming period was held to explore how this vision might become a reality.

The action plan

This section of the training curriculum usually had two dimensions. The first concerned the identification of necessary long-range actions, while the second placed emphasis on one or two short-range activities which could be completed by the group over the following two month period. The rationale here was that if the committee could successfully undertake a small number of projects in the immediate future, then the confidence of its members would be enhanced, allowing larger and more complex objectives to be pursued thereafter.

Modifications to the training program

The changes introduced into the training program during the course of the CRRP were not major, but rather adaptations designed to make the learning/action process more effective. In Year I the two day training session was convened on a regional basis involving the participation of three or four communities located in close proximity to each other. The interaction between these groups was a positive outcome in that ideas and resources were shared, and new contacts and friendships were created. However, the evaluation results demonstrated that a joint training curriculum was unable to address the specific needs of each community. Moreover, a two day block proved unpopular with some of the working people and total participation in the regional training was not achieved. Accordingly, in Year 2 the program was adjusted to allow for single community-based training. It was this change which prompted the introduction of the community survey, identified above. This proved to be an excellent learning/action training exercise for orientating committee members. But the absence of interaction with outside communities emerged as a weakness in this approach. In Year 3 the best of both experiences was combined, whereby the orientation and community survey work was undertaken on an individual community basis, and groups were then brought together for leadership training on a regional basis. This format required more staff time and was more costly, but the outcomes were deemed more satisfactory.

A number of other curriculum modifications were incorporated into the CRRP including additional material on group formation and team building in Year 3, personal and community visioning in Year 3, the preparation of development plans in Year 2 with further refinement in Year 3, and regional technical assistance training in Year 3.

Reflections on the training process

It is appropriate at this stage of the chapter to reflect on the operation of the training curriculum. The unfolding of several process phases or sequences can be identified.

First, the committees were usually not very excited at the outset about the training component. This partly reflected the fact that the volunteers were extremely busy people, with limited spare time, who had seen little productive work come out of past training efforts. Their preference was for outside expertise to diagnose problems and provide solutions. Nevertheless, the number of participants from each community that completed the leadership training phase of the Project was high. During the first and second year of the CRRP some 34 communities involved not fewer than 425 volunteers in training activities.

Second, as the committees began to discover the amount of work required of them, there was always some discontent and a few members opted to drop out. Comments such as "This committee could take over my life", or "I've already got a fulltime job", or "Some folks tried this several years ago and nothing happened" were not uncommon after the first few meetings. This became the shakedown phase that separated those who were willing to work from the dreamers and supervisors who wanted to tell others how community revitalization should be done.

Third, after three or four months, several committee members usually began to feel some ownership in the process. Others began to buy in as some of the short-term objectives were accomplished. After a small number of early projects had been completed, the wider community often began to get excited about the improvements and new volunteers indicated their interest in joining the team. Public recognition quite simply increased the momentum. At this point several different avenues opened up. In some cases the committee leadership was appointed to a town leadership position, thus diverting the committee's momentum and slowing down the short-term impact of the revitalization effort. In other cases the committee was given too much public recognition and was pressed into taking on more responsibility than could be handled. This resulted in burn-out and often triggered a major setback for that community. Occasionally, the leadership did not bond or the committee took on an unpopular task or issue. In the case of two communities the Project staff were obliged to return and conduct a second training program in an attempt to engage new leadership or initiate a new committee. In many instances, however, the committee was able to develop a cohesive team, to maintain owner-ship, and to work at a pace that produced real results with-out overstressing the participants.

Fourth, after the one year involvement in the CRRP, there was usually a reshuffling of committee personnel and a focusing of project work. This final phase often brought with it a new level of community ownership.

A focus on technical assistance

A second major component of the CRRP was the provision of technical assistance to communities which was aimed at making a contribution to action plan implementation. A budget of $2000 per community was held in the Project office to facilitate this work. But since most of this was provided on an in-house basis by drawing upon university and DOLA expertise, the small amount of grant aid was capable of stretching far beyond the normal contract costs for the type of work undertaken. The technical assistance phase usually commenced when communities embarked upon their short-term project activities. Many groups targeted their efforts on small signage, refurbishment or townscape enhancement schemes. These types of projects were encouraged by CRRP staff since they offered visual evidence of successful accomplishments by an improvements committee. Specific examples of projects and the technical assistance provided include the following:

1. The creation of new entrance signs for a small town; architecture students often helped to design these in consultation with community members and university faculty.
2. The design of a town theme; community planning or landscape architecture students would help with the preparation of ideas and drawings for community reaction.
3. Downtown beautification with an emphasis on one or two community buildings with historical significance; students and staff with structural engineering and architecture skills would draft plans.
4. The creation of new hiking/biking trails or recreation areas; this would usually involve students from the recreation and tourism school, with a design contribution coming from environmental planning students and staff.
5. Community promotion to attract new residents or tourists; journalism students would help design community brochures and media studies students would develop videos and slide tapes for the promotion of individual community attributes.
6. Infrastructure projects involving design work on street drainage, curbs, gutters and water/sewer systems; university staff or DOLA have given engineering assistance.
7. A study of the feasibility of a community waste recycling business; this unique request for technical assistance brought help from the business school and the College of Health Sciences.

As the work program of the CRRP progressed, the demand for technical assistance increased and very often groups began to focus on larger scale and more complex challenges. Thus, for example, several communities made a concerted effort to attract new businesses to their areas, while a number of other communities decided to collaborate on joint regional business ventures. An interesting illustration of the latter was a request for help to determine the feasibility of running a train between three rural communities as a new tourism product. Technical specialists in economics, business, tourism and recreation were consulted and a development assistance team was set up with expertise in obtaining business capital.

Table 9 Key community concerns, activities and outcomes related to Colorado Rural Revitalization Project: 1991

Topic	Number of communities
Basic community and leadership development	
• local communication, tolerance, bridging local differences	23
• local civic participation, cooperation and coordination	31
• local pride, identity and sense of community	22
• external relations/resources, e.g. access to grants, technical help	31
• capacity to explore, plan and manage the community's future	32
Beautification and hospitality	
• clean-up campaigns, streetscape design, building improvement	24
• community promotion; welcome signs/centers, brochures, videos	21
Community services and facilities	
• community center	7
• ecology; revegetation, waste recycling	4
• health, doctor recruitment, housing, safety, schools, libraries	21
• infrastructure: drainage, water, sewerage, landfill, sidewalks	14
Events, programs and celebration	
• arts/drama, local history/culture	6
• information/educational forums	14
• local celebrations, e.g. picnics, fairs, fiestas, marathons, bike races	18
Jobs/economic development	
• efforts to enhance/develop local businesses, local industry	16
• efforts to develop external business and industry	12
Recreation and tourism development	
• information, recreation and heritage centers	8
• preservation and development of natural areas, e.g. wetlands, trails	14
• parks, playgrounds and golf courses	14
• marketing brochures and campaigns	4
• recreation program development	9

All in all, the community revitalization committees uncovered a host of local concerns and mustered support for a wide variety of improvement activities (Table 9). At the conclusion of the CRRP, which overran into 1992, many projects had been completed as a result of this technical assistance, others were in progress or on local drawing boards. Technical assistance, in short, provided a crucial link between learning and action.

Evaluation of the Colorado Rural Revitalization Project

An independent *ex post* evaluation of the CRRP was commissioned in late 1991 (Kincaid and Knop, 1992) and responses to a series of questions were obtained from community participants, site managers and institution team members. In total, data were collected from 171 citizens drawn from 41 communities and from 30 site managers. Key points to emerge from this evaluation may be summarized as follows:

1. Some 92 percent of citizens and 90 percent of site managers suggested that the Project had yielded "somewhat" to a "great deal" of practical community benefit. This included the planning and implementation of specific local projects, cooperation through working together and organizing for action, and increased citizen awareness and community pride.
2. Some 95 percent of citizens rated the help given by the Project with local leadership team formation as "extremely" useful, 93 percent described the community/ leadership development workshops as "useful" and 92 percent rated the facilitation process during local meetings by the Project as "useful".
3. Some 91 percent of citizens gave values of "somewhat" to "a great deal" when asked the extent to which Project activities had increased local cooperation.
4. Some 57 percent of citizens and 45 percent of site managers suggested that local revitalization committee members had worked "extremely well" together during the Project.

5. Some 66 percent of citizens commented that the site managers worked "extremely well" with their communities, with a further 26 percent rating the assistance given as "rather well".
6. The technical assistance provided by the Project for the communities was rated by 95 percent of citizen respondents as "somewhat useful" or "extremely useful"; the corresponding approval rate from site managers was 90 percent.
7. When questioned about the turnover of committee membership, less than 15 percent of citizen respondents indicated that new people had not been added to the local teams, while nearly 55 percent indicated that a few members had joined. In all cases, most of the original committee members continued to serve their communities.
8. Citizen suggestions regarding adjustments in the operation of the Project included extending direct assistance beyond the period of one year, providing more leadership training, and offering greater funding and technical help.

An important dimension of the CRRP was its experimental approach to institutional collaboration between two universities and a state government department. As noted by the authors of the evaluation report "marginal differences in staff orientation produced a productive complementarity of perspectives, a need for flexibility that enabled creativity, and a dynamic of dialog which guided the Project's development toward a shared general vision of its potentials" (Kincaid and Knop, 1992, p. 40). A series of tensions was identified, however, which included the following matters:

1. There were some perceived ambiguities in project purpose and approach which required high level mediation among Project core staff.
2. There were some concerns that participants were caught between supporting a common Project agenda while at the same time remaining loyal to their parent institution missions. These do differ between the three parties with DOLA mandated to provide tangible services to local government, CSU stressing a rural service agenda and the UC working to a broad academic remit.

3. There was frequently expressed frustration that the contribution of key participants in the Project was undervalued by non-participating colleagues and superiors. Again, as the evaluation team commented, "many project participants based on the two campuses felt the applied nature of the work made it a low status activity in the eyes of their institutional peers, and the process emphasis of the work was often viewed as too intangible and academic within the Department of Local Affairs, which emphasizes highly applied visible work". (p. 46)

The operational experience of the CRRP and the results from this evaluation exercise allow for the identification of a suite of key issues, discussion of which may be subsumed under the banner of collaboration.

Collaboration

One of the most interesting aspects of the CRRP, which was canvased at the outset of the written proposal, was the specific commitment to collaboration. At the institutional level it was anticipated that the Project would bring the two universities and DOLA closer together at the community level. There were similar expectations that local people could be encouraged to work more closely together and benefit from stronger ties with agency personnel. While some expectations were met, others were not. In both instances valuable insights were gleaned into the challenges involved in initiating collaborative ventures.

At the institutional level it became clear that the complexity of the task and time involved in the creation of common cause between three partners was much greater than initially allowed for. In the late 1980s each of the sponsors came to the partnership as evolving, changing organizations. CSU, as a land-grant institution, possessed a well-developed Extension System that was focused primarily on agricultural matters. There had been no committed community development tradition in Extension, due in part to the creation of DOLA by the state legislature to work on economic and social development in rural communities. In the 1970s Extension budgets for community development had been redirected to DOLA to facilitate this technical assistance work. Nevertheless, there was still an interest at CSU in organizing campus resources to work in small communities drawing upon expertise, for example, in economics, tourism, sociology and social work. Accordingly, in May 1989, a Center for Rural Assistance was established at the university for that purpose. Initially DOLA was unwilling to contribute funds towards this initiative thus creating a continuing tension between the two institutions. Some three years later the issue was eventually mediated by the creation of posts for two Community Development Coordinators whose job description reflects the dual sponsorship of DOLA and CSU.

Institutional collaboration also suffered from important philosophical differences in community development approaches. While UC and DOLA stressed technical assistance as the means to community change, CSU placed greater weight on leadership training. This dichotomy can be distilled into a preference for product achievement rather than process development. CRRP exposed these differences, not appreciated at the Project's inception, and during many uncomfortable staff meetings the dividends of linking leadership training with an action component were slowly appreciated. This harmonization became one of the Project's best attributes and is given precept status by Kincaid and Knop (1992) in their *ex post* evaluation:

> When assisting communities to conduct community development or revitalization programs, it is important that the initiation, implementation, and where possible, the completion of specific improvement projects or events occur concurrently with training and other consultative activities to strengthen community volunteer leadership and other process abilities. In order to maintain the interest and motivation of volunteers to work together effectively as a core group of interested and dedicated community leaders, they need to see progress toward achievement of community improvement goals. Additionally, the visibility of tangible results is of significance in obtaining and maintaining the support of the community at large. (p. 21)

Finally at the inter-institutional level there were less prominent tensions on timing. Universities, by virtue of their teaching and research commitments, need considerable advance notice when they are providing technical assistance to individual communities, whereas within the DOLA an action response can be more immediate. Over time the CRRP tried hard to produce greater tolerance based on mutual understanding of these different conditions.

A second set of issues related to the collaboration agenda of the CRRP can be identified as having intra-insti-tutional significance. At the outset of the Project UC had established a strong reputation for working with small communities across the state through its Center for Community Development and Design in the School of Architecture and Planning at the Denver campus. It had provided help to communities to get organized and to pur-sue improvement goals. At the initiation of the CRRP pro-posal the university's interest was shifting from pursuing a public service mission to one more concerned with research and scholarship. This resulted in lowering the pri-ority of such community development work as the CRRP. A change in the Denver campus administration in September 1989 brought a new orientation, that of a regional university, and restored the public service com-mitment. The early years of the CRRP were thus caught up in this mission-related dilemma in UC, the internal resolu-tion of which allowed the Project to become part of a process of making the university system more accessible to rural Colorado. Internal collaboration provided for the establishment of a system-wide committee to facilitate access to university resources and to assist with the deliv-ery of technical assistance.

Internal tensions were also apparent within the CSU extension organization. Following the cut in funding from the state legislature noted above, the community develop-ment program was given lower priority and reduced resources. With the commencement of the CRRP, however, a higher demand for personnel time did not sit easily with what had become a casual involvement in community development. Extension agents, whose job descriptions could include development activities, were ironically, therefore, often less involved than UC faculty and DOLA staff who were invariably participating on a purely volun-tary basis. The internal collaboration being pushed for by the Project Director within CSU, whereby staff assumed more responsibilities for involvement in the CRRP, created its own pressure. In short, the increased workload was not always welcomed.

A number of more general insights can be offered about the involvement of individual staff members associated with the CRRP:

- Younger staff members seemed to be more open to working collaboratively than those who had developed a stronger institutional identity over time.
- Persons working by themselves in a single office setting often welcomed the opportunity to work collaboratively.
- People with political agendas were not usually very open or willing to pursue long-term collaborative work.
- After an initial experience of working collaboratively, staff usually volunteered for additional involvement in the Project.

At the interface between the partnering institutions and the participating communities, the collaborative agenda of the CRRP did prove to be especially useful. Rural communities, by tradition, are deeply skeptical of government sponsored programs. The high level involvement of the two universities in the CRRP helped to temper this distrust and to create a new climate of confidence among local people.

Finally, at the community and individual volunteer levels, the quest for collaboration by the CRRP progressed much more quickly than anticipated. The committee selection process demonstrated that many people in these rural communities felt isolated and welcomed the opportunity to become part of an active team. New friendships were created, new careers were initiated, and an abundance of work was completed through community collaborative teamwork. Moreover, it was demonstrated time and time again that as individual leadership skills increased, so also did the willingness to work collaboratively. It also became apparent that those communities with the greatest team diversity in terms of age, gender, ethnicity, profession and interests developed stronger cohesion and collaborative action.

Conclusion

The Colorado Rural Revitalization Project was both an innovative and timely response to the difficulties being experienced by many small communities during the latter part of the 1980s. When it formally concluded in 1992, the evidence points not only to substantial local project successes, but also to an enhanced capacity for community leadership in rural society. At the community level, volunteers and individual staff members were able to join together in effective collaborative work to generate these outcomes. At the institutional level, on the other hand, it is questionable whether the CRRP progressed much beyond communication and cooperation on the partnership continuum. An inability to build the intended collaborative front for rural development may well be a direct outcome of the Project's short life and the absence of any imperative to forge sustainable relationships by its sponsors. Indeed, it is noteworthy that support for continuation and elaboration of the CRRP at an equivalent level of funding is still lacking in late 1994. It is appropriate, therefore, that this matter should be revisited in the final chapter of this book. Before doing so, more detailed consideration of community involvement in the Project is necessary. Chapter 5 examines its impact and short-term legacy by means of a series of case studies.

5 A tale of six rural communities

Introduction

This chapter tells the stories of six communities (Figure 5) which participated in the Colorado Rural Revitalization Project. The previous account has given an overview of the working practices and achievements of the Project as a whole. Given that this book seeks to celebrate the contribution which rural communities can make to regeneration, it is only appropriate that a much deeper inquiry at a local level is included. Ultimately it is within the communities themselves that the challenges, tensions and accomplishments of the rural development process are most acutely experienced. The selection below is based on representative variation in geographical situation and perceived accomplishment at the conclusion of the Project. While useful insights can be gained from an analysis of failure in regard to product and process criteria, the tracking of community-led revitalization over later years may well be a fruitless exercise. Accordingly, this discussion relates to a number of communities which have been particularly active on the rural development front.

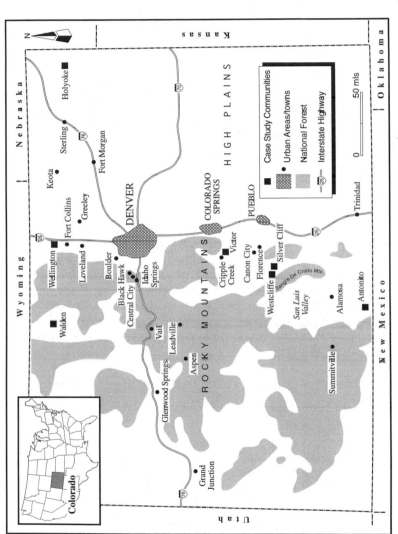

Figure 5 Location and context of Colorado rural community case studies

The structure of the narrative comprises, firstly, a short context-setting review for each community drawing upon historical and socio-economic data. The unfolding of the revitalization effort during the Project is then described and subsequent circumstances and achievements are reported. In each instance a key concern is the extent to which the presence or absence of collaboration has assisted or frustrated, respectively, these communities in achieving their development missions. A suite of issues arising from the analysis is advanced by way of conclusion. The content of the chapter draws upon the Project data bank and more recent interviews carried out with key informants in 1993 and again in 1994. The tracking of these six communities forms part of a longitudinal research project being carried out by the authors of this book. Key research questions being pursued comprise:

1. What factors are driving rural revitalization?
2. Who is stimulating rural revitalization?
3. How is rural revitalization being pursued?
4. What are the key revitalization goals of the community?
5. What are the process- and product-related achievements of this revitalization activity?
6. What difficulties are being encountered in regard to rural revitalization?
7. Has CRRP made any lasting contribution to rural revitalization efforts?

The chapter now considers each participating community.

Victor

> Where progress is our motto and prosperity our lot,
> Where our spirits never daunted are, and failure we know not,
> Where the people of all nations are as one in enterprise,
> Where as evidence of industry, towering smokestacks pierce the skies,
> There is the city of Victor, the "city of mines".
> *(The Cripple Creek Strike* by Emma F Langdon, 1904–05)

The City of Victor dates from the early 1890s at the time of the final mining bonanza of nineteenth-century Colorado. A gold rush brought thousands of people into the Cripple Creek Mining District on the southern slopes of Pikes Peak. As recorded by Abbott et al (1982) Cripple Creek emerged as the metropolis of the new gold region with production in the area climbing from $2 million in 1893 to $19.5 million by 1899. Of the 15 towns making up the division it was Cripple Creek which developed as the financial, political and social center, whereas most of the gold came from Victor. The latter became known as the "City of Mines" and by 1900 it recorded a peak census population of 4986, although unofficial estimates have put the population figure as high as 12 000 (Keener, 1993).

Victor today is still very much a mining town and, while its full-time resident population had shrunk to 258 by 1990, the contemporary townscape still offers positive proof of former greatness. Much of the community-led revitalization effort has been concerned with trying to arrest a high level of physical obsolescence which extends from buildings, to street surfaces, to basic infrastructure. Two factors have given added impetus to local initiative.

Firstly, Cripple Creek, only a few miles distant from Victor, received a franchise to offer limited stakes gambling. The issue had gone before Colorado citizens in November 1990, with a vote of 574 620 in favor to 428 096 against, allowing gambling to be used as an economic development tool for the first time in the state. Promises of historic preservation and town revitalization were key selling points. Two other towns west of Denver, Black Hawk and Central City, were also successful in winning support for gambling. Notwithstanding immediate problems of congestion, car parking, sewerage and the pricing out of many community retail services because of higher property taxes, the revenue raised through gaming has not been inconsiderable. In fiscal year 1993 some $30.5 million were distributed to the benefit of projects advanced by the state Historical Society and impacted counties and cities. The City of Victor is set for the first time to receive some $94 000 from the 1994 gaming revenues pool of $37.7 million. A key concern associated with the industry is the relative absence of locally available affordable housing, a problem highlighted by the fact that the 60 casinos in the three centers reported some 5300 employees on their payroll in June 1994. Accommodation shortages in Cripple Creek offer an opportunity for Victor to expand its population base and thereby begin to extend its restricted range of services.

A second factor underpinning local initiative in Victor is the existence of the Cripple Creek and Victor Gold Mining Company which in 1993 employed some 130 women and men. Not only has the mine been an important benefactor to the community with 1994 donations, for example, running in excess of $65 000 but it is also a key purchaser of water. Water sales at the time of writing net Victor more than five times its property tax collections which in 1994 are unlikely to exceed $45 000. In 1994 the company received new mining permits from the Colorado Division of Minerals and Geology and the Mined Land Reclamation Board to operate a 2500 by 1600 feet open pit mine with gold extraction by leach pad cyanide processing. Mindful of pollution problems elsewhere in Colorado, at Summitville (*The Financial Times*, 8 November 1993, p. 8), local concerns revolved around the initial location of the heap leach at only a quarter of a mile distant from Victor. Mediation and subsequent approval have paved the way for a project which will almost double employment and substantially raise property and production taxes. However, affordable housing for this expanded labor force again remains an outstanding issue.

It was within this context of a small, declining mountain community possibly about to be impacted upon by limited stakes gambling and mining expansion that local citizens in partnership with the city council agreed in November 1990 to become part of the Colorado Rural Revitalization Project. Calling itself the Victor Colorado Revitalization Committee, the group grew initially from 30 members to more than 50, with a core coordinating group of about 8. The formation of subcommittees followed on from a preliminary community assessment exercise and allowed community efforts to focus on identified projects and issues. These included a town opinion survey, zoning, historic preservation, centennial celebrations, recreation, housing and community facilities. By March 1991 the committee was able to present a vision statement for Victor which read as follows:

> Victor wants to create a thriving year round, cohesive, residential community, maintaining our small town atmosphere, with a collaborative, diversified economy; providing the essential necessary services; preserving our mining industry; promoting our heritage through tourism and providing appealing and accommodating recreational facilities and programs for all.

The results of the community survey identified significant objectives linked to this vision. Key improvements called for were the removal of rubbish, the painting of buildings, the renovation of vacant commercial premises, housing refurbishment, extended sewage collection, storm water drainage, better sidewalks and paved streets. An expansion of the historical zone was endorsed, together with land zoning for mobile homes and trailers. In order to achieve these aims the community participants in the CRRP gave strong support to local leadership team-learning activities and to technical assistance comprising planning and implementation. Inter-organization collaboration which brought together leaders and volunteers with university and state agency personnel was central to the change process.

In January 1992 Victor received formal congratulations on its one year anniversary with the Project. The development agenda after this milestone has continued to be heavily project driven but it has had to accommodate a series of disappointments in regard to federal and state grant applications. Nevertheless community representatives have endeavored to be innovative in regard to their team structure. During the spring of 1992 the formation of a new grassroots partnership was announced under the acronym of VICCI (Victor Goldfield Initiatives Consortium for Community Improvements). While its mission remains unaltered, membership allowed the revitalization effort to open out and include not only year-round and part-time residents but also former residents, outside business and corporate contacts, tourists and visitors interested in the welfare of Victor. Quite simply, the community has recognized the importance of looking beyond its own notional frontiers. All possible external assistance is actively sought in order to help make the community vision a reality. It is hoped that the gathering of a wider set of interested parties under a formal umbrella organization can secure not only greater opportunity but also enhanced legitimacy. Thus in October 1993 VICCI hosted a first ever community awards jamboree and acknowledged the contributions of some 150 people in making Victor a better place in which to live. Clearly there is a deeply held view that successful revitalization requires the energies of many people within and outside the city.

In late 1994 it was gratifying to report that there was now at last the prospect of significant change in Victor. Investments in water supply infrastructure, restoration of the city hall, completion of a wastewater project, the refurbishment of a show case commercial block (Plate 1), and restoration of the town hall in nearby Goldfield have received financial support. VICCI will continue to press for the conversion of a vacant church into a community center and will work with mining interests and public agencies to create a pool of affordable housing, both owner occupied and rental. The previous high frequency of committee meetings has been scaled down and a small cadre of committed community volunteers remains the driving force behind therepresentative body. Their enthusiasm has encouraged new people to become involved as others have decided to step down. In the final analysis the sustainability of VICCI will depend not only on mission successes but also on regular leadership renewal. One Victor resident, reported in the local newspaper, commented appropriately:

> 22 years ago when I moved to Victor, people in the community told me the things needed the most were economic development, a solid payroll and people working together. The mine has given us the first two. We need to do the rest.
>
> *(Gold Rush,* 11 August 1994, p. 7)

Plate 1   Victor: proposed showcase restoration block

Holyoke

> Colorado's outback: is there life down on the farm? You bet there is – and the folks on Colorado's Eastern Plains learned a long time ago to rely on their own brand of home-grown grit, faith and unswerving belief in the value of small town America. The result: economic development success stories that eclipse big-city coups.
>
> *(Colorado Business,* February 1994, p. 37)

Holyoke, located deep in the eastern plains of Colorado, is inextricably linked to the fortunes of agriculture. It originated as a railroad town on the line from Holdrege, Nebraska, to Cheyenne, Wyoming, with some 600 acres comprising the town site being offered to settlers in 1887. Holyoke was incorporated the following year and, with a 1888 census population recorded at 660, the evidence is that from its earliest days Holyoke was a thriving community. While the railroad brought initial prosperity to the town in its capacity as a railroad division headquarters until 1906, its future increasingly lay with agriculture. Access to water was crucial in the face of severe drought and, as noted by Green (1973), irrigated agriculture has played an important role in the historical development and population change of the region since the late 1800s. Vital here is the Ogallala aquifer which extends from southern South Dakota through to the Texas Panhandle. Some 30 percent of all irrigation water in the United States is pumped in the Ogallala region (Weeks, 1986). Most irrigation expansion has occurred since the 1950s following the invention of the center pivot irrigation system which brought rolling and hilly terrain into productive use. As a result Phillips County, within which Holyoke is located, is today one of the most prosperous agricultural areas in Colorado. Using data from 1987, Miller et al (1991) have identified Phillips County as one of 17 farm-dependent counties in the state, with over 20 percent of labor and proprietor income coming from farming. In fact, Phillips County ranked tenth with some 40 percent of total income coming from this sector, largely from cash crops such as corn, wheat and beans. However, the analysis also pointed to the crucial significance of direct payments to farmers and ranchers under government farm programs. In the farm-dependent counties such payments provided over 58 percent of farm earnings with the highest rate of support in the state being given to Phillips County where government assistance represented some 107 percent of farm income. Without this support Phillips County would have had a negative farm income with obvious adverse effects on the prosperity of Holyoke as the principal commercial and services center in the district.

There are over 200 businesses in Holyoke and the town has continued to attract new enterprises. In 1989, for example, a hog raising operation, named D&D Farms, decided to locate near the town instead of at the company's head-quarters in South Dakota. A family farm bill, approved by the South Dakota legislature, limited corporate ownership of hog raising facilities in that state. Some 120 jobs have been created and the hog production, set at 150 000 annually, draws upon 1.5 million bushels of locally grown surplus corn. The net result is that in a town of some 1900 persons, male unemployment in 1990 was recorded at only 2.9 percent compared with an average for rural Colorado of 5.1 percent. However, the median household income at $19 800 was substantially less than that for rural Colorado ($29 600); moreover some 15.7 percent of all persons were recorded as living below the poverty line in Holyoke compared with 11.6 percent in rural Colorado as a whole. Such evidence would suggest a marginally higher than expected level of privation in a local economy dominated by agriculture which itself is precariously dependent upon continued water availability and government support.

It was against this context that Holyoke became a third year community of the Colorado Rural Revitalization Project through the efforts of the school district superintendent, a citizen group interested in refurbishing the former local cinema as a youth center and the town council. The resulting Holyoke Revitalization Group initially consisted of 35 people who defined their boundary as the whole of the town school district. Some two-thirds of the community's families live within the town limits and the remainder in the surrounding agricultural area. The revitalization group was unable, however, to draw in sufficient numbers from the farming population and thus participation remained largely town based.

Under the guidance of the CRRP core staff, which included the County Extension Agent as site manager, the Holyoke group identified and prioritized three projects. Small task forces were established to look after a community assessment, community welcome signs and a community bike/hiking trail. Later two additional task groups were formed, one to refine a vision statement for Holyoke and the other to formulate an effective means for planning, coordination and cooperation. Here the community assessment results were useful in demonstrating that while citizens had a tremendous amount of community pride they were not working together in a unified effort for collective progress. The vision statement, adopted in July

1991, was designed to begin to address this issue. It reads as follows:

> Through broad participation of our citizens, Holyoke will be a community united together for Pride and Progress. A safe, healthy, pleasant and sustainable environment will be provided where each citizen can develop his or her potential. Holyoke will be a diversified and economically stable rural community committed to shaping its own future, developing leadership in people of all ages, and serving the interests, needs and values of this and future generations.

By the end of 12 months with the CRRP the community group had made substantial progress toward achieving its initial short-term goals. The completion of the comprehensive community audit was followed by the formal unveiling of four "Welcome to Holyoke" signs and the use of technical assistance to design the proposed recreation path. The community celebrated completion of the vision statement in several ways. A "Catch the Vision" campaign was launched and July 1991 became "Vision Month" culminating in the staffing of a booth at the county fair at which people were encouraged to discuss the statement and become involved in the revitalization effort. A copy of the vision statement, hand penned on a large parchment scroll, was signed by community members and presented to the Mayor at a special ceremony. Finally, the task force on implementation convened a day-long workshop entitled "Vision 2000" in order to focus collaborative efforts on achieving common goals.

What then, it may be asked, has been the legacy of the CRRP in Holyoke? By 1993 over 50 percent of the original committee had dropped out leaving a core group of 15 individuals active on a number of fronts. Incorporation of Holyoke Revitalization as a non-profit organization was still being pursued and had been achieved by the following year. The County Extension Agent had organized two follow-up leadership training sessions sponsored by a local utility company, K N Energy, and involving the expertise of the Nebraska Heartland Center as a facilitator; some 48 people signed up to attend. A further team-building program, designed to run over a period of 10 months, was also under consideration.

However, the fragility of all this work related to community visioning and its achievement was unexpectedly thrown into sharp focus by the tensions created by the Peerless Theater refurbishment project (Plate 2). While this was not part of the agenda of Holyoke Revitalization, a number of its proponents had been part of the Kellogg Program and still committed much time to community leadership activities.

Plate 2   Holyoke: proposed Peerless Theater
Youth Center

Stated briefly, the project supporters (organized as Golden Plains Recreation Center, Inc.) joined with DOLA through a Memorandum of Understanding signed in March 1992. By December of that year a business plan, a renovation cost estimate of some $640 000 and a scale model of the facility had been provided to the community under the Northern and Eastern Colorado Technical Assistance Program – a partnership between DOLA and CSU Cooperative Extension. It was anticipated that $300 000 could be drawn down from DOLA by way of an Impact Assistance Grant, the balance coming from donations and services in kind. But because funding regulations require applicants to be statutory units of local governments in order to insure that funds are going to a public facility rather than a private enterprise or individual,

Holyoke council was obliged to make the grant application
on behalf of Golden Plains Recreation Center, Inc. Concern
by the council that the project could subsequently impact
on its budgetary expenditures, if not self-sufficient, pro-
voked a special municipal election on the issue.

This was held on 16 November 1993 with voters turning
down the project by 347 votes to 177 – a total of 524 votes
from an electorate of 1177.

While the evidence points to the town council acting at
all times with due propriety, consultations with key informants during 1994 would suggest that the sponsors of the
project had handled the entire matter with some degree of
political *naïveté*. The resolution of technical issues had been
their overriding concern whereas more effort could perhaps have been directed at making the formal community
leadership, other influential citizens and the wider popu-
lace feel stronger affinity with the project. There is a clear
lesson here for other community-based non-profit groups
in the United States. It is heartening to record that in
December 1994, following participation by a group of volunteers in the Colorado Rural Cultural Facilities
Leadership Program, Golden Plains Recreation Center, Inc.
took a major step forward by acquiring the Peerless
Theater property from the local Credit Union. The project
sponsors have since regrouped, are again collaborating
with DOLA and other agencies to secure implementation
and are building a high profile of commitment to community. The Peerless Theater has also secured Colorado
Enterprise Zone status which will allow for capital donations to be used as tax credits.

Meanwhile Holyoke Revitalization, Inc. has been press-
ing on with a number of other projects. A Business
Retention and Expansion Committee has organized seminars on service marketing and advertising. It has published
a business directory specifically for the town since there is
no local Yellow Pages. A building improvements award has
been introduced, recipients of which are presented with a
banner carrying the town's motto "Pride and Progress".
Finally, a modest grant of $2000 has been secured in 1994 to
develop leadership skills among the Spanish speaking
members of the community; it is also proposed to promote
the more complete assimilation of this minority group by
teaching economic development skills and by establishing
three small businesses devoted to greenhouse horticulture,

childcare and house cleaning. It is important, however, to locate these rural development activities in their broader local context. Holyoke today is a thriving and active community where volunteerism runs high. It is evident in the sheer number of support groups, cultural, artistic and sporting diversity, and the breadth of its leadership across a wide range of civic and corporate infrastructure. The activities and legacy of CRRP have, in short, made a contribution to this dynamism. It is a contribution which continues to fit well with the consensus of contentment underpinning the community vision.

Antonito

> Antonito is more than a collection of buildings, it is more than a place on the map. From its earliest days, it has nurtured the lives and accomplishments of countless individuals – individuals united through the years by a common love for the place they call home. That deep sense of community, of responsibility toward one's neighbor and the common good, resonates through all cities and towns across America.
>
> (George Bush, President of the United States,
> 5 July 1989 in a letter to Antonito celebrating its centennial)

Antonito is located in southern Colorado just a few miles from the New Mexico state line. It was created in 1880 when the nearby town of Conejos, currently the county seat, refused to grant concessions on land to the Denver and Rio Grande Western Railroad. The establishment of a depot at Antonito to service the junction connecting Durango to the West, Espanola and Santa Fe to the south, and Denver to the north via Alamosa encouraged investment in homes and businesses. The town was incorporated in December 1889, though without a wider economic rationale for its existence, population growth remained relatively modest. The peak census year of 1950 recorded 1255 inhabitants. By 1990 the population had fallen to 875, with the abandoned railway depot now standing in lonely vigil within the town center.

Today Conejos County is one of the most disadvantaged areas in rural Colorado. Agriculture is orientated primarily to cattle and sheep ranching though the wider San Luis Valley has become a major potato producing region within the United States. In 1990, for example, farm net cash return in Conejos County was just over one-third of that recorded in Phillips County. The unemployment rate in the county recorded by the 1990 census was 21 percent; 34 percent of the population was living below the poverty level; median family income was just under half of that for Colorado as a whole. Within the town of Antonito 38 percent of the population was below the poverty level in 1989 and the median per capita income of $5867 was in sharp contrast to $14 028 for rural Colorado. Inevitably this condition of disadvantage spills over into the physical environment of the town. First impressions might well focus on unpaved and dusty streets, vacant buildings, neglected sidewalks along the main street, an overall town character which lacks cohesion and the absence of a strong positive image. Yet, notwithstanding the scale of these problems, Antonito is a "happening place". Community effort to build a better future is flourishing and it is the contribution of the CRRP which is commonly regarded as being the catalyst for change.

After six months of public meetings to canvass town interest, in October 1990 35 people met and agreed to work with the CRRP. Approximately 20 people participated in the capacity building program under the auspices of Antonito Revitalization, with a half dozen making up the active core. The initiative enjoyed strong support at the outset from the town government and from Save the Children, an internationally known family assistance organization active in the town.

A key concern of the team was to secure representation from all of the town's cultures and thus build consensus among ethnic groups. Some 90 percent of the local population is of Hispanic origin with the remainder from other ethnic backgrounds. The adoption of one primary goal (to raise the economic level of Antonito by relying on the existing resource base to attract tourists and provide recreational activities) helped facilitate the necessary support and participation. A number of opportunities have been pursued under this heading.

In the first instance the community sought to build upon its traditions as a railroad town. While the depot is now closed, the town still boasts one of the premier tourist attractions in southern Colorado – the Cumbres and Toltec Scenic Railway. Spiked down in 1880 to serve the mining camps in the San Juan Mountains this 64 mile track was scheduled for closure by Denver and Rio Grande Western Railroad in the 1960s. Local citizens responded by setting up a Save the Narrow Gauge Railroad Group. It changed its name in 1969 to the Colorado–New Mexico Better Transportation Association and became the foundation of a movement which persuaded both states to buy the line and establish a local management authority to operate it as a tourist attraction. In 1993 some 56 000 passengers were carried during the season extending from Memorial Weekend to mid-October.

A key limitation of this enterprise for the prosperity of Antonito is its location on the fringe of the town. The revitalization committee examined, with technical assistance, the feasibility of establishing a stronger link between the town center, the vacant station and the scenic railroad base. But in order to achieve something with immediate impact on residents and visitors the group promoted, in May 1991, the first Antonito Spring Steam Festival. This drew a crowd of some 200 to enjoy a day of train rides, a pancake breakfast, an arts and craft show, a chuckwagon supper, entertainment and fireworks. Since then the annual event has grown from strength to strength and was extended to two days in 1994 when several hundred people participated in a program which included an outdoor Catholic mass, music and dancing. Underpinning its success is strong collaboration between the revitalization committee, the town council and the Chamber of Commerce; in 1994 a new and innovative grassroots organization known as Arco Iris Center for Creative Development was a partner in and co-sponsor of the project. The significance of this latter group for the economic regeneration of Antonito is discussed below.

A second area of activity with which Antonito Revitalization has concerned itself is an improvement in townscape quality. A town clean-up in 1991 gained widespread participation. Again with technical assistance from the CRRP, the committee worked with a university landscape architect to draw up proposals for a downtown facelift. One element comprised the architectural unification of storefronts along the main street. The idea was to present an Old West theme by adding uniform signage, old fashioned names for businesses and decorative wood trim to building façades. A related project called for the greening of downtown which included window boxes, hanging baskets and tree planting. The revitalization committee has placed new trees outside the post office and town hall as the first stage in plowing back profits from the Spring Steam Festival into the community (Plate 3). Further planting is scheduled and the fact that these first trees have not been vandalized suggests that they are strongly symbolic of community regeneration. In 1994 the committee engaged the Colorado School of Mines to prepare a phasing plan and model for the enhancement of the town center. From the federally funded Intermodal Surface Transportation Efficiency Act (ISTEA), under the Department of Transport, the town council has received a grant of $300 000 for new street kerbs, sidewalks and storm water channels. Antonito is located on the 129 mile Los Caminos Antiguos Historic and Scenic Byway and the incorporation of the town's history into an interpretative plan dealing with the Hispanic influence on the cultural heritage of the region is anticipated to bring further financial support.

Finally, the CRRP gave technical design assistance to a very active museum committee which had obtained property adjacent to the railway for future premises. Since registered as a non-profit organization, the Conejos Parks, Education and Heritage Foundation of Conejos County purchased a building in 1993 to house the museum and cultural center. A loan of $3700 was obtained from the town council to facilitate the acquisition.

Plate 3 Antonito: new planting and sidewalk

Antonito Revitalization is itself now a non-profit organization with its monthly meetings giving way to more frequent get togethers as the Spring Festival approaches. Its committee of 10 people was headed in 1994 by three individuals who were part of the Kellogg funded revitalization project. Their principal concerns remain the ongoing greenscaping of Antonito and the organizing of the festival. The effort associated with this agenda is focused and has been sustained over time. But perhaps most importantly, this group has realized that there is little merit in seeking to claim territorial control over all the social and economic challenges facing Antonito. The emergence of complementary organizations has been welcomed and accepted as strong evidence of a healthy community dynamic. Two alliances are especially noteworthy.

Firstly, an Antonito Gaming Committee has tried, since limited stakes gambling was permitted in Colorado in 1990, to have Antonito added to the select list of towns. In 1992 72 percent of Colorado voters refused to allow gambling in Antonito and 13 other gateway towns. The matter did not die at that stage and a new petition drive was launched for the 1994 ballot. This fell foul of a state Supreme Court decision which ruled that the adopted ballot title was misleading, thus postponing the vote to 1996. Within Antonito, as might be expected, there are very strongly held views for and against the proposal. Proponents argue economic growth, opponents respond with concerns about impact on quality of life. In 1992, 54 percent of residents voted against gambling, which would suggest that a subsequent local vote could go either way. Much will depend on how informed the electorate is about these issues, but the fact that there is debate within the community is an encouraging sign. As outlined in Chapter 1 an acceptance of controversy and a political focus on issues and policies are essential characteristics of an entrepreneurial community.

A second community group which has emerged in the town is Arco Iris Center for Creative Development. At its inaugural meeting in February 1994 there were 35 people in attendance from whom a committee was elected. This non-profit organization seeks to provide self-help opportunities and to empower the community through cultural arts, small business development, training and financial assistance programs. In regard to its mission a spokesman has commented as follows:

Occasionally individuals can make changes, and if they fit together and recognize common goals, the chances for creating those goals increase dramatically. People do support what they help create and Arco Iris wants to help create an atmosphere to support the people of Antonito to implement changes we want to make in our community.

It is perhaps significant that one of the visionaries in this group has been a recent participant in the Colorado Agricultural Leadership Program established in 1983 to strengthen the pool of trained leaders available to serve rural Colorado. In its short time of existence Arco Iris has hosted a Small Business Administration seminar, produced a newsletter, organized arts workshops and sought to establish a Conejos County Mission Tour with an accompanying video. Again consistent with the characteristics of an entrepreneurial community this group demonstrates a commitment to network widely, draws upon reflective and innovative leadership, and provides a high level of information about its activities.

In short this brief analysis would suggest that while the needs of Antonito are many, its process and product achievements are not inconsiderable. Antonito is well placed to face the challenges of the immediate future.

Custer County

The Valley's civic leaders of just a decade ago would be amazed at what has happened along the Main Streets of Westcliffe and Silver Cliff. These days, we've got two bed-and-breakfasts and even an espresso bar; there are two feed and tack stores and a saddle shop; a clothing store; an antique emporium; arts and crafts galleries; all this in addition to Westcliffe's and Silver Cliff's long-established businesses. Long gone are the days when empty storefronts outnumbered the going concerns. When Gov. Romer visited Westcliffe earlier this year, he and his staff were impressed with the strength and vitality of the local business community.
(Editorial, *Wet Mountain Tribune*, 2 December 1993)

Custer County in south central Colorado extends eastwards from the Sangre de Cristo range across the high grassland country of Wet Mountain Valley to the Wet Mountains beyond. Its contemporary ranching and tourism-oriented economy masks a former greatness associated with gold and silver production. From 1870 homesteaders arrived in significant numbers only to be followed

by a rush of prospectors and miners. Mining towns in the
area have come and gone and today there are only two settlements of significant size.

The first, Silver Cliff, was the third largest city in
Colorado at the 1880 census with a population of 5040.
Only Denver with 35 629 residents and Leadville with
14 820 residents were larger. However, by 1882 the mining
boom was over and the population steadily declined.
Many businessmen and homeowners moved to nearby
Westcliffe to escape the higher taxes of its sister city and
hastened this decline. During the 1880s Westcliffe developed as a railroad town for the supply and transportation
needs of local ranchers and farmers. It was incorporated in
1887 and became the county seat of Custer County in 1928.
Relative prosperity was again followed, however, by
steady decline. The Denver and Rio Grande Railroad abandoned its line in 1937 leaving the valley area isolated. A
further slump during the 1950s brought business closure
and population loss. Thus, for example, in the 1940s
Westcliffe had five grocery stores, two drug stores and a
bank. By 1975 there was only one grocery store and the
bank and drug stores had closed.

Some twenty years later, however, Custer County has
been rediscovered with local prosperity strongly under-
pinned by a combination of recreation, tourism and a
thriving ranchette property market. In 1994 there were no
fewer than eight real estate companies and some 45 con-
struction-related businesses in the twin towns. The boost-
erism associated with the current boom is strikingly
displayed by the following advertisement:

> Prime 35 acre parcels in an Alpine setting, located at the very base
> of the Rocky Mountains. Excellent tree coverage consisting of
> Aspen, Ponderosa Pine and Blue Spruce. The parcels feature close
> up views of the Rocky Mountains to the West, and the views to
> the East look over a lush Valley to the Wet Mountains and to
> Pike's Peak in the distance. Nearby National Forest and
> Wilderness access. Abundant wildlife is seen on the Ranch. Power
> has been distributed to each parcel. The roads at the Ranch have
> been deeded to the County. Live creeks traverse some of the
> parcels. Fourteen parcels have already sold and there are prime
> parcels remaining! Parcel prices range from $125 000 to $146 000.
> (*Wet Mountain Tribune 1994 Real Estate and Builders' Guide*)

The editorial comment at the outset of this section thus
correctly identifies the transformation that has taken place

in the fortunes of Custer County. Population has almost doubled from 1120 to 1926 over the period 1970–90. The 1995 estimate was for 2333 persons. The unemployment rate in July 1994 was posted at 3.5 percent reflecting summer job peaks associated with the agriculture, tourism and construction industries. Clearly a key challenge for the local community has been the formulation of appropriate management of change strategies. The CRRP was set, therefore, to enter the area at a crucial point in this planning process and while a number of initial successes were achieved, the unfolding of more recent events points to some significant tensions accompanying the realization of a policy-loaded agenda.

Custer County was invited to join the Project in July 1988, following the initiative of a County Commissioner who was keen to bring about closer collaboration between Silver Cliff and Westcliffe on revitalization efforts. Concerns about a local economic downturn at that time had been linked to the closure of a nearby 3000 acre ski area after 15 years of operation. Twenty-four volunteers came forward to serve on the Custer County Revitalization Committee representing broad interests from both towns. However, soon after attendance at a regional leadership training program and a local follow-up session on strategic planning, participation began to decline owing to competing commitments and differing opinions about the group's direction. Nevertheless, 15 active members continued to meet twice a month and went on to establish a suite of 12 goals. These may be listed as follows:

1. To develop a means for retaining water rights in the county in an equitable manner.
2. To develop permanent, full-time job opportunities, including more businesses in all sectors.
3. To retain quality of life features of the present county and communities when planning for growth.
4. To improve communication, coordination and cooperation throughout the county.
5. To develop a successful four season resort and ski area.
6. To remove Sangre de Cristo and Green Horn Mountain areas from proposed wilderness designation.
7. To develop activities to enhance existing agriculture.
8. To develop additional cultural and recreational activities, including a community recreation center for both residents and tourists.

9. To develop more youth programs.
10. To retain and take advantage of Custer County's authentic western atmosphere.
11. To explore the feasibility of merging Silver Cliff and Westcliffe town governments.
12. To establish a community foundation as a means of financing county improvement projects.

In order to secure legitimacy for these goals with the wider community a questionnaire was distributed to 650 residents to which a response rate of over 87 percent was achieved. Support for these goals, rated as "strongly agree" and "agree", was within a band of 76 to 90 percent. The analysis indicated that a large majority of Custer County residents was very supportive of the deliberations of the Revitalization Committee. Two community meetings to discuss the survey results and a community workshop to develop action plans for economic development based on agriculture, recreation and tourism were then convened. Thus, throughout the period the committee appreciated the importance of information sharing (a newsletter was published) and increased community participation, if these initial capacity-building measures were to be sustained.

On the project outcome side the committee was successful in procuring the appointment of a peripatetic services administrator for both towns and in securing equipment storage premises again shared by Westcliffe and Silver Cliff. Collaboration with the local Chamber of Commerce prompted the hiring of a Community Activities Coordinator who helped develop a calendar of local events and design a summer recreation program. Finally, two other projects resulted when committee personnel pursued individual interests for the betterment of the community. One member has been working on the refurbishment of the old Westcliffe schoolhouse as a museum and youth center (Plate 4). Several other members who call their group "All Aboard Westcliffe" have established an historic railroad district, acquired and fitted out a caboose to use as a visitor center and secured the listing of the Denver and Rio Grande Engine House in Westcliffe in the State Register of Historic Properties. It is difficult to untangle the contribution made by the CRRP from the personal interests and abilities of those involved in an assessment of these two very successful projects. The engine house listing was only achieved in December 1993. Refurbishment of the schoolhouse commenced in August 1994 having drawn down contributions of \$34 000 from the Colorado Department of Local Affairs, \$13 500 from the Colorado Historical Society and \$13 000 from the Gates Foundation. Notwithstanding the winding-up of the Revitalization Committee after only one year, the momentum to implement both projects has continued unabated. At the very least the capacity-building program of the CRRP is perceived by their proponents to have enhanced their personal confidence in working through complex long haul agendas.

Plate 4   Westcliffe: schoolhouse, museum and youth center

Fresh efforts to reawaken community participation in a county-wide strategic planning process began again in January 1993. The combined energies of the County Extension Agent and the Colorado State University Community Development Specialist for the region eventually facilitated a working session the following April at which some 30 citizens reviewed progress toward the goals set five years earlier and began to think about future improvement activities. At a follow-up meeting in May, residents were selected to work on four theme committees comprising economic development, social development, quality of life and agriculture. However, while the commitment of participants was well intentioned, the initial flourish of activity was quickly dissipated. Undoubtedly the

transfer of the County Extension Agent to another part of
Colorado removed an important catalyst from the community, but also important was a combination of turf protection by other interests and the involvement of committee
personnel in highly controversial public policy issues. Brief
mention may be made of two matters.

The first concerned a proposal by the Colorado Air
National Guard to establish a Military Operations Area
over the Wet Mountain Valley and portions of the Sangre
de Cristo mountains. Its approval would permit low level
military aircraft training. Locally perceived adverse
impacts on the county economy and human health
prompted the formation of the Custer County Action
Association to coordinate and present community objec-
tions. The Revitalization Committee was inevitably drawn
into this debate thus placing the Extension office as a
"cooperating public agency" in a difficult position regarding advocacy one way or the other.

A second issue attracting controversy is the subdivision
of ranches. Many hold the view that this process has
helped revitalize the local economy; others bemoan the loss
of traditional ranching lifestyles. The instrument for mediation comprises the zoning resolution for the county. During
1993 and 1994 both state and county administrations considered proposals which would significantly have changed
land use policy by increasing the smallest parcel a
landowner could sell from 35 acres to 160 acres and by
increasing the minimum acreage for new homes in the floor
of Wet Mountain Valley from 80 acres to 160 acres. While
both propositions were eventually defeated, one consequence in Custer County was the tension created between
the Revitalization Committee on the one hand and the
more powerful land-holding interests of the Colorado
Cattlemen's Association and the Custer County Stock-
growers' Association on the other; the former had adopted
a goal of ranching preservation while the latter were
opposed to tighter land zoning policies. The possibility of
fewer new homes in the future also ran counter to the
interests of the Chamber of Commerce and the Valley
Merchants and Community Association of Westcliffe/Silver
Cliff even though the Revitalization Committee had
adopted a goal of creating yet another business development committee to foster economic development. Again
the Extension agent as a key catalyst for the Revitalization
Committee faced a daunting lose–lose scenario in regard to

credibility with ranching and business interests. Not surprisingly the community revitalization aspect of the agency agenda has been quietly dropped as a priority in Custer County. Without this leadership the activities of the Revitalization Committee did lose momentum.

The value of this case study lies with the insights offered into the *realpolitik* of community-led revitalization which in this instance pitched highly motivated volunteers against more powerful institutional and sectoral interests. Community leadership must not only be alive to the need and opportunity for change but also be acutely sensitive to the reality that protest-led actions may be counterproductive when the development agenda is richly multifaceted by overlapping themes and fractured by multiple interest groups. Agency personnel who become involved in such an arena need the skill to deal effectively with complex public issues.

In late 1994 a third wave of community participation in building a better future began to assert itself. An umbrella organization called Custer County 2020 has sought to redefine a shared vision, prepare a development strategy with as full a representation of stakeholders as possible, and move forward to project implementation. It is anticipated that this planning process will qualify the community to benefit from an endowment of up to $100 000 from the Colorado Trust under its Healthy Communities Initiative. Again the involvement of new leadership in this work is significant. Vociferous opposition from a small group of citizens concerned about the perceived moral agenda of the Colorado Trust will test its resilience. In short the Custer County experience underlines the principle that strategic planning cannot be viewed as a purely technical activity. It requires close integration with community development processes which seek to heal division through understanding and collaboration.

Walden

And, in a larger way, what is the matter with community spirit, community force, community character? North Park spirit, force, character? That is what you need. And the way to get it is to keep your brains, your energy, your money, working at home for your good and the community's good. Whoever helps the community, helps you.
(From an advertisement of the early 1900s, reported in the Jackson County Star Centennial Edition, 8 November 1990)

Walden is located in Jackson County, commonly known as North Park, which comprises a high, isolated intermontane basin opening north into Wyoming. The enclosed physical geography and the one-time great number of buffalo which used to summer in the area led the Ute Indians to coin the name Buffalo Pen for this part of rural Colorado. While the discovery of gold, silver and copper brought settlers to North Park, the growing prosperity of the area in the early twentieth century owed much to the mining of good quality lignite coal and fluorspar. This was also ranching territory and it was from the need for a centrally located trading post that Walden eventually emerged. The original plat was recorded in 1889 and the town was incorporated on 2 December 1890. The railway arrived in 1911 as a result of a project linking Laramie to Coalmont for the purpose of transporting coal. The contemporary local economy is still very much dependent upon the natural resource utilization which prompted the settling of the area in the first instance. Ranching, lumber, coal and latterly tourism are key wealth-creating sectors. Relative isolation has, however, continued to hold back population growth with the 890 residents recorded for Walden in the 1990 census representing some 55 percent of total population in Jackson County. The downsizing of mining employment during the 1980s and uncertainty in the lumber industry have made job creation a longstanding community priority. Thus, the involvement of the CRRP in Walden was well timed since the community had already begun to address the challenge of local economic development.

In 1987 the volunteer memberships of the North Park Economic Development Council and North Park Chamber of Commerce joined with the Walden Town Council and the Jackson County Board of County Commissioners to produce a five year economic development action plan for the area. Funding was provided by the Colorado Department of Local Affairs, Division of Commerce and Development. Six major objectives were identified comprising business development, recreation, community enhancement, retaining the railroad, agriculture diversification and community capacity building. Local morale was further boosted when also in 1987 Walden was selected to provide the 1990 Christmas tree for the Capitol in Washington thus coinciding with the celebration of Walden's centennial.

It was upon this foundation that Walden was selected in 1988 as a Year 1 CRRP community. Ten volunteers came together to form the North Park Revitalization Committee. During the interim its membership has seen changes; for various periods the committee has been able to draw upon town board members, town staff, county commissioners, residents, business people, ranchers and county administrators. This mix of public, private and voluntary sector participation is an important feature of the internal dynamic of the committee and has allowed new leadership to become involved; at one stage, for example, the Chair was held by the District Ranger of the Forest Service whose involvement was totally consistent with the 1990 Farm Bill provisions on rural revitalization, as outlined above in Chapter 2.

At the outset the committee examined the various opportunities available for revitalizing the local economy. Five goals were established which may be listed as follows: to develop materials and methods for promoting the area; to identify and develop the area's potential for natural-resource-based industry and tourism; to expand medical services for present residents and in order to attract new residents; to enhance and extend leadership abilities in local people; and to beautify and clean up the town. As with other CRRP communities, training was needed to help build the capacity of participants to bring about effective action, but in the case of Walden a more direct link between process and product was achieved. During the 25 hours of regional training, convened in December 1988, the committee was given the task of presenting a slide show on the personality of its area. This was subsequently developed into two promotional videos for tourism which were then used to recruit a doctor for the town. A $40 000 Forest Diversification Grant had financed this project and by using the remainder of the funds, together with technical assistance from the CRRP, the group went on to publish a tourism brochure, design a town signage package, produce a town marketing plan and prepare proposals for a wetlands recreation park and information kiosk; the kiosk was completed in the summer of 1990 (Plate 5).

The committee also played a key role in advancing proposals for a regional visitors' environmental center. A public–private sector partnership was formed comprising four federal and four state agencies, the local utility company, banking, mining, forestry and agribusiness industries, the Chamber of Commerce and the North Park Revitalization Committee. In November 1991 a formal memorandum of understanding was signed among all parties collaborating in the construction and operation of the interpretative center. Two years later, however, little progress had been made on taking the project forward. In March 1994 the Colorado Department of Parks and Outdoor Recreation announced its intention to build a visitor center and moose viewing platform close to Walden, with funding of some $300 000. It would seem highly unlikely that two major visitor centers can in the short term be supported in the area. Undoubtedly the profile of the North Park Revitalization Committee would have been considerably enhanced through an association with the former development. Its non-implementation would suggest the presence of local tensions associated with ownership and constituency loyalty which are battled out beneath any agreement to collaborate on a project.

Plate 5　Walden: visitor information kiosk

But even if this matter is set to one side, it still remains the case that the activities of the Revitalization Committee have been affected by internal and wider community tensions. During its formative stage there was a perception held by some members that the group was seen as operat-

ing in a rival capacity to the already established Economic
Development Committee. Relations with this body were
not always easy, especially when information sharing by
the Economic Development Committee would have been
mutually beneficial. Secondly, there has long been an
absence of common purpose among different interest
groups in the community, a condition which spilled over
into the activities of the Revitalization Committee. Thus,
for example, ranchers were frequently less than enthusias-
tic about tourism development, town business people
showed reluctance to commit investment, residents contributed to trade leakage beyond the town into Fort Collins
and Laramie, and many employees of the logging industry
did not sufficiently integrate into the community because
of their transient lifestyle. Building consensus across this
spectrum, including town and county political representatives, has been difficult. Thirdly, there has been difficulty
in sustaining the involvement of trained participants in the
revitalization process with the result that by 1993 only two
members of the group remained from the panel involved
in the capacity building program of the CRRP. Finally, a
credibility gap had begun to emerge in regard to the
accomplishments of the committee and its potential to
bring about change given the large-scale nature of the economic development challenge. A feature article in the local
newspaper in December 1993 boasted that the
Revitalization Committee was alive and well and went on
to list key actions undertaken during the previous 12
months: the 75 percent restoration of a railway caboose
whose further siting and use will be put to the community
for consultative input; the commissioning of conceptual
designs for townscape improvements along Main Street;
collaboration with the Jackson County Board of
Commissioners on signage for the information kiosk; the
preparation of information displays inside the kiosk; the
erection of Welcome to North Park signs; and research on
commemorative plaques for historic buildings in Walden.

It certainly would be unfair to suggest that the
Revitalization Committee is operating on the margins in
terms of major impact; these activities are totally consistent
with the goals established at the outset of the CRRP in
1988. That the Revitalization Committee is in existence at
all, given some deep structural difficulties, speaks well of

the commitment of its membership. But there is a danger that those efforts may be allowed to drift at this level and that potential contributors to a broader revitalization agenda may not identify strongly with these actions, thus depriving the collective push for change of fresh citizen involvement.

It is significant, therefore, that in April 1994 members of the community went back to basics and started again to build a vision for the area, based on a search for consensus and greater breadth of activities. Upwards of 40 people met to begin the strategic planning process with technical facilitation provided by expertise from the Northwest Colorado Council of Governments – a voluntary association of 32 local governments in a six county region, constituted in 1972 to provide a range of regional services including community development. The rationale for this fresh initiative was captured well by one of the conveners from the North Park Revitalization Committee:

> ... the community has no vision. Without a common vision the community cannot decide where to go next or what to do first. There is a great need for the community to draw together and determine where it wants to go so that our limited resources are focused on the right future.

Perhaps a key insight from this case study is that development processes are not necessarily linear in character moving easily from initiation through to maturity. The pattern of progression is much more complex and can include some winding around for a period of time at a level beyond basic animation and with modest accomplishments building confidence. It then requires a people-led response, perhaps stimulated by controversy or misfortune to restart the push upwards on the development scale. It is interesting that Walden has recently experienced such a combination of provocative circumstances, which has given implementation of projects an unprecedented urgency.

In 1993 the Wyoming and Colorado Railroad Company filed for abandonment of the line from the state border to Walden. A previous application in 1991 had been withdrawn. Local suppliers of coal, lumber and fluorspar again argued that shipping arrangements would be adversely affected by closure. Also in 1993 rangeland reforms announced by the Bureau of Land Management and the Forest Service proposed the replacement of the then existing grazing fee formula across the United States. Locally within North Park, where there are extensive tracts of land under the control of both agencies, the response by ranchers was hostile as expected. Further controversy towards the end of that year was prompted by a proposal to build a 4200 acre all-season resort near Walden, with an employment potential for 500 jobs. The Colorado State Land Board, perhaps mindful of the opposition of the Governor to the project, rejected the proposal. A substantially modified scheme, involving only 80 acres, was re-submitted in the spring of 1994. At that time Rocky Mountain Natural Gas announced that its wells, used to supply Walden, had been virtually depleted. This has necessitated the connection of the town to a transcontinental pipeline near Laramie and could increase average customer bills almost threefold. But, arguably, of greatest immediate significance for the economy of Walden has been the decision by the Louisiana Pacific Corporation to close its timber processing mill in the town in July 1994 on the basis of falling stocks of raw material and higher input costs; some 65 employees have been offered transfer opportunities.

The fresh vigor injected into the revitalization effort in Walden has undoubtedly been sharpened by opinions and impacts connected with these events. Particularly significant is the determination of the town council which has recently opened an economic development office staffed by a part-time project manager and assistant. Their joint brief is the determined completion of those projects which have originated in part from earlier community visioning exercises, and in part from more recent economic development necessity. This high profile focus on performance and results contrasts with the more passive stance adopted contemporaneously by Jackson County. In Walden there is a clear need to work towards an agreed vision which draws upon wider participation and closer collaboration among those whose interest and brief is rural development in North Park.

Wellington

In small towns like ours, town government only performs the nuts and bolts functions that keep the town going. In our community, CRRP pulled together a group of people willing to spend time and energy to do something creative for the betterment of the town.
(Cited in Colorado State University Cooperative Extension (1992)
Visions in Action)

Wellington, described as the northern gateway to Colorado, is located just beyond Fort Collins and adjacent to Interstate Route 25 which connects Denver with Cheyenne. It was incorporated in 1905 and, during the early decades of the twentieth century, developed as a railroad, farming and oil-dependent town. Today Wellington is an expanding bedroom community; in 1990 a peak census population of 1340 was recorded. Development pressure in Fort Collins, where the estimated 1993 population of 95 000 was some 6000 more than the 1990 figure, makes it inevitable that growth management strategies will continue to push this small town population upwards. The significant contribution made by a group of local volunteers as a result of their involvement with the CRRP is helping to improve the quality of life in Wellington for long-term residents and newcomers.

In 1988 the Wellington Town Board applied for assistance through the CRRP and, following selection, some 12 people attended the leadership training sessions. The group organized as the Community Awareness Participation Program (CAPP) and adopted primary goals of overcoming local lethargy and improving the town's image. At first CAPP tried to encourage some residents to develop a quilting cottage industry, but after finding little community enthusiasm for this project it turned its attention to developing an agricultural museum. A similar facility in Fort Collins was visited and contact was made with Burlington Northern Railroad to obtain information on the history of Wellington. By putting together a display, CAPP members hoped to spark community interest in local history and thus begin to gather support for the museum. However, they again met with little enthusiasm.

The group subsequently turned its attention to town enhancement and sponsored a clean-up effort called Trash Busters. A measure of breakthrough was achieved with the 12 person committee organizing and implementing the event in the first year being joined by a total of 75 volunteers some three years later. Town beautification thus emerged as the operational niche for CAPP, a mission which was still being pursued in 1994 though the committee had reduced in the interim to five persons. Technical assistance provided by the CRRP produced a design for a pedestrian walkway along four blocks of Wellington's main street linking a recently renovated park with a river

along the southern edge of the town. Funding this walkway proved difficult initially and out of 86 proposals only
one generated a positive response: a local business
donated $500. The committee then applied for Energy
Impact Assistance from the state and received $50 000. The
continued soliciting of moneys allowed a package of $64 000
to be assembled. Some $45 000 was spent on a range of
streetscape improvements including tree planting, the siting of flower beds and the introduction of new street furni-
ture (Plate 6). Local participation in maintaining the
planting was encouraged through an Adopt a Barrel
scheme. Now registered as a non-profit organization this
small cadre of volunteers, who share strong bonds of
friendship, would acknowledge that the CRRP was instru-
mental in bringing them together to work on community
service. Their ambitions go no further than creating a
greenbelt and bike path along the river corridor, but what
they have learnt is how to engage necessary people, funds
and material resources to stay with and complete a highly
visible project for community betterment.

Plate 6   Wellington: townscape improvements

This type of safe, non-threatening project would seem to be an ideal way by which local leadership capacity can be nurtured. The alternative model involving a large-scale project with significantly greater capital and recurrent costs is undoubtedly more controversial especially when there are real or perceived implications for the public purse and future local taxation. The Wellington community was drawn into such an arena during 1993 when a new non-profit organization comprising public representatives and residents advanced a proposal for a $2.5 million cultural center and museum. The group, calling itself the Cultural Conservancy, was keen to focus on the multiethnic heritage of the area whose history includes American Indian and German Russian settlers. A seed grant of $1300 from the Larimer County Commissioners combined with $600 from residents allowed the proponents of the project to undertake some preliminary investigations. These included conceptual design of the buildings, a funding search and a community survey to raise awareness and to begin gathering support. Preliminary results from the latter were positive and encouraged the Cultural Conservancy to press ahead. However, a combination of circumstances conspired against progression of the initiative beyond December 1993. A vociferous but small minority in the town continually expressed open concern about the long-term viability of the project and its consequences for the town budget. Suspicions that the proposed site included some 5.4 acres of public land, which could be better used to generate liquid revenue, added to the controversy. Crucial was the loss of a number of very supportive town trustees from the municipal council who, having moved residence outside the jurisdiction, had to resign their seats. Without this political patronage the advocacy of the project within the local decision-making arena was irreparably undermined. The work of the Cultural Conservancy was brought to an abrupt halt during public debate in the Council Chamber.

As a case study Wellington provides a useful illustration of the need in rural development to arouse the involvement of a much greater number of the silent majority in communities. The early activities of CAPP suffered from an acknowledged community indifference and the townscape improvements have attracted, at best, quiet appreciation. Had the sponsors of Cultural Conservancy been able to turn these into open support then the potential of the project and its associated leadership would not have been lost to the community. Perhaps the single greatest challenge in community-led rural development is turning this key of apathy.

Key issues

In the previous chapter a suite of institutional and operational issues associated with the Colorado Rural Revitalization Project was identified. The discussion in this chapter is set at the local level and has concerned itself with tracing the community impact of the Project and the subsequent short-term legacy. It is difficult to disentangle cause and effect relationships over time given the changing nature of participation and circumstance. The case studies related above have not been designed specifically for that purpose, but rather to provide insights into process trends within communities which share a common process baseline. Some issues particular to each case study have already been raised in the analysis and in this section it is intended to deal with some overarching themes. Seven main and related matters can be identified.

The importance of capacity building

From the outset the CRRP was conceptualized as a social change system composed of university and state agency personnel, working with a recipient system comprising residents participating in a local community, through a change nexus of a committee structure. Anticipated effects were activities (action espisodes), specific happenings or attainments (events) and the creation of new social relationships (linkages). The case studies identify both process and product outcomes related to this catalytic conceptual framework. However, the withdrawal of the formal social change system at the conclusion of the Project has required community adaptation and the refocusing of former dependency upon external change agents. This adjustment has involved a shift from comprehensive and concentrated assistance over a period of time to aid which is more selective but predominantly product biased. The net result is that the leadership training dimension to capacity building effort has seldom been revisited (except notably in Holyoke) or has been piecemeal and individualistic. Yet with new personnel on community committees, with new challenges and opportunities, this would seem as necessary as at the outset. Sustainability of effort and achievement cannot be divorced from continuity of community development training measures facilitated by outside expertise.

The role of partnership

The case studies underscore clearly the need for volunteer committees to work closely with public and private sector interests. Community-led revitalization, in particular, cannot be regarded as an alternative to elected local governance. It exists, rather, in a complementary role. While a weak public partnership perspective can frustrate a project (the Walden interpretative center was rejected as a recipient of Forest Service grant aid because of the reluctance of Jackson County to commit support to the project), the analysis also demonstrates that close working relationships can generate major dividends (for example, the successful Antonito Spring Steam Festival or the streetscape improvements in Wellington).

The need for staying power

The case studies demonstrate that initial accomplishments under the CRRP have not always provided the platform for additional immediate action episodes or events. Because of technical requirements or funding the gestation period is frequently long. It is interesting that communities faced with these blockages have continued to promote the bonding of existing social relationships and the creation of new ones (for example, the community jamboree in Victor, the 1994 vision setting of Walden, the formation of Arco Iris in Antonito). Very often the importance of these linkages is undervalued when measurements of success deal only with visible capital investment outcomes. It is a truism that rural development is a long-haul operation. Staying power has much to do with the renewal of community interaction and how this can be harnessed to enhance the local participative culture. At times the onus may be on a few key individuals to sustain the development agenda. In these circumstances the synergy created between community leadership and pursuit of a pet project, particularly if it is at implementation stage, can be a powerful antidote to volunteer burn-out (for example the restoration of a train engine shed in Westcliffe or the provision of a youth facility in Victor).

The value of flexible implementation

Much of the evidence in this book attests to the value of community-led rural development which draws upon the visioning and implementation efforts from volunteer committees. While a community strategic plan, agreed at the outset and perhaps rolled forward during subsequent years, charts a necessary development path, it is often the case that local circumstances derived from domestic politics and personnel availability, together with operational factors linked to resources, priorities and timing, can hold back the delivery of projects sponsored initially by a community revitalization alliance. The Walden example demonstrates the potential value of altering the implementation approach by internalizing it for a period within local government in order to attempt to achieve results more quickly, to demonstrate visible success and to rebuild volunteer enthusiasm and initiative. It would seem important, however, that this municipal input to the implementation process should not run ahead of community consensus.

The practice of inclusion

Communities are not homogeneous entities which can secure quick and easy agreement on development directions. In small rural communities an outspoken and hostile minority can often have a major impact on shaping the local development agenda, either to prompt change or to maintain the status quo. The case studies demonstrate the need for community initiatives to practice inclusion through open and constructive processes of working together and through providing full and unbiased information to all interested parties. The challenge here is to deal with diversity through mutual understanding. Discussion, sensitive leadership and creativity are essential ingredients in practicing inclusion and building strong intra-community collaboration.

The legitimacy of the objectives

Being mindful of the questionable legitimacy of a volunteer revitalization committee in its community, there was a requirement from the designers of the CRRP that participants receive a local government mandate. Wider consultation with residents on goals and objectives (for example in Custer County and Wellington) was also used to enhance this imperative of public accountability. But difficulties can arise with projects which involve a high capital expenditure. *Vis-à-vis* a high order shared goal for economic development, community groups may be unwilling or unable to move beyond low cost/low risk ventures. Again difficulties can arise when certain objectives, even if they command popular support, run counter to the objectives of more powerful interests. This is particularly the case when a community group moves beyond projects to public policy-related concerns and in so doing, perhaps unwittingly, changes its role from positive advocate to negative adversary. For professional agency personnel working with development committees this situation can be especially troublesome. On both counts the search for more inclusive arenas of debate, a stronger focus on issues and not personalities, and the gathering of broader commitments to investment-led local strategies would seem useful in beginning to address the legitimacy dilemma.

A balanced development agenda

As mentioned at the outset of this book the imperative of job creation has prompted many communities to become involved in self-help activity. The challenge of rural development, however, is much broader, a point well illustrated by the analysis of CRRP activities as a whole in Chapter 4 above. There is a potential in revitalization activity for the agenda to be dominated by more powerful interests associated with capital – to the detriment of those who could be regarded as socially excluded in local society (the old, the young, the unskilled, those in need of affordable housing). The case studies do pick up on these concerns and signal the need to be wary of local elitism in both needs assessment and project implementation.

Conclusion

This chapter completes the main empirical content of the book by dealing with community-led rural development matters at the local scale. While there is a rich diversity of experience across the six communities, there is also sufficient common ground from which to generate matters of wider relevance. In the final analysis these may be distilled into process- and product-related concerns.

At the outset of the CRRP it was broadly the case that participant committees could be measured in terms of low process capacity and low product achievement. The combination of training, technical assistance and project accomplishment was designed to realize a collective potential and begin to shift a low performance condition towards higher levels of attainment. In the interim some groups have developed more along the process axis, while others have remained more firmly rooted in the product side. Common to all, however, is the realization that a "go it alone" development approach is not conducive to progression in either sphere. Time and time again the case studies returned to the fundamental principle of collaboration as the mechanism by which a positional advantage can be secured.

At a broader level it could be argued that collaboration based on community interaction, community collaboration with other partners and collaboration between institutional and agency personnel, and with political representatives, amounts almost to a paradigm shift in rural development. It is appropriate, therefore, that the final chapter should now turn to examine more closely the rationale for and implications of a collaborative approach to the revitalization of rural America.

Rediscovering rural community through collaboration

6

Now Main Street's whitewashed windows and vacant stores
Seems like there ain't nobody wants to come down here no more
They're closing down the textile mill across the railroad tracks
Foreman says these jobs are going boys and they ain't coming
     back to your hometown
Your hometown
Your hometown
Your hometown.

(Bruce Springsteen: *My hometown* (1984))

Whither rural communities?

On 16 August 1989 *The Wall Street Journal* featured a report about life on the Great Plains which included the following account of Keota, Colorado:

Brooding beneath its black water tower, alone amid an immense stillness, this near ghost town is a reminder – and perhaps a portent.

Something terrible happened here. Deserted sidewalks, pathways to nowhere, thread past yawning cellar pits of homes that no longer exist. The town bristles with boarded up buildings and don't tread on me signs – "Keep Out", "Private", "No Trespassing" and at least one don't tread on me resident who tells a visitor to "get the hell out of here". The land itself, sometimes the sickly color of window putty, sometimes blown away to expose fist sized rocks is a dust bowl wound still healing over with grass. Here is a landscape so vast that only its titanic thunderheads, boiling up in the slanting afternoon sunlight, seem in scale. Yet there is something mesmerizing about its sweep and its solitude. The Indian word Keota, by one definition, refers to a fire died out. And so it symbolizes the question overhanging this least known, least appreciated region of the US.

Is the fire dying out in the Great Plains? (p. 1)

In September 1990 Rob Gurwitt wrote about Baker, Montana, in *Governing*:

Not too long ago, there were four farm implement dealers; since Gary Bottsford closed down the Massey Ferguson dealership, there have been none. The oil field jobs that used to be available to hundreds of local residents have all but disappeared, accelerating the decline in population. Hardware stores, clothing stores, auto dealerships and lumber yards have shut their doors over the last decade ... the churches are still there, but half the bars are gone. A tenth of the houses are for sale, and that doesn't include ones taken off the market for lack of demand. ... Like other rural communities across the country, it is caught up in a fundamental restructuring of the economy that is making its old ways of life obsolete.

On a cool mid June evening, Baker's loosely knit group of development minded citizens signaled what they thought of all this at a meeting. The problem with dollars and cents dismissals of towns like Baker is that they don't take into account groups such as this one. ... These are people who are living in Baker, and intend to do whatever it takes to stay. ... The activists in Baker are doing their best. They are full of ideas. ... And suddenly it seems that Baker's small size could turn out to be a source of strength. (pp. 35–38)

Notwithstanding a wide variation in the circumstances of rural communities across the United States, these two illustrations encapsulate the stark choice between atrophy and adaptation being confronted by many small towns. Keota manifests itself as an apocalyptic vision of a community which has simply surrendered to overwhelming environmental and economic catastrophe. If the heady emotion of the prose is set to one side, the fading away of this rural community remains a reality which foreshadows the prospects for those places condemned today by the politics of indifference and the economics of utility. Advocates of settlement triage, concerned with ensuring the most efficient and effective utilization of limited resources, argue that the number of rural settlements should be reduced. An academic rationale posits the view

that the dynamic changes in the contemporary rural landscape should not be constrained by a plethora of anachro-
nistic cultural relics. But, as the example of Baker confirms,
there is an intimate relationship between place and culture
which expresses itself as human attachment, shared identity and civic responsibility. The empirical evidence presented in previous chapters of this book confirms that
citizenship and community are highly valued aspects of
rural living and that there is an enthusiasm to promote
transformation as an antidote to public policy neglect and
market failure. The high standing of this more humanist
perspective on rural society compared with mechanistic
and bureaucratic responses has been captured succinctly
by Wendell Berry (1993):

> A culture capable of preserving land and people can be made only
> within a relatively stable and enduring relationship between a
> local people and its place. (p. 171)

The challenge handed down here is how such a relationship between local people and place can be sustained.
Berry's espousal of local economic strategies and local
economies strikes a familiar chord. This new localism
means that rural areas must take responsibility for their
own economic well-being and find their own niches in the
changing global market (Center for the New West, 1992).
Indeed the implementation of the provisions in the North
American Free Trade Agreement and the General
Agreement on Tariffs and Trade gives an urgency to the
task of finding creative responses which fit with these concerns. In their review of opportunities, threats and challenges from processes of globalization, Glasmeier and
Conroy (1994) emphasize the involvement of community
groups in development decisions as one of a suite of policy
needs which span national and local concerns. A special
plea is made for the identification of appropriate representatives from citizens' groups to participate in projects for
economic growth in rural America.

Here again the illustration of Baker, Montana, provides a
useful reminder of the necessary courage and commitment
required from small town residents. While this sits
squarely with the experience to date of the six Colorado
communities examined in Chapter 5, the accompanying
behavioral shift required within any rural community
should not be passed over glibly. Kathleen Norris (1993), in

her powerful evocation of contemporary life on the Great Plains, gives eloquent voice to this issue:

> Like ethnic peoples all over the world, Dakotans are in danger of becoming victims of their own mythology. As our towns are failing and our lives here become less viable, many Dakotans cling stubbornly to a myth of independence and local control that makes it difficult for us to come together and work for the things that might benefit us all. We've been slow to recognize that our traditional divisiveness (country versus town, small town versus city) makes us weak, not strong. As one North Dakota official recently put it, "We talk about a global society . . . for crying out loud, we have to open our eyes and become a state society first." (pp. 32–33)

Local activeness can effect growth (Humphrey and Wilkinson, 1993). What would seem important, therefore, is that this effort engages in linkages which are not only horizontal as between local leaders, but also vertical as between community leaders and external private investment, and state and federal officials. In short, the key to unlock the development challenge is partnership, which expressed in its richest form equates with collaboration. The rugged individualism and pioneering spirit, which, as noted above, comprise the traditional paradigm for rural society, look increasingly redundant. Within an interdependent world it would seem that the meeting of rural needs over the years ahead can best be approached through collaboratively inspired policies and actions.

Collaboration revisited

In Chapter 1 collaboration was defined (after Borich, 1994) as being concerned with the following processes:

1. Interdependent stakeholders dealing constructively with differences.
2. Interdependent stakeholders having joint ownership of the decisions involved.
3. Interdependent stakeholders assuming collective responsibility for future joint action.
4. Interdependent stakeholders creating alternative power systems which complement rather than promote the termination of existing institutions.

The evidence presented in this book identifies collaborative efforts as being both multilevel and cross-cutting: col-
laborations lie individually on and enclose the local, state
and federal scales. This interconnectedness both overtly
(say, through memoranda of understanding) and with
great subtlety (through inclusiveness, negotiation and consensus building) is reshaping the governance of rural
America. Not all the historical baggage of traditional government has been jettisoned and inertia, at the very least,
still insures that almost all rural policy formulation and
implementation take place within the confines of program-
specific goals. However, the management of public policy
within broader program structures (Mandell, 1994)
whereby people, not necessarily under the control of a
lead agency, move beyond information sharing to doing
something together, has the potential to emerge as an
exciting feature of administrative action. The activities of
the National Rural Development Council, the State Rural
Development Councils and small town municipal volunteer alliances are being steered in this direction as they
seek to understand and address differences in a constructive manner.

But the extent to which it is possible to shift from a public policy agenda dominated at present by problem searching and solving deliberations through to the creation of
alternative but complementary power systems remains
problematic, especially above the community scale. It is
recognized that the activities of the National Rural
Development Council require high level policy maker
patronage if they are to move forward from mere discussion to the securing of collective responsibility for program
area decisions. Again it is uncertain how far the activities of
Rural Development Councils can mature at state level and
still receive the benediction of the Governors' offices and
the highly influential National Governors' Association.
Even at town level collaborative action, which promotes
collective responsibility between elected representatives
and revitalization committee volunteers, is unlikely to be a
tension-free process. Gray (1989) offers a useful insight on
these dilemmas by arguing that collaboration is essentially
an emergent process rather than a prescribed state of organization. What is important is that early interactions are
skillfully managed, thus laying the groundwork for subsequent higher order relationships to be envisioned and

enacted. By adding this dynamic or evolutionary quality to the processes identified by Borich, the collaboration paradigm becomes instantly less threatening. It is predicated on deepening trust and mutual agreement.

Collaboration, at whichever process stage it is undertaken, is not an end in itself; the process is not the product. As a feature of government action it has to be designed to insure that disadvantaged rural communities can prosper. In this regard the outcomes of the Rural America Program, discussed at an aggregate level in Chapter 3, at a project-specific level in Chapter 4, and at a community case study level in Chapter 5, are significant. It is reported frequently that people and agencies have made an effort to cross their personal boundaries, notwithstanding institutional differences, turf battles in small communities, political agendas and negative attitudes. Time and patience are essential elements in building these relationships.

University expertise, especially through the Extension System, emerges from the discussion in this book as having had a crucial role to play in building linkages between state and local government and community. While inter-institutional partnerships are weighted more often to communication and cooperation, as evidenced by the Colorado Rural Revitalization Project, the evaluation research does point to the realization of many truly collaborative outcomes at the individual community level. Leadership capacity building, in particular, has engaged extensive local participation and has promoted a deeper sense of commitment and ownership. Within the traditional model of community development, the contribution of facilitators in brokering interactions is widely valued. The Rural America Program has responded to this need by transforming dependency on others into connectedness with others for shared gains. Current funding limitations have, however, precluded further enhancement of these collaborative processes at an equivalent rate.

What then are the challenges which confront effective collaboration for rural development in the United States? Gray (1989, p. 270) has expressed more broadly the necessary revision in thinking and problem solving: "Essentially, we need to switch from an image of individual sovereignty over a problem domain into one of shared ownership."

Bryson and Crosby (1992) have in turn explicated this principle in *Leadership for the common good: tackling public problems in a shared power world.* They seek to move beyond conventional organization-based thinking (for example, corporate strategic planning) to collaborative action which eclipses agency boundaries. This book, perhaps more than any other, has provided the conceptual guidance to evolving rural development structures in the United States; it fits well with the current political interest in reinventing government. In tandem with Gray the authors identify leadership as the critical variable for constructive change in a context of shared power which is defined as shared capabilities exercised by interaction between or among actors in order to achieve separate and joint aims. They emphasize that authority is not merged and that participants, whether individuals, groups or institutions, still retain the right of exit. Shared power relationships, they suggest, exist on the mid-range of a continuum:

> At one end of the continuum are organizations that hardly relate to one another, or are adversaries, dealing with a problem domain that extends beyond their capabilities. At the other end are organizations merged into a new organization that contains a problem domain, pursues shared objectives and operates cooperatively. In the mid range are coalitions of organizations that have characteristics of both extremes. As in a situation in which the problem outstrips organizational abilities, no one is fully in charge; but the organizations communicate directly and share objectives as in a merged organization. In addition, although participant organizations hope for a win–win situation, as do those in a merged organization, they will settle for a reduced gain in exchange for a reduced loss. (p. 13)

The rural development challenge could be described usefully as a "wicked" problem (after Rittel and Webber, 1973) the solving of which is beyond the capabilities of any single organization. The sheer breadth of the rural agenda has clearly created a condition whereby no one is fully in charge, where there is competition for resources, rivalry for ownership and, arguably, a preoccupation with institutional assertiveness which often relegates the constituency being served to a residual role. Leadership is crucial to redressing this imbalance and as Bryson and Crosby (1992) state:

> In shared power situations, however, leadership that encourages the participation of others must be emphasized because only it has the power to inspire and mobilize those others. (p. 21)

Essential requirements at both institutional and community levels are the vision and courage to agree to new ideas, and approaches for rural society which are supportive of mutual gain. Leadership and collaboration are inextricably linked and offer potential for the rediscovery of rural community. There are two themes which an alliance of leadership and collaboration might usefully pursue: contracting with rural America and engaging with rural communities. The remainder of this chapter discusses each matter.

Contracting with rural America

Politics is not merely a matter of personalities and political dealing: it is also a matter of ideas and of their transformation into policies and programs. Addressing the development problems of rural America requires this political consciousness to come through strongly at national, state and local levels. The review in this book of progress made over the past decade would suggest that rural issues have largely been riding a public policy elevator, moving up and down between Administrations, Congress and agencies and picking up along the way an assemblage of ideas, initiatives, policies and actions. Certainly it is easy to identify emergent themes which focus on the importance of collaboration, community and the potential contribution of human capital localism to rural revitalization. But identifying the extent to which these preferences are articulated in an agreed and resourced long-term strategy is more elusive. It could be argued that the political process is as much a wicked problem as rural development.

Adaptation of the critique of planning fashioned by Rittel and Webber (1973) offers some useful insights on this troublesome relationship. Firstly, there cannot be an exhaustive set of potential solutions to rural disadvantage; many can be formulated, but others remain at any one period of time to be discovered. Political judgment of economic feasibility and social acceptability influences the selection of those solutions which can be pursued and implemented. Thus program expenditures must be weighed against the setting of taxation thresholds and the reduction of the federal deficit. Secondly, it is vital that problem resolution is placed on as high a level as possible, given that low level action may exacerbate conditions by treating only the symptoms of a problem. When extended over space and time a preference for small steps can make it much more difficult to address effectively the structural weaknesses of rural society and economy. This should not be interpreted as being dismissive of very local action; what is important is the strategic context within which this type of activity is located. Finally, solutions advanced in an agenda for rural revitalization will be subject to varying perceptions of their merits from the wide variety of stakeholders. Such solutions may be deemed good or bad, and better or worse than previous or existing initiatives. However, by locating a desired course of action within a strategy which looks forward over a period of years, an environment can be created for negotiation and accommodation on the basis of shared power relationships. Rural America needs urgently the political will and action capacity associated with this operational outline.

Two major opportunities present themselves at the time of writing (December 1994) for the formulation of appropriate responses. These comprise: firstly, the drafting by the National Rural Development Council of an Intergovernmental Partnership Compact for rural America which is designed for the support of the Clinton Administration; and, secondly, the forthcoming 1995 Farm Bill with its anticipated rural development measures.

As outlined in Chapter 2, much of the current wave of public policy interest in rural development can be attributed to initiatives instigated during the period of the Bush Administration. In January 1990 President Bush announced a six point action plan which led to the formation of State Rural Development Councils and eventually to the broader National Rural Development Partnership. The White House, under President Clinton, has kept its distance from the specific issues facing rural America although by mid-1994 there was evidence that the domestic agenda of this Administration was beginning to turn to these concerns. By August 1994 a strategic rural development vision had been drafted as follows:

> The vision of the Federal role in rural development should be to assist communities, based on inclusive development initiatives, to become more competitive in a world marketplace, through creating sustainable economic opportunities for all residents. Given limited resources, the Administration has three priorities for its rural development efforts:

- reduce long term poverty in the poorest rural counties
- increase the viability of rural communities in areas of long term decline
- assist rural communities experiencing short term difficulty from rapid structural change due to shifts in public policy, the international marketplace, and natural disasters.
(Intergovernmental Partnership Compact of the National Rural Development Partnership, 6th Draft, 23 August 1994)

The Administration was, moreover, being invited at that time to actively support the National Rural Development Partnership by, inter alia, developing a policy linkage between the Partnership and a senior federal rural development policy maker group; reactivating policy level involvement in the National Rural Development Council; providing for reasonable funding support from multiple federal agencies; encouraging federal agencies to be involved in the Partnership as a system which provides for the flow of policy, program and management information, as well as a forum for holding discussions on rural issues and pending initiatives of interest to local, tribal, state and federal stakeholders. Quite clearly, the drafting of the Compact is an attempt to deal with the practical limitations of the National Rural Development Council as identified by the General Accounting Office. A White House mission statement on rural development, where previously there was nothing, and strong approbation of the collaborative work of the National Rural Development Partnership provide an all too necessary foundation upon which to build outcome actions.

The 1995 Farm Bill represents a related and early opportunity to begin to define more tangible objectives related to rural development. The eventual passage of the previous 1990 legislation demonstrated that rural concerns were much more than agriculture. During the interim the reinventing government initiative, the restructuring of the United States Department of Agriculture, the experience of agencies working together, and the prominence of community-led regeneration linked to capacity building have gathered momentum as features of change on the policy landscape. New challenges are also emerging from competition within the international marketplace, from the need to promote sustainable rural development through environmentally friendly investment, and from the need to plan and implement resource-based actions through

regional initiatives. All these matters would seem appropriate for inclusion in a new Farm Bill, but with the proviso
that they should contribute to a coherent strategy for the
well-being of rural America.

The final shape of the Bill will be largely influenced by
the preferences of House and Senate Republicans who
now command a majority within Congress. Their legislative agenda is aimed at ending Big Government and significantly includes an amendment to the Constitution which
would compel the Administration to balance its books. The
Congressional Budget Office estimates that to balance the
federal budget by 2002, as the Republicans propose, would
mean finding some $1200 billion in savings or extra rev-
enue over the intervening period. With the entire annual
federal budget set at $1500 billion and with the new House
Speaker ruling out further cuts in defense spending and
promoting tax cuts over the remainder of the decade, it
would seem inevitable that many federal programs will be
cut back. Welfare and health care are likely sectors to be
affected. But there is also the prospect that rural interests
could become further disadvantaged through a shrinkage
of resources.

In their mission for the first 100 days following the mid-
term elections and the swearing in of the 104th Congress,
the Republican members of the House of Representatives
have advanced a suite of new Bills in their *Contract with
America* (1994). Scant mention is made specifically of rural
America. However, remarks made by Representative Newt
Gingrich by way of a postscript are interesting. His comments relate to the potential of distance medicine, distance
learning and distance work for revolutionizing the quality
of life in rural America thus creating "the greatest explo-
sion of new opportunity for rural America in history". The
rhetoric is superficially appealing. What is most important
here, but remains unstated, is that, if these opportunities
are to become realities, rural areas in the United States
must not be left behind in the quality of information technology infrastructure, nor be disadvantaged by deregulation systems and commercial practices, nor be
underprivileged by lack of quality education and training.
Civic responsibility must partner public intervention. The
1995 Farm Bill will be a preliminary test of how the
Republican majority in Congress perceives the rural constituency. Ultimately the extent to which an appropriate

form of contracting with rural America emerges will be shaped by the interplay between the Democratic Administration and the Republican-controlled Congress. But getting beyond the inevitable wrangling in this legislation and agreeing a joint vision and resourced strategy for rural society must remain the ultimate challenge.

It is beyond the scope of this book to articulate the desired shape of a vision and strategy for rural America. Nevertheless, since a central theme of the discussion is "community", it would seem only proper to return once again to the significance of this geographical and cultural phenomenon for the future well-being of rural society.

Engaging with rural communities

The reciprocal of the needed contractual commitments by government to rural America, as discussed in the section above, is on-the-ground involvement with rural people. Communities cannot promote change in isolation from external agencies or even from neighboring communities. The experiences of the Rural America Program in general and the CRRP in particular demonstrate clearly this need for interdependency. Planning, based on an ability to envision the future, prioritize measures, and agree action, also emerges as a central process in community development. It is a dynamic activity which can be revisited frequently to take account of new challenges and opportunities, and to promote wider community inclusiveness.

Three models of community development are explored by Flora et al (1992) in *Rural communities: legacy and change*. These comprise a self-help model which places weight on process and looks to people within a community working together to arrive at group decisions and take improvement actions; a technical assistance model which is project oriented and draws upon expert advice for feasibility assessment; and finally a conflict model which prompts those without power in a community to organize as a group and achieve their objectives by using their numerical strength to put pressure on political and economic institutions.

The case studies in Chapter 5 display interesting evidence of these models in operation – either individually or in more complex sequential and concurrent arrangements. But the important point which Flora et al make in regard to the performance of these three models is their common association with external linkages and the planning process. Engaging with rural communities must encompass both these dimensions. The Colorado community case studies underscore this point.

While the sweep of community actions can range from social provision to local economic development, it is increasingly apparent that broad-based participation within rural communities is concerned first and foremost with the latter. However, as demonstrated by the CRRP, there is a deep relationship between basic community development processes and the achievement of economic development objectives. By beginning with local people and by enhancing their leadership capacity through externally facilitated training activities which are action orientated, it is possible to build out into the achievement of more ambitious job-creating or income-generating projects. Capacity building provides the necessary confidence and ability to achieve economic development successes.

Thus it is within this context of linkage, planning and capacity building for economic development that the discussion can now move to examine briefly the potential contribution of the Cooperative Extension System to rural revitalization by way of its national initiative, Communities in Economic Transition. This organization, as demonstrated by analysis of the Rural America Program, could act as a key player in rural development given adequate resources and deeper commitment.

A White Paper published in 1992 (Williams and Landfried, 1992) commented that although the Cooperative Extension System has a history of rural development programming, it has lacked this serious commitment to the issue. Past efforts have depended on targeted funding sources and the assistance given by the Kellogg Foundation. (In this regard the Rural America Program is significant.) However, with the passage of the 1990 Farm Bill, the Extension System was charged with important mandates for rural development and in particular was given major responsibility for advancing economic development initiatives in rural communities through education and training. Such concerns were in fact anticipated in the drafting of the Revitalizing Rural America National Initiative from the mid-1980s, as outlined in Chapter 1 of this book. Notwithstanding the fact that some states had submitted plans of work under this initiative for the period 1992–96, the White Paper was stinging in its criticism of the capacity for implementation:

> Base programs such as Community and Economic Development, Agricultural Competitiveness and Profitability, Leadership and Volunteer Development, and Natural Resources and Environmental Management provide a minimal level of support for the mandates expressed in current legislation. Staffing with specific expertise is thin. The ability of Extension administrators to articulate program justification, program direction, program authority, and program impact is limited. Many Extension specialists working in rural development at the state level have been retrained from other disciplines and lack the subject depth and experience needed to command the credibility the organization must exhibit within the community and among state level economic development professionals. The cadre of area development specialists recruited during the funding initiative of the 1972 Rural Development Act has largely disappeared from Extension's ranks. With the blending of funds in 1980, most of these budget dollars have been redirected to support other Extension program areas. (p. 17)

The Extension System, however, has a high potential to assist rural communities. It can reach into almost every county unlike other federal agencies; local agents have knowledge of their communities and enjoy the trust of rural residents; and the system can draw upon additional professional expertise from faculty and staff in land-grant institutions. In building on these strengths and responding to the weaknesses cited above, the White Paper advanced the proposition that Extension should move with an action-oriented agenda which included fostering new partnership arrangements. It was suggested that economic development efforts should be pursued through four objectives: leadership training, strategic planning, networking and capacity building, and business development.

The establishment of the Communities in Economic Transition National Initiative, to run to 1998, is designed to respond directly to this analysis. The project has been set up initially on a pilot basis and will involve 12 community sites in the six southwestern states of Arizona, Colorado, New Mexico, Oklahoma, Texas and Utah. There are two primary components: community strategic planning for economic development and rural entrepreneurship. By engaging seven National Design Teams to prepare educational materials, for example, on value added agriculture, small firm manufacturing, youth entrepreneurship, retailing and tourism it is anticipated that an innovative base for education and technical assistance can be created. It is intended that the utilization of this output will then be tested within the pilot communities through the preparation of strategic economic development action plans. An additional element of the initiative will be the training of a panel of county extension agents in these different specialist subject areas to support strategic planning actions.

Without doubt the style of this new initiative has been heavily influenced by the experiences derived from the Rural America Program though unfortunately the funding available pales significantly by comparison. Nevertheless, the achievements of Communities in Economic Transition deserve close scrutiny over the coming years, particularly since the initiative signals a more *implementation*-orientated approach to rural development which goes beyond preparing for readiness. There is a welcome focus on tangible outcomes as required by the Government Performance and Results Act of 1993; this mandates that by the year 2000 federal agencies report annually on actual achievements compared to goals on the basis of yearly plans. Communities in Economic Transition has been selected to pilot the approach intended by this legislation. What also comes through very strongly from the combined objectives of strategy preparation, enterprise development and business assistance is the wide sweep of sectoral activity and the search for integration opportunities. At a conceptual level this desire for creativity in economic diversification among rural communities, linked to education and training, fits well with the opening discussion of Integrated Rural Development in Chapter 1. However, it would be quite wrong to overemphasize this initiative, important though it is. At the present time there is a difficult choice to be made by the Extension System between on the one hand paying only lip service to engaging with rural communities and possibly even withdrawing from that arena, and on the other hand building on its reputation for rural development. What is clear is that its future role as a committed team player depends on being able to move beyond relatively low budget pilot programs. More resources targeted specifically at community-led rural development have the potential to reinvigorate the Extension System and to allow it to join more effectively with other agencies inside the USDA and with strategic partners from other federal and state agencies and the private and voluntary sectors in the revitalizing of rural America.

In late 1994 the Cooperative Extension System of the United States Department of Agriculture published its strategic plan for community resources and economic development (USDA, 1994). This is an important manifesto for change and deserves to be widely read and supported by policy makers. It reaffirms the challenges facing rural America and identifies closely with community aspirations reported in this book. One sentence encapsulates the argument advanced in the paragraph above:

> Enthusiasm and commitment must start at the top and must be characterised by a willingness to take reasonable risks and to support others who do so. (p. iv)

A positive response to this challenge is essential for revitalizing rural America.

Conclusion

The challenges facing rural America in the mid-1990s are serious and demand a high level of national responsiveness. Rural America is diverse, its problems have many dimensions, yet policies are piecemeal and resources are constrained. Rural development is becoming ever more strongly identified with community-led regeneration initiatives. It is this commitment to the future of rural society by local people which this book celebrates.

Rural development in the United States has drifted for decades across a policy landscape dominated by agricultural interests and now the extent to which it may continue to drift on the rhetoric of a community-led ticket must remain a concern. But where there is resourced initiative the evidence time and time again is that rural communities can and do act. Capacity building processes linked to action outcomes can be effective mechanisms for the unlocking of citizen potential and the realization of development opportunity. Initial accomplishments may be modest, but over time these can translate into ever greater successes.

Empowerment is a much abused concept and is frequently measured only by visible outcomes. This is a shallow interpretation since true empowerment must come through the forging of collaborative relationships between all whose brief and interest is rural development. This book has demonstrated the necessity of linkage between stakeholders and has pointed to both practical difficulties and visible rewards. Collaboration has the potential to be the new engine for governance extending from federal down to state and local levels. A commitment to and an engaging with rural society must interact with community abilities and efforts. Under these circumstances rural America enjoys the prospect of being rediscovered!

References

Abbott, C, Leonard, SJ and McComb, D (1982) *Colorado: a history of the centennial state*. Colorado Associated University Press, Boulder.

Albrecht, DE (1993) The renewal of population loss in the non-metropolitan Great Plains. *Rural Sociology*, 58(2), 233–246.

Andrews, M et al (1994) *Rural America cluster evaluation – final report*. Michigan State University, East Lansing.

Baker, H (1993) *A thought piece on collaborating*. Paper presented at the International Community Development Society Professional Training Workshop, Milwaukee, Wisconsin, 18 July.

Barlett, PF (1993) *American dreams, rural realities: family farms in crisis*. The University of North Carolina Press, Chapel Hill.

Basler, A (1979) The concept of Integrated Rural Development. *Intereconomics*, July/August, 190–195.

Beale, C (1991) *Preliminary 1990 census counts confirm drop in non-metro population growth*. USDA Economic Research Service, Washington DC.

Berry, W (1993) *Sex, economy, freedom and community*. Pantheon Books, New York.

Bohan, H (1979) *Ireland green: social planning and rural development*. Veritas Publications, Dublin.

Bonnen, JT (1992) Why is there no coherent rural policy? *Policy Studies Journal*, 20(2), 190–201.

Borich, TO (1994) Collaboration: a different strategy for rural economic development. *Economic Development Review*, winter, 18–21.

Bowman, A and Pagano, M (1992) The state of American federalism, 1991–1992. *Publius: The Journal of Federalism*, summer, 1–19.

Brodnax, D, Heasley, D, Korsching, P and Youmans, R (1992) *1992 combined report: four regional rural development centers, selected research and extension projects*. Western Rural Development Center, Oregon State University, Corvallis.

Brown, DL and Deavers, KL (1988) *Economic dimensions of rural America*. Paper presented to Rural Development Policy Options Workshop.

Bryden, J and Scott, I (1990) The celtic fringe: state sponsored versus indigenous local development initiatives in Scotland and Ireland. In Stohr, WB (ed.), *Global challenge and local response: initiatives for economic regeneration in contemporary Europe*, pp. 90–132. Mansell, London and New York.

Bryson, B (1990) *The lost continent: travels in small town America*. Sphere Books, London.

Bryson, JM and Crosby BC (1992) *Leadership for the common good: tackling public problems in a shared power world*. Jossey Bass, San Francisco.

Buxbaum, S and Ho, R (1993) *Innovation and collaboration: challenges for state rural development councils*. A paper on the National Initiative on Rural America presented at the International Community Development Society Meeting, Milwaukee, Wisconsin, 21 July.

Byrne, JV (1989) Rural America: the land-grant university's greatest challenge. In *New alliances for rural economic development: colloquium proceedings from land-grant universities' presidents and science and education/United States Department of Agriculture administrators*, pp. 14–18. Northeast Regional Center for Rural Development, The Pennsylvania State University, University Park.

Cantlon, JE (1989) The land-grant university and economic development. In *New alliances for rural economic development: colloquium proceedings from land-grant universities' presidents and science and education/United States Department of Agriculture administrators*, pp. 3–9. Northeast Regional Center for Rural Development, The Pennsylvania State University, University Park.

Center for the New West (1992) *Overview of change in America's new economy*, A report to the Ford Foundation and the Aspen Institute, Center for the New West, Denver.

Christenson, JA and Robinson, JW (1989) *Community development in perspective*. Iowa State University Press, Ames.

Clark, C and Clark, J (1992) Federal aid to local governments in the West: an irony of the Reagan revolution. *Policy Studies Review*, 11 (1), 91–99.

Clinton, W and Gore, A (1992) *Putting people first*. Times Books, New York.

Clout, H (1993) *European experience of rural development*. Rural Development Commission, Salisbury.

Colorado State University Cooperative Extension (1992) *Visions in action: Colorado community cases*. Colorado State University, Fort Collins.

Commins, P (1983) *Community based cooperatives and rural development in the West of Ireland*. Paper presented at the conference – Changing Problems and Policy Responses in Rural Development, Regional Studies Association, Newtown.

Conlan, T (1988) Federalism after Reagan. *The Brookings Review*, autumn, 23–30.

Contract with America: the bold plan by Rep Newt Gingrich, Rep Dick Armey and the House Republicans to change the nation (1994). Times Books, New York.

Cooperative Extension System (1986) *Revitalizing rural America: a cooperative extension system response.* University of Wisconsin, Madison.

Cooperative Extension System (1994) *National initiatives: communities in economic transition.* USDA Extension Service, Washington DC.

Davidson, OG (1990) *Broken heartland – the rise of America's rural ghetto.* Doubleday, New York.

Dawson, A (1978) Suggestions for an approach to rural development by foreign aid programmes. *International Labor Review,* No. 117, 391–404.

Deavers, KL (1988) Scope and dimensions of problems facing rural America. In *Rural development issues of the nineties: perspectives from the social sciences,* The 46th Annual Professional Agricultural Workers Conference Proceedings, Ch. 2, pp. 33–42. Tuskegee University, Alabama.

Deavers, KL (1992) What is rural? *Policy Studies Journal,* 20(2), 184–189.

Denenberg, RV (1992) *Understanding American politics.* Fontana, London.

Economic Policy Council Working Group on Rural Development (1991) *Rural economic development for the 90s: a presidential initiative.* USDA, Washington DC.

Ennis, E and Hage, D (1993) Concept of responsive initiators, in Sanderson, DR (ed.), *Adjusting the course: redefining the national council's mission and roles.* National Rural Development Partnership, Washington DC.

Etzioni, A (1993) *The spirit of community: rights, responsibilities and the communitarian agenda.* Crown Publishers, Inc., New York.

Finkelstein, J (1992) *The American economy: from the Great Crash to the Third Industrial Revolution.* Harlan Davidson, Inc., Arlington Heights.

Fitchin, JM (1991) *Endangered spaces, enduring places: change, identity and survival in rural America.* Westview Press, Boulder.

Flora, CB and Flora, JL (1990) Developing entrepreneurial rural communities. *Sociological Practice Community,* 8, 197–207.

Flora, CB, Flora, J, Speers, J, Swanson, L, Lapping, M and Weinberg, M (1992) *Rural communities: legacy and change.* Westview Press, Boulder.

Freshwater, D (1991) The historical context of federal rural development policy. *Western Wire,* Spring, 1–12.

Galstan, W (1992) Rural America in the 1990s: trends and choices. *Policy Studies Journal,* 20(2), 202–211.

General Accounting Office (1992) *Rural development: rural America faces many challenges.* Washington DC.

General Accounting Office (1994) *Rural development: patchwork of federal programs needs to be reappraised.* Washington DC.

Glasmeier, AK and Conroy, ME (1994) *Global squeeze on rural America: opportunities, threats and challenges from NAFTA, GATT, and processes of globalization,* A report of the Institute for Policy Research and Evaluation, Graduate School of Public Policy and Administration, The Pennsylvania State University, University Park.

Gray, B (1989) *Collaborating: finding common ground for multiparty problems.* Jossey Bass, San Francisco.

Green, DE (1973) *Land of the underground rain: irrigation on the Texas High Plains, 1910–1970.* University of Texas Press, Austin.

Green, GP, Flora, CB and Schmidt, FE (1990) Local self-development strategies: national survey results. *Journal of the Community Development Society,* 21(2), 55–73.

Green, GP, Flora, JL, Flora, CB and Schmidt, FE (1993) Community-based economic development projects are small but valuable. *Rural Development Perspectives,* 8(3), 8–15.

Greer, JV (1984) Integrated rural development: reflections on a magic phrase. *Pleanail,* 1, 10–15.

Grindle, MS (1981) Anticipating failure: the implementation of rural development programs. *Public Policy,* 29, 51–74.

Gurwitt, R (1990) A small town's choice: change or fade away. *Governing,* September, 32–38.

Hady, T and Ross, P (1990) *The diverse social and economic structure of rural America – an update.* USDA Economic Research Service, Washington DC.

Harrington, D (1986) New Deal farm policy and Oklahoma populism. In Havens, AE (ed.), *Studies in the transformation of US agriculture,* Ch. 6, pp. 179–205. Westview Press, Boulder.

Hedge, DM and Scicchitano, MJ (1992) Devolving regulatory authority: the federal and state response. *Policy Studies Review,* 11(1), 81–89.

Huillet, C and Van Dijk, P (1990) Partnerships for rural development. *OECD Observer,* No.162, February/March, 19–22.

Humphrey, CR and Wilkinson, KP (1993) Growth promotion activities in rural areas: do they make a difference? *Rural Sociology,* 58(2), 175–189.

Hustedde, RJ (1991) Developing leadership to address rural problems. In Walzer, N (ed.), *Rural community economic development,* Ch. 8, pp. 111–123. Praeger, New York.

Hyman, D (1991) Rural development policy: promises made and promises denied. *The Rural Sociologist,* 11(2), 9–12.

Johnson, KM (1993) Demographic change in non-metropolitan America 1980 to 1990, *Rural Sociology,* 58(3), 347–365.

Keener, JOB (1993) Victor: city of mines. In *Victor Centennial Commemorative Book 1893–1993,* pp 9–14. Victor.

Kemmis, D (1990) *Community and the politics of place.* University of Oklahoma Press, Norman.

Kerouac, J (1955) *On the road.* Viking Press, New York.

Kettl, DF (1993) *The new governance and rural development.* New Governance Discussion Paper Series, No. 2. National Rural Economic Development Institute, Madison, WI.

Kettl, DF (1994) Beyond the rhetoric of reinvention: driving themes of the Clinton Administration's management reforms. *Governance: An International Journal of Policy and Administration,* 7(4), 307–314.

Kettl, JD and Walcott, E (1993) *Reinventing government for rural development: principles, examples and action.* National Academy on Public Administration, Washington DC.

Kettl, JD, Dyer, B and Lovan, WR (1994) What will new governance mean for the federal government? *Public Administration Review,* 54(2), 170–175.

Khan, A (1977) Integrated rural development. *Philippine Journal of Public Administration*, **21**, 20–34.

Kincaid, JM and Knop, EC (1992) *Insights and implications from the CRRP 1988–1991*. Colorado State University, Fort Collins.

King, DS (1992) The changing federal balance. In Peele, G, Bailey, CJ and Cain, B (eds), *Developments in American politics*, pp. 190–209. Macmillan Press, London.

Lapping, MB, Daniels, TL and Keller, JW (1989) *Rural planning and development in the United States*. Guilford Press, New York.

Leistritz, FL, Rathge, RW and Ekstrom, BL (1989) Farm families in transition: implications for rural communities. *Journal of the Community Development Society*, **20**(2), 31–48.

Leupolt, M (1977) Integrated rural development: key elements of an integrated rural development strategy. *Sociologia Ruralis*, **17**, 7–28.

Luloff, AE and Swanson, LE (1990) *American rural communities*. Westview Press, Boulder.

Luther, V and Wall, M (1989) *The entrepreneurial community: a strategic leadership approach to community survival*. Heartland Center for Leadership Development, Lincoln, Nebraska.

Lyson, TA (1989) *Two sides to the sunbelt*. Praeger, New York.

McGuire, M, Rubin, B, Agranoff, R, and Richards, C (1994) Building development capacity in non-metropolitan communities, *Public Administration Review*, **54**(5), 426–433.

McGranahan, D (1991) *Can the rural economy be competitive? Lessons from the data*. Annual Agriculture Outlook Conference, USDA, Washington DC.

McGranahan, D and Salsgiver, J (1993) Recent population change in adjacent non metro counties. *Rural Development Perspectives*, **8**(3), 2–7.

McWilliams, R, Saranich, R and Pratt, J (1993) The Forest Service's investment in rural communities. *The Annals of the American Academy of Political and Social Science*, **529**, 128–139.

Mandell, MP (1994) Managing interdependencies through program structures: a revised paradigm. *American Review of Public Administration*, **24**(1), 99–121.

Mattessich, PW and Monsey, BR (1992) *Collaboration: what makes it work*. Amherst H Wilder Foundation, Saint Paul.

Mayer, LV (1993) Agricultural change and rural America. *The Annals of the American Academy of Political and Social Science*, **529**, 80–91.

Mazie, SM and Killian, MS (1991) Growth and change in rural America: the experience of the 1980s and prospects for the 1990s. In Walzer, N (ed.), *Rural community economic development*, Ch. 1, pp. 1–19. Praeger, New York.

Miller, TA, Gray, SL and Trock, WL (1991) *Colorado's farm and food system: farm and agribusiness contributions to the Colorado economy*. Bulletin 551A, Colorado State University, Fort Collins.

Moe, RC (1994) The reinventing government exercise: misinterpreting the problem, misjudging the consequences. *Public Administration Review*, **54**(2), 111–122.

Murray, M and Greer, J (1992) Rural development in Northern Ireland: policy formulation in a peripheral region of the European Community. *Journal of Rural Studies*, **8**(2), 173–184.

Murray, M and Greer, J (eds) (1993) *Rural development in Ireland: a challenge for the 1990s.* Avebury, Aldershot.

National Commission on Agriculture and Rural Development Policy (1990) *Future directions in rural development policy.* USDA, Washington DC.

National Governors' Association (1988a) *New alliances for rural America: report of the task force on rural development.* Washington DC.

National Governors' Association (1988b) *A brighter future for rural America? Strategies for communities and states.* Washington DC.

National Governors' Association (1992) *State–federal collaboration on rural development.* Washington DC.

National Governors' Association (1993) *An action agenda to redesign state government: reports of the state management task force strategy groups.* Washington DC.

National Initiative on Rural America (1992) *Rural development for the 90s.* USDA, Washington DC.

National Initiative on Rural America (1993) *Briefing book: reinventing government in rural America.* Washington DC.

National Rural Development Partnership (1994) *A strategic plan for the National Partnership Office.* Washington DC.

Newlands, CA (1981) Local government capacity building. *Urban Affairs Papers*, 3(1).

Nordhaus, WD (1991) The United States. In Llewellyn, J and Potter, SJ (eds), *Economic policies for the 1990s*, Ch. 2, pp. 25–51. Blackwell, Oxford.

Norris, K (1993) *Dakota: a spiritual geography.* Houghton Mifflin, Boston.

Osborne, D and Gaebler, T (1992) *Reinventing government: how the entrepreneurial spirit is transforming the public sector.* Plume, New York.

Peters, BG and Savoie, DJ (1994) Reinventing Osborne and Gaebler: lessons from the Gore Commission, *Canadian Public Administration*, 37(2), 302–322.

President's Council on Rural America (1992) *Revitalizing rural America through collaboration: a report to the President.* US Government Printing Office, Washington DC.

Pulver, GC (1989) Developing a community perspective on rural economic development policy. *Journal of the Community Development Society*, 20(2), 1–14.

Pulver, GC and Somersan, AC (1989) Building an economic development outreach program in a land-grant university. In *New alliances for rural economic development: colloquium proceedings from land-grant universities' presidents and science and education/United States Department of Agriculture administrators*, pp. 24–27. Northeast Regional Center for Rural Development, The Pennsylvania State University, University Park.

Radin, B (1991) *Managing rural policy initiatives in the intergovernmental system.* Annual Agricultural Outlook Conference, USDA, Washington DC.

Radin, B (1992) Rural development councils: an intergovernmental coordination experiment, *Publius: the Journal of Federalism*, 22(3), 111–128.

Radin, B, and Romzek, B (1994) Accountability and the National Rural Development Partnership. *New Governance Discussion Paper Series*, No. 8. National Rural Economic Development Institute, Madison, WI.

Reed, BJ and Blair, R (1993) Economic development in rural communities: can strategic planning make a difference? *Public Administration Review*, **53**(1), 88–92.

Regan, C and Breathnach, P (1981) *State and community: rural development strategies in the Slieve League peninsula, County Donegal.* Occasional Paper Series No. 2. Geography Department, Maynooth College, Ireland.

Report of the National Performance Review (1993) *From red tape to results – creating a government that works better and costs less.* US Government Printing Office, Washington DC.

Rhodes, RAW (1994) Reinventing excellence: or how bestsellers thwart the search for lessons to transform the public sector. *Public Administration*, **72**, summer, 281–289.

Rich, MJ (1991) Targeting federal grants: the community development experience, 1950–1986. *Publius: the Journal of Federalism*, **21**, winter, 29–49.

Rittel, HWJ and Webber, MM (1973) Dilemmas in a general theory of planning. *Policy Sciences*, No. 4, 155–169.

Robinson, JW and Silvis, AH (1993) *Community actualization: mirage or reality? fantasy or feasible?* Paper presented at the Annual Meeting of the Community Development Society, Milwaukee, Wisconsin, 21 July.

Roselle, SA (1992) *Governing in an information society.* Renouf Publishing, Ottawa, Canada.

Rural Information Center (1992) *Federal funding sources for rural areas.* United States Department of Agriculture, National Agricultural Library, Beltsville, Maryland.

Rural Sociological Society Task Force on Persistent Rural Poverty (1993) *Persistent poverty in rural America.* Westview Press, Boulder, Colorado.

Ruthenberg, H (1981) Is integrated rural development a suitable approach to attack rural poverty? *Quarterly Journal of International Agriculture*, **20**, 6–14.

Sanderson, DR (1993) *Adjusting the course: re-defining the National Council's mission and roles: a report of the October 1993 retreats of the National Rural Development Council.* National Rural Development Partnership, Washington DC.

Sedjo, RA (1991) Forest resources: resilient and serviceable. In Fredrick, KD and Sedjo, RA (eds), *America's renewable resources*, Ch. 3, pp. 81–119. Resources for the Future, Washington DC.

Self, P (1993) *Government by the market? The politics of public choice.* Macmillan Press, London.

Shaffer, R (1993) *State Rural Development Councils: do they offer a chance?* Paper presented at the 13th biennial meeting of the Pacific Regional Science Conference Organization, Whistler, British Columbia, 11–14 July.

Shaffer, R (1994) State Rural Development Councils and the National Partnership for Rural Development. *New Governance Discussion Paper Series*, No. 7. National Rural Economic Development Institute, Madison, WI.

Smith, B (1994) Colorado's outback: is there life down on the farm? *Colorado Business*, February, 36–43.

Sokolow, AD (1986) Local governments in rural and small town America: diverse patterns and common issues. *New dimensions in rural policy: building upon our heritage, studies prepared for the use of the Subcommittee on Agriculture and Transportation of the Joint Economic Committee*, pp. 372–379. Congress of the United States, US Government Printing Office, Washington DC.

Steinbeck, J (1939) *The grapes of wrath*. Viking Press, New York.

Stinson, T, Fortenberry, J, Sigalla, F and Conlon, T (1986) *Governing the Heartlands: can rural communities service the farm crisis?* US Congress, Washington DC.

Summers, GF (1991) Poverty persists. *Western Wire*, winter, 1–4.

Summers, GF, Horton, F and Gringeri, C (1990) Rural labor market changes in the United States. In Marsden, T, Lowe, P and Whatmore, S (eds), *Rural restructuring: global processes and their responses*, Ch. 5, pp. 129–164. David Fulton Publishers, London.

Swanson, LE (1991) The rural development dilemma. *The Rural Sociologist*, 11(2), 4–8.

Tickameyer, AR and Duncan, CM (1990) Poverty and opportunity structure in rural America. *Annual Review of Sociology*, Vol 16, pp. 67–86.

Unruh, T (1991) State and federal policy initiatives in rural development. In Walzer, W (ed.), *Rural community economic development*, Ch. 9, pp. 125–139. Praeger, New York.

USDA (1976) *The face of rural America*. US Government Printing Office, Washington DC.

USDA (1987) *Rural economic development in the 1980s*. Agriculture Information Bulletin No. 533, Washington DC.

USDA (1988) *Rural economic development in the 1980s: prospects for the future*. Rural Development Research Report No. 69, Washington DC.

USDA (1989) *A hard look at USDA's rural development programs: the Report of the Rural Revitalization Task Force to the Secretary of Agriculture*, Washington DC.

USDA (1990) *Rural economic development for the 90s: a presidential initiative*. Washington DC.

USDA (1991) *Putting the pieces together: annual rural development strategy report*. Washington DC.

USDA (1992) *Rural economic development for the 90s – a presidential initiative*. Washington DC.

USDA (1993a) *Rural conditions and trends*, 4(1).

USDA (1993b) *Team USDA summary*. Washington DC.

USDA (1993c) *Rural conditions and trends*, 4(3).

USDA (1994) *Strengthening communities: a strategic plan for community resources and economic development*. Washington DC.

USDA, Forest Service (1990) *A strategic plan for the 90s: working together for rural America*, Forest Service, Washington DC.

Van Der Plas, L (1985) *Rural development and conservation: new approaches*. Seminar report, Peak Park Study Center, Losehill.

Varley, T (1988) *Rural development and combating poverty*. Research Report No. 2, Centre for Community Development Studies, Social Sciences Research Centre, University College, Galway, Ireland.

Varley, T (1991) On the fringes: community groups in rural Ireland. In Varley, T, Boylan, T and Cuddy, M (eds), *Rural crisis: perspectives on Irish rural development*, pp. 48–76. Centre for Development Studies, University College, Galway, Ireland.

Weeks, JB (1986) High plains regional aquifer-system study, *US Geological Survey Circular 1002*. Government Printing Office, Washington DC.

White, SE (1992) Population change in the High Plains Ogallala Region: 1980–1990. *Great Plains Research*, 2(2), 179–197.

Wilkinson, KP (1986) Communities left behind – again. *New dimensions in rural policy: building upon our heritage, studies prepared for the use of the Subcommittee on Agriculture and Transportation of the Joint Economic Committee*, pp. 341–346. Congress of the United States, US Government Printing Office, Washington DC.

Wilkinson, KP (1991a) *The community in rural America*. Greenwood Press, New York.

Wilkinson, KP (1991b) *Social stabilization: the role of rural society*. Paper presented to International School of Rural Development, University College Galway, Ireland.

Wilkinson, KP (1991c) The future of the community in rural areas. In Pigg, KE (ed.), *The future of rural America: anticipating policies for constructive change*, Ch. 5, pp. 73–89, Westview Press, Boulder, Colorado.

Williams, MR and Landfried, TC (1992) *Communities in economic crisis: looking ahead to extension program opportunities in community and economic development*. An Extension White Paper, USDA Extension Service, Washington DC.

WK Kellogg Foundation (1993) The language of hope – communities in action. Annual Report, WK Kellogg Foundation, Battle Creek.

Wood, WC, Harbaugh, DR and Bowen, LH (1993) Critical barriers in total community development and practical steps to overcome them. *Economic Development Review*, spring, 6–13.

Wulf, R (1978) On the concept of integrated rural development. *Economics*, 17, 63–80.

Appendix 1:
Portfolio of Rural America Projects partly funded by the WK Kellogg Foundation

Leadership for Economic Development: Developing Leadership in Rural Communities – Auburn University

The Alabama Cooperative Extension Service and the Economic Development Institute at Auburn co-sponsored this project at Auburn University. In total, there were 17 collaborators: seven units within the university, six Alabama governmental agencies, others in private business, and representatives of Tuskegee University who cooperated for the success of this project. The project's three goals were to: (i) develop a replicable multimedia rural leadership program; (ii) improve leadership skills in rural communities; and (iii) establish a mentoring/support system. The project focused on five counties in southern Alabama that had been identified as extremely poor and with a very high ratio of blacks to whites. Five teams, one from each of the five counties, attended six 2½ day workshops over a two year period. Teams were matched with at least one mentor/supporter who could give them access to university resources and meet with them in the county. A total of 58 rural leaders and 28 resource persons participated. Two of the major challenges that the project faced were to: (i) encourage a collaborative interdisciplinary team at the university level to work together; and (ii) have that team adapt to citizens with whom they typically did not work. Each workshop was evaluated with instruments that measured the participants' response to the subject matter, materials, the training session itself, and the multimedia presentation. Pre- and post-testing were used to measure skills and knowledge gained, the effectiveness of the mentoring system, and local problem solving. The rural leaders involved in this program gained skills and knowledge concerning group dynamics and economic development issues in their specific communities. They applied those skills to solve major local problems in race relations and subsequently watched black and white leaders work together and greet each other on the street. As a direct result of this project, the president of Auburn University announced a major initiative to address community development in western Alabama to build on the leadership base developed by this program.

Palmetto Leadership – Clemson University

The Cooperative Extension Service at Clemson University created and sponsored Palmetto Leadership. The leadership program gathered a staff of 17 faculty members, 7 newly hired community development agents, and local community development agents already on staff. This project was a leadership and community development program that assisted mostly rural counties in South Carolina in addressing economic, social, governmental and quality of life issues. Phase 1 offered a 35 hour course that included a retreat. Following the course, participants attended in-county seminars for 2½ hours one night a week for 8 to 10 weeks. These seminars focused on: (i) personal skills development such as communication and leadership; (ii) group skills development such as problem solving; and (iii) community development activities such as needs assessments. In Phase 2, participants were divided into task forces that began strategic planning and implementation of their visions for the county. Phase 3 enabled the experienced participants to identify and work with new, emerging leaders from the Phase 1 program. New task forces were formed as needed and the network continued as a number of community projects resulted – for example, county-wide recycling, the establishment of a 911 emergency phone system, and the creation of county-wide chambers of commerce. Leaders representing business, education, religion, civic and governmental sectors participated in the sessions. Approximately 1000 people have graduated since the program began. One of the challenges was the difficulty in finding instructors at the university who had experience and were effective with local residents.

This project showed that it is possible to train and support Agricultural Extension agents to work effectively in community development. Extensive effort was given to multiple evaluation strategies covering both the educational sessions and the technical assistance work with the counties. For example, benchmark data and end of session data were obtained from the participants of the leadership program and from the participating communities to assess the effectiveness of the program. Focus group interviews held with participants throughout South Carolina were a component of one of the mini studies that contributed to the overall cluster evaluation.

Colorado Rural Revitalization Project – Colorado State University

This project was a joint effort between three institutions: (i) the Cooperative Extension Service of Colorado State University; (ii) the Center for Built Environment Studies of the University of Colorado; and (iii) the State Department of Local Affairs (DOLA). The project had three purposes: (i) to enhance the capacity of local communities to better manage their own affairs by providing them with new skills, knowledge and technical expertise; (ii) to enable communities to work together; and (iii) to help communities make better decisions about their futures. There were 800 people from 47 small communities with populations under 5000 in this project. In each community, a leadership team was formed of 10 to 20 people, including two town council members. A site manager from one of the three institutional partners was assigned to each team and was responsible for supplementing the materials and mini lectures on such topics as: group dynamics, methods for community self-study, goal setting and evaluation. A $2000 technical assistance fund was reserved for each community to provide funding for a variety of projects such as studies of rural tourism, trash recycling programs and grant writing assistance. Students were often used as consultants on community projects. The three institutional collaborators faced a challenge in learning to work together and to sort out their roles. For example, the Cooperative Extension Service has been out of the business of community development for a number of years and the DOLA was not accustomed to working with small communities. The project required a large commitment from both local volunteers and project staff. Outside evaluators used inputs from the community action teams and the internal evaluation team to design an overall summative evaluation. As a result of this project, increased communication across groups within communities was noted. These small communities were able to access external resources for their own ends, which suggests an increase in confidence and capacity.

Creating Opportunity for Rural People and Places: a State Rural Economic and Community Development Policy Academy

This rural policy academy was sponsored by the Council of Governors' Policy Advisors, a non-profit organization affiliated with the National Governors' Association in cooperation with the Aspen Institute (a foundation), the Corporation for Enterprise Development (a non-profit organization), the Western Governors' Association, and the US Department of Agriculture's Economic Research Service and Extension Service. The project's purpose was to: (i) translate research results on rural issues into a form useful to state governments; (ii) build the states' capacities to craft and implement comprehensive strategies tailored to their unique circumstances; (iii) help states assess the barriers to and opportunities for rural development; (iv) support state efforts to set appropriate policy goals; and (v) provide ideas and rural policy initiatives that might improve the quality of life in rural communities. Before materials were developed for the academy's sessions, a round table discussion was held to diagnose rural economic problems. A group of governors and other state decision makers spent time defining which high priority rural issues were to be addressed. During academy sessions, teams of top level policy makers from participating states obtained substantive information about rural economic development, worked closely with leading experts in the field, and developed their own strategic policy recommendations. The teams shared and critiqued their current policies and future plans. The best of the policies were collected into a handbook *Rural competitiveness: policy options for state governments*. It summarizes some of the most promising state strategies to improve the economic competitiveness of rural communities and includes most of the materials presented at the academies. The evaluation of this project included internal and external monitoring of the progress of each activity by making use of qualitative data, by tracking the products produced and by identifying the actual changes in a state's policy or policy-making process. As a result of their participation in the academy, several states enacted legislation, revised state programs, improved services and increased opportunities for rural communities.

Rural Revitalization Initiative – University of Georgia

The Rural Revitalization Initiative was a project shared by seven different service units within the University of Georgia. They were: (i) Carl Vinson Institute of Government; (ii) College of Journalism and Communications; (iii) Cooperative Extension Service; (iv) Georgia Center for Continuing Education; (v) Institute of Community Leadership Development; (vi) J W Fanning Community Leadership Development Center; and (vii) Small Business Development Center. The purpose of the project was to improve economic development in 12 rural counties in Georgia and to improve the problem-solving skills of the local elected officials and leaders. In addition, the project was intended to strengthen the development of collaborative efforts between city and county governments and the University of Georgia service units. There were six areas of focus: (i) governmental management; (ii) community development; (iii) rural heritage; (iv) economic development; (v) rural media; and (vi) training simulations with interactive video. A total of 1309 individuals and representatives of 26 local governments and 15 cities participated in the many activities that were offered by the project. Some of those activities were retreats, workshops, seminars, a state conference, a national conference, and a community simulation center. Fostering collaboration between the seven university service units with their diversified missions presented a major challenge. Another dynamic was added at the community level by the high turnover of local elected officials. The project had two major evaluation reports. The first reported that the community participants were very satisfied with their involvement. The second report identified commitment to carry on the collaborative efforts as an issue at the university level. The project created significant impact on participants in the various community programs. It remains to be seen if the on-campus units involved will continue to collaborate and coordinate efforts.

Helping Small Towns Survive: a Training Program for Community Development Practitioners – Heartland Center for Leadership Development, Lincoln, Nebraska

The Heartland Center for Leadership Development, a non-profit educational and community development organiza-tion, served as host of this project. The Heartland Center gathered a group of professionals and community devel-opment practitioners from the four states of Colorado, Kansas, Nebraska and Wyoming to participate in the pro-ject. The program had three goals: (i) the introduction of successful strategies for small town survival; (ii) the provi-sion of links between community leaders and community development specialists; and (iii) the provision of follow-up coaching visits. An extensive needs assessment revealed that training was being sought by community develop-ment professionals. Therefore 65 community development professionals received scholarships to meet for two 5 day workshops. The training was in response to the audience requests for strategies to assist rural leaders to manage community change, ideas about using local resources effec-tively, and methods to develop the economies of the com-munity. The training built individual capacity in group processes, interpersonal skills, identifying and developing leaders, understanding and managing change, and com-munity analysis/assistance. Participants were tracked, sup-ported and visited in the interim between the workshops. Owing to the large size of these states and the uneven population distribution, the Center was challenged to assemble a group that was reasonably representative of each state. Each workshop session was accompanied by an on-site evaluator. Facilitators received immediate feedback from the evaluators so changes could be incorporated. At the end of the workshop the evaluators wrote an overall report and conducted phone interviews with the partici-pants concerning their reactions to the support efforts and the site visits. The presenters enjoyed being able to use the feedback from both the evaluators and the audience to improve subsequent segments of the program. Participants were asked to prepare specific plans to implement after they returned home.

Rural Partners: Helping Rural Communities Prepare for Economic Development – University of Illinois at Urbana–Champaign

This state-wide project highlighted the collaboration of the University of Illinois Cooperative Extension Service and the Illinois Coalition for Rural Community Development, known as Rural Partners, whose membership includes approximately 120 public and private sector organizations that are interested in rural Illinois. The purpose of the project was to establish, with the assistance of the local boards of coordinators, a comprehensive system of information resources for county, municipal and township officials, and to provide those resources in face-to-face courses or by remote delivery methods. There were 18 counties selected to participate. Each county established a board of coordinators which consisted of four to six members from private business, electric cooperatives, the Farm Bureau and volunteers. Faculty in seven university units developed 20 Community Action Modules emphasizing education, local leadership, and long-range community development. The 108 participants of these courses were full-time and part-time elected and appointed officials. Challenges existed in the formation of the county coordination teams and in their ability to internalize the program goals, to mobilize resources to provide support in each county, and to establish a team effort. The evaluation focus was formative. A consulting team was hired after the first 18 months to identify areas that needed improvement. In summary, 20 modules focusing on community and economic development were developed and delivered in the 18 counties. Additionally, a process of community development and economic development was established in these counties. The establishment of linkages continued to evolve with time.

Tomorrow's Leaders Today – Iowa State University

Tomorrow's Leaders Today (TLT) began as a project sponsored solely by the Iowa State Cooperative Extension Service within Iowa State University. Collaboration with community colleges and private colleges evolved over time. The project focused on a process called "clustering", drawing rural communities together to form multicommunity development organizations that shared resources and worked together towards common goals to improve the quality of life in small communities in rural Iowa. To date there have been 1200 participants from 200 communities in TLT. The program, consisting of 11 sessions, was delivered over the course of a year. Sessions 1 through 5 dealt with matters of personal development, new leadership roles, creating the capacity for action within the communities, networking, community knowledge and involvement, and continuing education. Sessions 6 through 10 were customized to reflect local needs and specific projects. Evaluation was built into the program's final session, called Back to Reality. There was a "great debate" where people were given the opportunity to highlight positive and negative conclusions and brainstorm program improvements and possible future events. Two of the major challenges faced by the project were: (i) the establishment of cooperation among state agencies and other educational providers; and (ii) selling the concept of clustering as a developmental strategy for small towns. A variety of end of session and end of program evaluation strategies was used. The project incorporated the focus group interview technique as an evaluation format. By increasing the capacity of the local human resource base, these communities were able to make better decisions and mobilize resources to create new opportunities and new relationships.

Building Community-based Leadership for Economic Development – Kansas State University

This project was undertaken by the Kansas Center for Rural Initiatives at Kansas State University (KSU). The overall purposes were to: (i) make the resources of KSU available to rural communities throughout Kansas; (ii) nurture and cultivate existing and emerging leadership in rural/small town Kansas; and (iii) create ongoing service linkages to rural Kansas by merging the talent of KSU, community colleges and the communities. KSU developed the following four objectives: (i) to extend the Community Service Program in which students (approximately 75 over three years) worked with communities on community identified projects; (ii) to involve nine non-Cooperative Extension KSU faculty in community research; (iii) to engage staff and faculty from seven community colleges in a series of in-service seminars in conjunction with hiring local coordinators from the communities; and (iv) to provide support for many outreach programs and the dissemination of information through newsletters, luncheons, publications and conferences. In all, 38 counties, 150 participants, 20 collaborators and 45 resource persons were involved. A significant evaluation effort was devoted to the Community Service Program (student service). It provided the impetus to make changes in the Community Service Program curriculum. Also, there were reaction surveys at the end of sessions and interviews with community college personnel. The community colleges changed their organizational behavior and their vision of economic development for rural Kansas. They became more interactive with their respective communities and were committed to keeping that link with their communities as a vital part of their program. There was also a significant change in the lives of individuals who interacted with the communities.

The Appalachian Civic Leadership Project – University of Kentucky and Berea College

The Appalachian Civic Leadership Program was sponsored by the Appalachian Center at the University of Kentucky (UK). The project brought together the leadership efforts of the Brushy Fork Institute at Berea College and the five community colleges in the region, which are also part of the University system. There were seven partners in all. The project was designed to: (i) build a stronger civic infrastructure in eastern Kentucky by training leaders; (ii) increase the level and quality of public talk; and (iii) increase the level of commitment, collaboration and involvement in rural development by institutions of higher education in the region. Four major components were developed to reach 450 leaders, students and citizens in 49 counties. The Commonwealth Fellowship Program gave financial support to emerging leaders to take part in a two-year series of workshops. The Appalachian Student Leadership Program involved students from the UK, and five eastern Kentucky community colleges, and Berea College. The Brushy Fork Institute at Berea College provided a leadership development program for community representatives from four central Appalachian states. The Community Issues Gatherings were open to all eastern Kentuckians to discuss controversial issues and learn the process of public talk. As a result, the audience of the project was multigenerational and socio-economically diverse.

Appalachians had frequently been exposed to materials, curricula, representatives of institutions and others who were not culturally sensitive. Thus residents had become very suspicious about getting involved in opportunities offered to them. It was discovered that developing a civic infrastructure and altering highly structured institutions was a process, not a product, and that the expectations of both staff and participants had to be based on this fact. Before and after, personal assessments were used to track formal participation. Records were kept of the number of communities and citizens and mailed questionnaires were used to canvass the entire population served. Participants were extremely positive and excited about the programs. Many strides were made in breaking down the barriers between this local population and the institutions involved. It was realized that these efforts would require continued support over a long period of time.

Community Leadership in Maine: Ensuring a Viable Future for Small Communities – University of Maine

This community leadership project was implemented by the Cooperative Extension Service of the University of Maine. Its purpose was to encourage more responsibility and participation in local decision making. The project sought to: (i) establish a leadership development opportunity for communities of less than 4000; and (ii) develop leadership skills in communities by working with local individuals as facilitators and educators. Three clusters of communities within four entire counties and portions of two others were established. In these clusters locally controlled and operated leadership programs were developed that placed heavy emphasis on the value and implementation of cooperation, collaboration and inclusion. The project provided the necessary resources for the development, presentation and evaluation of a program consisting of 7 to 10 workshops and symposia. During the life of the project 1184 people participated. Each region received funding for and developed a network within the region adapted to local needs as it worked on issues of government, gender, youth and schools. It was a challenge to listen to residents' and participants' needs before designing programs and then to shape programs to address the participants' concerns. It was also a challenge to integrate a new, innovative project with the existing institutional structure. Each project component received a systematic evaluation and a cumulative qualitative evaluation that included feedback from participants, advisory boards, Extension agents, project staff and significant others. The project provided data on three distinct models of community-based activities. Site visits confirmed initial local impact and many spinoffs; for example, after the training, fuel for the area schools and road salt and sand were purchased collectively rather than separately. It was felt that the project had great potential to benefit other sections of Maine that were not in the initial clusters.

Financial Management for Local Government Officials and Community Organizations – University of Maryland

This project was managed by the Institute for Governmental Services, a 31-year-old unit within the University of Maryland. The institute traditionally provided technical assistance to small communities. With this project the institute was able to expand its service to training. The goal of the project was to offer training in financial management to small local governments and non-profit organizations to enable their members to better understand and manage their financial obligations. A needs assessment, conducted with local government professional associations such as the Maryland League of

Cities and Towns, suggested topics for the training sessions. Grantsmanship, financial planning, budgeting, investment systems and capital improvement plans were some of the concepts that were developed into an integrated series of nine modules. A total of 400 officials from 155 municipalities attended one or more training sessions. Evaluation centered on pre- and post-testing of the participants' skills and knowledge as well as end of session reflections. A random sample of participants was contacted as a follow-up assessment. Attracting non-profit groups to the sessions was a problem. Different marketing strategies were examined by an outside firm. Participants found new ways to approach their financial management problems and they incorporated these new ideas into their current operations. Networking was an important result of this project. Neighboring cities and counties began contacting each other to share ideas and exchange information, and many local government officials began to see the whole university as a resource as their skills in accessing information grew.

Leadership and Local Government Education Project – Michigan State University

This project was a joint effort between Michigan State University's Cooperative Extension Service, Department of Agricultural Economics and Department of Resource Development. Other collaborators were three professional associations of local government officials and three community colleges in the southwest region of the state. The project's goal was to enhance the capacity of local leaders, officials and institutions to provide necessary services to residents in seven southwestern Michigan counties. This region was identified as suffering from economic distress due to declining agricultural land values and shrinking governmental revenues. The project had three components: (i) to increase leadership capacity in rural communities; (ii) to improve officials' skills in accounting, budgeting, finance, assessing, computer use and program analysis; and (iii) to increase collaborative efforts in providing services. Nine unique projects were initiated by Cooperative Extension personnel in response to significant issues in their counties. A total of 450 participants engaged in activities ranging from the establishment of small leadership development groups, regional leadership meetings, computer training sessions, and the development of collaborative agreements between governmental units to share services to their publics. Maintaining the active involvement of the community colleges was a challenge. Likewise, with such broad involvement, coordination was an issue. This project succeeded in involving Cooperative Extension staff in non-traditional programming, which increased local support for the Service. There were 244 local units of government involved in some phase of either the technical training or collaborative efforts. Six new intergovernmental agreements were developed as a direct result of this project.

Montcalm Tomorrow – Montcalm County Board of Commissioners

The County Board of Commissioners of rural Montcalm County (population 50 000, located in central lower Michigan) directed this project with assistance from Michigan State University Extension and Montcalm Community College. The purpose of the project was to engage citizens in seeking ways to assist in economic development and to enhance the quality of life in rural areas. The Board of Commissioners invited 50 county residents to attend a forum to discuss and identify important issues that affected the county. Out of that discussion rose a twofold objective: to create a set of task forces, and to develop a leadership training program. The board appointed a seven member steering committee to direct five task forces involving 75 citizens. Each task force focused on one topic: (i) education, (ii) health care, (iii) the environment, (iv) economic development and (v) quality of life issues. The leadership program, under the direction of the Montcalm County Cooperative Extension Service, consisted of nine sessions attended by 45 people. Interest was high, so the steering committee added an advanced class for an additional 20 people. Those involved in the task forces found that process was important. It took an unexpectedly long time to develop a sense of community for these groups; however, the steering committee held to its philosophy of non-interference, allowing the groups to grow and function at their own pace. As one participant put it, "Something has to happen within the people before anything can happen in the project". Each task force investigated the status of the issues under its jurisdiction and presented a plan for future action. Evaluations were developed by graduate students of Michigan State University, Department of Resource Development. They used personal interviews and telephone interviews with participants and submitted reports to the project steering committee. Through the task force process, networks and relationships were established. Spinoffs included an arrangement by two communities to share one city manager and the development of a parks commission.

Property Tax Assessment Computerization Project (PTACP) and the County Educational Forum (CEF) – Kirtland Community College and Michigan State University

This project had two distinct components. PTACP was a cooperative effort between the Department of Resource Development at Michigan State University and Kirtland Community College in Roscommon, Michigan. Its goal was to train tax assessors in small communities to use computer technology in the assessment of property for tax purposes. Some 429 assessing units, mostly townships, received software and attended group training sessions conducted by the software manufacturer. A principal difficulty with the project was the lapse of time between training and the first use of the software. Additionally it was discovered that some assessors did not have the data that the software needed to make its computations. The project staff learnt that this was not simply a matter of teaching people a new technology. The project required basic computer literacy lessons, basic assessing lessons, and then the specific training for the software. The CEF was the second component of the project. It was carried out in cooperation with MSU, Kirtland Community College and the United County Officers Association – a coalition of many different professional associations representing county officials. A series of training sessions was provided. The subject matter of the program was classified into two main categories. One was personal growth and development which offered programs such as "Care and feeding of the lifelong mind" and "How to stay cool in the hot seat". The other set featured topics directed at improving job-related skills and knowledge. "Demystifying the law" and "The user-friendly courthouse" were some of the topic titles. Records of attendance were kept and upon the completion of 135 classroom hours, participants received a certificate of completion. There were 1085 graduates, 20 percent of whom were black and 41 percent of whom were female. The CEF Project broadened the subject matter that county officers were accustomed to consider appropriate to them. It demonstrated the importance of education in building organizations and it conditioned many of the newer members to expect sound educational programs at their regular meetings.

RECLAIM (Rural Education for Community Leaders Aimed at Improved Management of the Environment) – Midwest Assistance Program (MAP)

MAP, a non-profit organization that serves nine midwestern states, developed the RECLAIM project based on its extensive background experience in providing training and technical assistance on water and wastewater systems. RECLAIM focused on solid waste management issues in three states – Nebraska, North Dakota and Missouri. MAP's mission was to serve the most disenfranchised groups, the smallest and least prepared communities. To begin this project, MAP's staff educated themselves on solid waste management and then assembled a library of relevant materials and developed a four module training manual for local officials. MAP conducted RECLAIM along the lines of their water/wastewater programs, using informational meetings and workshops and then working on an individual level with specific communities in a technical assistance mode. There were 259 workshops for local officials and 24 technical assistance projects. These programs were attended by local and state officials, rural community leaders, private recyclers, trash haulers and interested citizens. Initially staff felt daunted by the challenges of developing their expertise and connections in the solid waste arena and making presentations to local groups. However, the strong need for this type of assistance overcame any hesitancies. Evaluation of the project was informal, utilizing feedback from the communities, from the MAP board of directors, and workshop evaluation forms. As a result of this project, MAP enlarged its capacity to deal with solid waste issues and sparked interest not only in local and state officials but also in other regional agencies which considered using RECLAIM as a model for other regions. At the community level, North Dakota consolidated its solid waste management sites, began to discuss solid waste policies and legislation, successfully passed new legislation and created awareness of larger environmental issues. Across the communities there was an enormously increased awareness that recycling was preferable to land-filling for solid waste management.

PRO-MISS: Promoting Rural Opportunity in Mississippi – Mississippi State University

The PRO-MISS leadership development project was originally conceived by the Cooperative Extension Service at Mississippi State University and later transferred to the College of Agriculture for administrative leadership. The purpose of PRO-MISS was to prepare participants to provide leadership to their rural communities in governmental and economic affairs and to enable them to access the resources of Mississippi State University. Two major groups led the project: the advisory board that was committed to the sustainability and long-lasting effects of the project and the design team which created and implemented the curriculum. A series of eight different workshops was rotated through seven different locales. The "home" team at each locality played host to the 30 participants for three to four days. A total of 90 rural leaders participated from 21 Mississippi communities. These workshops provided knowledge and individual skills necessary for the group to become effective community leaders and team members. Participants were given the opportunity to use their skills in practical contexts through the development and implementation of a community project. Because extensive time away from work and home was required, participants negotiated contracts with their employers and spouses to clarify their commitments. Challenges were met at both the university and the participant level. The change in ownership of the program led to some delay in the project's start-up and the participants proved to be at a higher learning level than the design team originally had estimated, which led to adjustments. An outside evaluator met with the advisory board every three months to determine what data were needed from the participants. The participants were then interviewed and a community profile emerged. The workshops themselves were also evaluated and necessary changes were incorporated. The concepts of a design team and a working advisory board have worked well for this project, instilling a great sense of ownership at the administrative level. Involving spouses and employers as well as the participants created a similar feeling of ownership at the community level.

Missouri Rural Innovation Institute (MRII) – University of Missouri

MRII was created with project support as an outreach unit of the University of Missouri Cooperative Extension Service. Its mission was to increase the capacity of rural leaders to deal innovatively with change and thereby improve the quality of life in their communities. Its tools of choice in accomplishing this mission were creativity and collaboration used both by the projects' developers and the rural participants. MRII developed four core projects to address the problems of lack of coordination of the delivery of human services to rural Missouri.

1. A satellite broadcast gathered 2000 rural health care providers into their first ever joint dialog. This method provided many important spinoffs, including networking partnerships and a sense of ownership for the participants.
2. The *Rural Community* magazine, with a subscription list of 12 000, featured stories of the forward strides of rural communities.
3. Program EXCEL brought leadership development to 60 towns and 2000 people.
4. The CONNECT telephone answerline provided a means for people to stay connected to the university as a resource.

These and other projects reached people in all 114 counties and involved 15 partner organizations and 615
resource persons. The amount of time and energy the staff
needed to bring people together in the various activities
and especially for the satellite broadcast was a challenge.
There were philosophical challenges as well in helping
staff and partners understand the mission of the institute.
Innovation was a worthy goal but took courage to implement. The use of a 28 member Program Leadership
Council helped to legitimize and imbed the program in
key institutions. A variety of evaluation processes was used
to monitor the activities of the project. Feedback was an
important element in maintaining collaboration and
momentum. This project succeeded in building stronger
alliances, enhancing the abilities of individuals to respond
to change, and providing both the impetus and tools for
comprehensive community improvement. The MRII's support for innovation encouraged creativity, risk taking and
new models of thinking. It made rurality important in the
context of both the university and the rest of the state.

Mon Valley Tri-State Leadership Academy – Mon Valley Network, Inc. (at West Virginia University)

The Monongahela River carves a valley through three
states: Pennsylvania, West Virginia and Maryland. In this
region, local units of government, civic organizations, businesses and 10 universities joined together to form a non-
profit organization called the Mon Valley Network. This
organization sponsored the project called the Mon Valley
Tri-State Leadership Academy, headquartered on the
University of West Virginia campus. The academy's purpose is to create for the region dynamic, visionary leaders
who can improve planning and economic development
strategies, increase employment, and enhance the quality
of life of valley residents. Both faculty and practitioners
brought their perspectives together to frame four educational modules focused on collaboration, leadership, communication skills and increased awareness of the region's
resources. The original target audience was economic
development professionals but it was discovered that the
program had a wider appeal and the audience became

more diverse. Thirty-eight participants from 18 counties graduated from the program series over a two-year period, although up to 70 individuals participated in some aspect of the training. While in the program, participants were asked to plan and implement economic development projects specific to each of their communities. More than 35 action projects were initiated. The academy sought to create unique models and concepts with the thought of copyrighting them to generate revenue for the project. A continuing challenge is adapting these programs for use in multiple settings. A train the trainer program will be developed to accompany the curriculum modules. The program has benefited from the involvement of faculty from 10 universities and of a rich array of local professionals. Feedback from the faculty and the board of directors of Mon Valley Network contributed to design decisions. End of session evaluations and focus group interviews with both faculty and participants provided insights to improve ensuing sessions. Participants developed a strong sense of common destiny and recognized the importance of working together across the region to accomplish things they previously thought they could not do. Joint efforts across more than one community were common. Three new leadership development programs were funded, and enthusiasm for the potential of the region has grown.

Training for Local Government Officials: Local Government Center – Montana State University

Montana State University's Department of Political Science developed the Local Government Center as a pathway for providing training and resources for rural communities to enhance their capacities for self-governance. Three key elements of the project were to: (i) form advisory committees of 13 state, county and city officials' associations to determine their educational needs; (ii) conduct annual and serial workshops to train officials including three year certification programs for municipal clerks, county treasurers and clerks of court; and (iii) involve the political science faculty and students with the center's training programs. Montana is a large state with widely separated communities. Yet distance became an ally to the project. More than

700 participants from 86 counties and towns welcomed the chance to socialize and develop personal networks and often verbalized the thought that "I realized that I wasn't alone with my problems. Others have these problems too." Because a large number of the local officials in Montana were women, the trainers recognized and explicitly addressed the need to develop their confidence and competence so that they could work effectively with their local authority structures which were staffed primarily by men. The certification programs did much to legitimize the role of women in local government. One challenge was maintaining rapport with colleagues in the Department of Political Science. The linking of the Local Government Center to the academic agenda was a very conscious effort. Participant questionnaires and end of session reflections provided insight and feedback for evaluating the project. At the end of the project an external evaluator provided a comprehensive program review. As a result of this project the professional skills and standing of local officials were advanced and their communication networks were strengthened. Additionally the Local Government Center was able to establish a policy council to address state policies concerning local governments.

Grassroots Government Educational Program – National Association of Towns and Townships (NATaT)

The National Association of Towns and Townships, a non-profit membership organization, developed this project to provide easy, low cost access to practical and appropriately scaled public management information, training and resources for rural public officials. The project had two primary goals: (i) to develop and distribute training modules on high priority rural issues; and (ii) to organize and enhance a national network of rural technical assistance providers to disseminate those materials. The training modules were patterned after NATaT's previously developed successful program, Harvesting Hometown Jobs, an economic development module. The new modules consisted of a substantial instructional guidebook, a 15 minute motivational video tape, and a meeting planner's guide. Assisted by NATaT's 12 member advisory committee and

853 technical advisors from a wide range of public and private agencies, the project staff researched and developed four educational modules: *Why waste a second chance?*, which covered recycling issues; *Accidents will happen*, a small town's guide to planning for hazardous materials response; *Innovative grassroots financing*, a guide to fund raising and cost cutting; and *Getting out from under*, which described underground storage tank alternatives. NATaT's monthly journal kept the technical advisors abreast of the project and encouraged their input in the module development. The project encountered some difficulty with the production schedule of the modules. A longer time frame was needed than was originally projected to accommodate the extremely thorough research needed to maintain the quality that NATaT sought to achieve. An external evaluator with a background in adult education provided input to tailor the presentations to the needs of adult learners and analyzed in detail both the target audiences of the program and the marketing strategies needed to reach them. Mailed questionnaires and telephone interviews provided feedback from the module users on the ease of using the modules and the level of technical difficulty. Some of the target audiences were the USDA Extension Service officials, circuit riding town managers, local government organizations, rural electric cooperatives, economic development districts, community colleges and non-profit development groups. In all, 5084 sets of educational materials were distributed.

Leadership Institute for Small Municipalities (LISM) – National Forum for Black Public Administrators (NFBPA)

LISM was sponsored by the National Forum for Black Public Administrators, a professional organization dedicated to the advancement of black leadership in the public sector. Faculty from Arkansas State University and Mississippi State University helped develop the curriculum. The institute was housed on the campuses of North Carolina Central University and the University of Georgia. The purpose of the project was to empower black administrators of small city and county governments by making them more effective managers and leaders in their communities through intensive skills training and peer networking for advice and consultation. Participants from eight states, Alabama, Arkansas, Louisiana, Missouri, Florida, Georgia, North Carolina and South Carolina, attended five 3 day weekend training sessions over a period of three months. Critical management and professional development topics central to the curriculum included: budgeting/financial management, communication skills, economic development, ethics, grantsmanship, managing public services, problem solving, team or coalition building, use of small computers and visionary leadership. This group of small town and county public officials presented a challenge to the project in that a large percentage of them was required to work outside of their official capacities in either full- or part-time employment. This resulted in holding the training sessions over the weekends and, in some cases, reimbursing airfares for those who lived at too great a distance to drive to the sites without compromising time at work. Peer networking was greatly facilitated by the intimate size of the participant groups which developed close, friendly, almost family-like relationships. End of session evaluations were done and follow-up telephone interviews were used to assess the impact of the officials' training on their communities. An external evaluator collected data to assess the number and types of grant applications made and received. Respondents to the follow-up survey also listed a wide array of new resources that were brought into their communities – for example, backhoes, computers, police cars, police and firefighting equipment, a new tutorial service for high school students, a senior citizen housing project and equipment for housing demolition.

Transformational Leadership Training (TLT) – State University of New York at Binghampton

This project was a joint effort between the College of Economics at the Binghampton campus of the State University of New York and the Cornell Cooperative Extension Service. The purpose of TLT was to strengthen community development in designated small cities and towns in New York State by strengthening the leadership skills of their individual leaders. TLT was designed to: (i) apply what has been learnt about transformational leadership to the education and development of community leaders; (ii) develop a comprehensive and intensive leadership program that could be administered efficiently (within a six day time period) using appropriate follow-up sessions to generalize the effects of training in community organizations; and (iii) evaluate the impact of the transformational leadership training program at the individual, group, organizational and community levels. Participating teams of leaders attended a three day workshop during which they were introduced to the transformational model. They were given tests to measure their own personal leadership behaviors and develop their own leadership plans. These personal plans were then entered into a software program on a computer network so all of the participants could examine each other's plans on-line, although each person's anonymity was protected. In a second 3 day workshop, which was held three months later to allow an interval for practice and growth, participants re-evaluated their personal plans, received additional information about personal characteristics relevant to improving their performance and learnt strategies for further development. The program graduated 450 people. One of the challenges was to find and measure correlations between the leaders' training and the events that happened within their communities during a significant economic downturn in the region. The evaluation of this project was of major interest to the cluster evaluation. The participants were tracked at every intersection of their learning and their community's actions. This was the only research-oriented project in the cluster using a very specific leadership model and using a control group.

Community Voices: Leadership Development for Public Decision Making: a Multi-state Project for a Limited-resource Audience – North Carolina Agricultural and Technical State University

Community Voices was sponsored by the Cooperative Extension Service at North Carolina Agricultural and Technical State University. Since the project's main purpose was to act as a pilot, four institutions in the region participated by receiving curriculum materials and training regarding the activities. This project's three purposes were to: (i) develop new strategies and methods for teaching and training a limited resource audience; (ii) train other institutions to use these new methods; and (iii) provide educational services to a limited resource/disadvantaged citizen audience in North Carolina. The project focused on emerging community leaders with incomes below 80 percent of the average in the geographic area and with an education level of high school or lower. The project developers created modules specifically to address this audience. The modules dealt with the topics of leadership, public decision making, public policy analysis, group dynamics, situational analysis, needs assessments, and community organization and change. The participants were 500 new leaders from 17 counties in Alabama, Arkansas and Texas. An additional 1200 new community leaders participated in the training in North Carolina. A major challenge for the project was attracting professionals with the skill and sensitivity to work with this audience. A self-administered evaluation procedure and audience feedback resulted in a constant modification of materials and methods. An outside evaluator was hired to present an unbiased view, but it was determined that because of the evaluator's incompatibility with the audience, the documents produced were less valuable than the in-house evaluation strategies used. Statements made by a large number of participants suggested there had been a significant impact on individuals' community involvement. This project touched participants' lives and increased their understanding of and involvement in creating change.

Dakota LEADers (Dakota Leadership Education and Development) – University of North Dakota

Dakota LEADers was jointly administered by the Center for Rural Health and the Division of Continuing Education within the University of North Dakota. The project's goal was to build capacity for economic development in rural communities by establishing an effective leadership training program, helping to create stable coalitions of rural leaders, enhancing networking at local, regional, state and national levels, and increasing economic development activity at the local level. The project leaders targeted 32 small communities in North and South Dakota and asked each of them to select a six person team of leaders who represented six critical sectors of the community: primary industry (agriculture, energy, mining, manufacturing and tourism), commerce, religion, education, health care and government. These 192 community leaders participated in two 3 day workshops and a series of seminars on community development. Community teams were expected to develop action projects. A closing symposium was held to showcase and celebrate the end of the project and what each team had been able to accomplish. There were differences of opinion between the states as to what constituted economic development. Consensus building became a major activity. County grants proved to be effective tools for encouraging leadership development and invigorating local economic development. Quantitative and qualitative data were collected from participants and teams concerning the context of the training, its presentation and the type of outcomes in the community. Focus group interviews with participants were conducted in three locations and the final report was a set of cases studies. During the course of these interviews, many long-term impacts and spinoffs were reported, such as the opening of a fitness center, a day care facility, and a mini mall containing eight businesses.

Training for Rural Officials – Ohio University

The Department of Political Science of Ohio University developed the Institute for Local Government Administration and Rural Development (ILGARD). This group provided information and statistics to state officials and the university system and was in a good position to sponsor the Training for Rural Officials project. The goal of the project was to provide training for local officials in the Appalachian region of south and southeastern Ohio in skills essential to perform their jobs and assist them to make sound local decisions. The three areas of focus were: (i) solid waste management; (ii) capital improvement planning; and (iii) effective use of computer software applications such as spreadsheets, data bases and automated mapping. ILGARD assembled a faculty team of 15 people from three colleges within Ohio University who developed a series of day-long training workshops on each of the three topics. Over a three-year period, 980 officials from all levels of government participated. Personal recruitment methods were used. Staff visited the counties to discuss the workshops and follow-up material explaining the programs was mailed to all government officials and other interested people. As a result, the audience represented a broad cross-section of officials from 29 counties in south and southeastern Ohio. A challenge to the project was that the target audience of the Appalachian region of Ohio had paid little attention to technological advances and seemed resistant to acknowledging that they needed training. Another challenge was involving faculty from campus in working with this audience. A great deal of evaluation was done on the training programs. A telephone survey six months after the workshops showed that a majority of the participants were pleased with the training programs, the quality and usefulness of the manuals and the help they received to deal with local issues: 78 percent reported referring to the technical manuals after the programs and 96 percent recommended the programs to others. In total, the project was successful in linking ILGARD resources to rural communities, forming a training and technical support network (MicroNet), providing training through distance education technologies, changing a university faculty ethic towards service, and enlarging the capacities of local officials in a resource-poor area of the state.

Program for Local Government Education (PLGE) – Washington State University

PLGE represents a mutual effort between WSU's Cooperative Extension Service and the Division of Governmental Studies and Services and three of the state's governmental associations – the Association of Washington Cities, the Washington Association of County Officials, and the Washington State Association of Counties. The project's purpose was to increase educational support for elected and appointed officials in smaller jurisdictions in Washington State by building capacity in local governments, strengthening local governmental associations and improving the ability of WSU to respond to the needs of local governments. The PLGE project received leadership from an eight member policy council made up of elected and appointed local officials, one staff member from each of the associations, and three WSU administrators and faculty. The council prioritized cutting edge topics for the workshops, seminars and materials. Some of these were "Negotiation and Dispute Resolution Seminar for County and City Officials", "Mason County Criminal Justice Working Team", "Grand Coulee Dam Area Project", "Risk Management for Rural Counties" and "Local Government Growth Strategies Forum". The project reached an audience of 803 participants from 68 cities and 35 counties. The Cooperative Extension Service evaluation specialist organized many of the evaluation approaches to meet the needs of both the association practitioners and the WSU faculty. A series of case studies and pert chart type monitoring devices provided insights on community change. There was a challenging period while the associations and the university personnel learnt to work with each other, which ultimately led to the associations taking a lead role. As a result of this project, the three associations recognized the power of working together in lobbying, two of the associations changed their opinions, and trust was built between the university and the associations which enabled new working relationships.

The Wisconsin Leadership Development Program – University of Wisconsin

This project was developed by the Cooperative Extension Service of the University of Wisconsin. Its purpose was to develop, test and implement strategies that would increase the numbers of African American, Latino, American Indian, and Southeast Asian community leaders and their levels of commitment in six southeastern Wisconsin counties. The project provided opportunities for these participants to expand their understanding about how the community works, how people work together effectively around common concerns, and how leaders and others influence community decisions, especially in urban neighborhoods. This was the only project in the cluster evaluation that had such a broad multicultural audience. Project staff implemented two types of leadership development for 450 participants: (i) workshops with a series of 12 sessions were held throughout the year in targeted communities; and (ii) selected graduates of these workshops were invited to participate in four week-long traveling seminars held within a two-year period of time. A major challenge of this project was trusting the development of human relationships long enough to allow such a diverse group of people to listen to and respect the ideas of others. Qualitative data were readily available since debriefing sessions and reflection were built-in components of this project. The project documented topics of interest to the participants and many of the lessons learnt had valuable application in other settings. Seminar participants said that this project significantly improved their effectiveness as leaders in their respective neighborhoods and significantly increased the networking in each neighborhood. They were better informed, had a better understanding of the process of "getting things done" and, most of all, they listened to and understood their colleagues better.

Appendix 2: Products of Rural America Projects partly funded by the WK Kellogg Foundation

Institution and Host	Title	Product Type	Year Produced	Contact
Auburn University Cooperative Extension	Community Assessment Profile Manual	Assessment manual		**Dr R. Warren McCord** Auburn University, 104 Duncan Hall Auburn, AL 38649
	Leadership for Economic Development	Application packet		
	Leadership for Economic Development Workshop #2	Workshop curriculum		
Colorado State University	Colorado Rural Revitilization Project	Training manual		**Sheila Knop** Colorado State Univ. 234 Aylesworth NW Fort Collins, CO 80523
	Community Assessment Guide	Assessment guide		
	Visions into Actions	Colorado case studies		
Council of Governors Policy Advisors	Academy Manual	Seminar curriculum	1990	**Tom Bonnett** Council of Govs. Policy Adv. 400 N Capitol St. Washington DC 20001
	"Strategies For Rural Competitiveness: Policy Options For State Government"	Book	1993 ($19.95)	
University of Georgia	Collaboration Evaluation	Collaboration report evaluation		**Melba G Cooper** University of Georgia Hoke Smith Annex Fanning Leadership Center Athens, GA 30602
	It's in Your Hands: An Interactive Exercise in Decision-Making	Leader's Guide		
Heartland Center	Heartland Center for Leadership Development	Workshop activity manual and agenda	1992	**Milan Wall & Vicki Luther** Heartland Center 941 O St, Suite 920 Lincoln, NE 68508
	20 Clues to Rural Community Survival	Flyer		
	Vision into Action: The Critical Path to Small Town Development	Poster/sign		

Institution and Host	Title	Product Type	Year Produced	Contact
Heartland Center (*continued*)	6 Myths About the Future of Small Towns	Publication of the Heartland Center for Leadership Development		
	Resources for Community Survival	Pamphlet		
University of Illinois	Helping Rural Communities Prepare for Economic Development	A brochure describing the program		**John C Van Es** University of Illinois 305 Mumford Hall 1301 W Gregory Dr Urbana, IL 61801
	Motivation Sequence Steps	Information sheet		
	Why Community Development Must Precede Economic Development	Speech	1991	
	Leadership Roles in Community Groups	Community action module	1991	
	Conducting Needs Assessment Studies in Your County	Program manual	1991	
	Conflict Management in Community Groups	Program manual	1991	
	Developing County Economic Profiles	Program manual	1991	
	Analyzing the Retail Trade Market of Your Community	Program manual	1991	
	Strategic Planning for Community and Economic Development	Program manual	1991	
	Committees – A Key to Group Leadership	North Central Regional Extension Publication	1980	
	Team Skills in Community Groups	Booklet	1977	
	Helping Rural Communities Prepare for Economic Development	Information sheet	1980	
	Identifying and Recruiting Leaders for County Development Groups (AE 4672-1)	Community action modules		Laboratory for Community and Economic Development, University of Illinois at Urbana–Champaign (217) 333-5509

Institution and Host	Title	Product Type	Year Produced	Contact
	Conducting Needs Assessment Studies in Your County (AE 4672-2)	Community action modules		
	Leadership Roles in Community Groups (AE 4672-3)	Community action modules		
	Strategic Planning for Community and Economic Development (AE 4672-4)	Community action modules		
	Working with Communities (AE 4672-5)	Community action modules		
	Conflict Management in Community Groups (AE 4672-6)	Community action modules		
	Retaining and Expanding Local Business and Industry (AE 4672-7)	Community action modules		
	Developing a Labor Force Profile for Your County (AE 4672-8)	Oommunity action modules		
	Developing County Economics Profiles (AE 4672-9)	Community action modules		
	Maintaining Participation Community Organizations (AE 4672-10)	Community action modules		
	Analyzing the Retail Trade Market of Your Community (AE 4672-11)	Community action modules		
	Helping Entrepreneurs Initiate Businesses (AE 4672-12)	Community action modules		
	Developing Business Targeting Skills (AE 4672-13)	Community action modules		
	Analyzing Economic Impacts (AE 4672-14)	Community action modules		

Institution and Host	Title	Product Type	Year Produced	Contact
University of Illinois (*continued*)	Marketing Your Community and County to Others (AE 4672-15)	Community action modules		
	Presenting Your Community and County to Others (AE 4672-16)	Community action modules		
	Assessing and Developing Tourism Resources (AE 4672-17)	Community action modules		
	Developing an Inventory of Resources and Products (AE 4672-18)	Community action modules		
	Analyzing Social Impacts of Development (AE 4672-19)	Community action modules		
	Communicating with the Public (AE 4672-20)			
Iowa State University	Tomorrow's Leaders Today	Program overview #TLT2	1990 & 1991	**Betty Wells** Iowa State University 303 East Hall Ames, IA 50011
	Tomorrow's Leaders Today: Continuing the Leadership Challenge	Training Manual #TLT26 $15.00	1990	
	Communities Creating Their Futures	Booklet (Facilitator's Guide) #TLT30	1991	
	Why Cluster?	Pamphlet #TLT14	1989	
	Communities Creating their Futures (TRT: 21:46)	Video tape #75688	1990	
	Building Group Skills: Forming a Group (TRT: 14:36)	Video tape #75623	1989	
	Building Group Skills: Agendas & Meeting Environment (TRT: 11:20)	Video tape #75602	1989	
	Building Group Skills: Delegating (TRT: 12:47)	Video tape #75621	1989	

Institution and Host	Title	Product Type	Year Produced	Contact
	Building Group Skills: Using Networks (TRT: 13:46)	Video tape #75622	1989	
	Group Phases (TRT: 9:15)	Slide/Tape Sets #007955	1989	
	Group Member Roles (TRT: 8:15)	Slide/Tape Sets #001125	1989	
	Difficult People in Groups (TRT: 8:30)	Slide/Tape Sets #007965	1989	
	So Much to Gain – Community Clusters (TRT: 16:05)	Slide/Tape Sets #002045	1990	
	Tomorrow's Leaders Today	Program materials list #TLT29	1991	
Kansas State University	KCRI Publications	List of Publications and prices		**Sue Maes** Kansas State University College Court Building Manhattan, KS 66505–6001
	Kansas Center for Rural Initiatives	Brochure		
	Community Services Program Evaluations	Project evaluation forms	1990	
	Community-based Leadership/Community College Leadership Workshop – 1	Manual	1991	
	Self-development: Profiles of Kansas Communities	Publication/booklet		
	Rural Data Resources	Publication/booklet		
	Rural Resources Directory	Publication/booklet		
	Strategic Planning Guidebook	Publication/booklet		
	Strategic Planning Resources Directory	Publication/booklet		
	Reach for A S.T.A.R. (Senior Talents and Resource)	Seminar material		
	Kansas Center for Initiatives	Organizational chart		

Institution and Host	Title	Product Type	Year Produced	Contact
Appalachian Center at the University of Kentucky	Commonwealth Fellowship Program	Program application		**Ronald Eller** University of Kentucky 641 S Limestone Lexington, KY 40506-0333
	Jobs and Economic Development: Meeting the Needs of Appalachian People	Booklet	1991	
	1990 Commonwealth Fellowship Program Application	Booklet	1990	
University of Maine	Taking the Land	Leadership tips from the Cooperative Extension		**Deb Burwell** University of Maine 110 Libby Hall Orono, ME 04469
	Community Leadership in Maine	Workshop curriculum	1992	
University of Maryland	A Report from the Institute for Governmental Services	Report describing project and the Institute for Governmental Service (IGS)	1987–90 & 1993 update	**Barbara S Hawk** University of Maryland Suite 2101 Woods Hall College Park, MD 20742
	Financial Management Training for your Local Government	2 volume set consisting of 8 training texts in financial management for rural governments $15.00/volume	1993	
Michigan State University	Evaluating Rural Development Projects: Action Researching as Empowerment Evaluation	Paper	1993	**Mary P Andrews** Michigan State University 109 Human Ecology East Lansing, MI 48824
	Conceptualization: A MUST	Paper	1992	
	Responses to the "End-of-Session Group Evaluation Networking Conference", May 1992	Paper	1992	
	Gaining Institutional and Organizational Support for Community Leadership Programs	Paper	1993	

Institution and Host	Title	Product Type	Year Produced	Contact
	Lessons Learned about System Changes from Twenty-Eight Rural Development Projects	Paper	1994	
Midwest Assistance Program	Reclaim the Environment	A program of rural education for community leaders aimed at improved management of the environment		**Kenneth Bruzelius** Midwest Assistance Program PO Box 81 New Prague, MN 56071
	Reclaim the Environment	Workshop curriculum		
University of Missouri Cooperative Extension	EXCEL	Notebook curriculum		**James O Preston** University of Missouri 529 Clark Hall Columbia, MO 65211
	Developing Community Leadership the EXCEL Approach	Program development and implementation curriculum booklet	1992	
	The Missouri Rural Innovation Institute	Booklet	1990–92	
Mon-River Coop. Dev. Net. WVU	Modules 1–4	Workshop curriculum		**Paul Fendt** West Virginia University 918 Chestnut Ridge Suite A8 Morgantown, WV 26506
	Happy Reading... Various newsletters	Workshop curriculum		
Montana State University	Reflections on Tribal Governance in Montana	Book	1990	**Kenneth L Weaver** Montana State University Local Government Center Bozeman, MT 59717
	Montana Solid Waste Handbook	Handbook	1990	
National Assoc. of Towns & Townships	How to Begin Solving Your Town's Most Crucial Problems – Right Away – For Less Than You Ever Thought it Would Cost	Cost-saving and time-saving curriculum from NATaT (booklet)		**Hamilton Brown** Nat. Assoc. of Towns & Townships 1522 K. St, NW Suite 260 Washington DC 20005
	Order form for booklet described above	Order form		

Institution and Host	Title	Product Type	Year Produced	Contact
National Assoc. of Towns & Townships (*continued*)	NAT & T: Innovative Grassroots Financing	Video tape		
	NAT & T: Why Waste a Second Chance?	Video tape		
	NAT & T: Accidents Will Happen	Video tape		
	NAT & T – Kellogg Technical Assistance Program	Module topic selection plan		
	Grassroots Leaders Have Always Had to Deal with a Log of Garbage (Recycling Program)	Information sheet		
	Order form for recycling guide	Order form		
	Innovative Grassroots financing	Audio-visual facilitator's guide		
	Accidents Will Happen	Training guide/booklets		
	Why Waste A Second Chance?	Training guide/booklets		
	Innovative Grassroots financing	Training guide/booklets		
State University of New York	Kellogg Leadership Program	Brochure		**Bernard M Bass & Bruce Avolio** State University of New York PO Box 60000 Binghampton, NY 13902-6000
	Multifactor Leadership Questionnaire	Leadership evaluation		
	Self-scoring Directions for Questionnaire	Scoring sheet for leadership evaluation		
	My Leadership Development Plan	Information sheet to be filled out by participants		
	Kellogg Leadership Program	Conferences curriculum		
	Transformational Leadership Development Training Program	Information sheet		
	Styles of Leadership	Information sheet		

Institution and Host	Title	Product Type	Year Produced	Contact
North Carolina A & T	Community Voices	Brochures		**Dr Shirley M Callaway** North Carolina A & T State University PO Box 21928 Greensboro, NC 27420
	Executive Summary	Information sheet about community development		
	Recruitment Strategy	Booklet		
	Site Selection	Booklet		
	Plan of Action	Booklet		
	Marketing Strategy	Booklet		
	A Multi-state Leadership Development Project	Booklet		
	Tool Kit	Booklet		
	Is Community Voices a Program for Me?	Conference curriculum		
	Co-Facilitator's Guide (Sessions 1–8)	Booklet		
	Audience Analysis	Booklet		
North Dakota	Dakota LEADers Goals	Information sheet		**Kim Nesvig** University of North Dakota 501 Columbia Rd Grand Forks, ND 58203
	Your Leadership Behavior	Self-evaluation/work shop curriculum		
	Community/County Profile	Format used for profile requirements		
	Development in the Dakotas	Dakotas case studies		
	Workshop Evaluation	Evaluation materials		
	Variable List Dakota LEADers Model	Booklet		
	Guide to Economic Development	Booklet		
Ohio University	Passport to Governmental Regulatory Requirements	Manual for local government officials	1992	**Patricia Dewees** Ohio University 302 Tupper Hall Athens, OH 45701-2979
	Rural Communities Legacy & Challenge	Information brochures		

Institution and Host	Title	Product Type	Year Produced	Contact
Ohio University (*continued*)	Working Today for a Better Tomorrow in Rural Ohio	Workshop curriculum		
Washington State University	How to Apply Deming's Quality Improvement Principles to Public Sector Sevices and Administrative Operations	Booklet for conferences and institutes	1992	**Ronald Faas & Greg Adranovich** Washingon State University Cooperative Extension Pullman, WA 99164-6230
	Human Development Programs	Booklet		
	Tools and Techniques for Evaluation and Assessment Operations	Booklet	1992	
	Applied Research Roles and Uses in Evaluation PLGE Learning and Lessons from the field	Booklet	1992	
	Risk Mangement	Brochures		
	Sensing Interviews Questions for Grand Coulee Dam Area Project	Interview questions		
	Survey of Eligible Participants	Booklet		
	Instructions for Conducting/Reporting Sensing Interviews	Booklet		
	Innovative Programs and Management Practices Survey	Evaluation		
	Community/Family Leadership Evaluation Project Interviewer Instructions	Booklet		
	Program for Local Government Education Evaluation	Booklet		
	Questionnaire for Local Government Education Evaluations	Guideline sheets		
	Chart A Bold Course!	Program support workshop	1991	

Institution and Host	Title	Product Type	Year Produced	Contact
	Program for Local Government Education	Instructions for conducting/reporting sensing interviews	1990	
	Tools and Techniques for Evaluation and Assessment: Monitoring of Second-Order Change	Evaluation tool for second-order change	1992	
	Applied Research: Rules and Uses in Evaluation: PLGE Learnings and Lessons from the Field	Paper prepared for RACE Networking Conference, May 1992 in New Orleans	1992	
	Project Design for PLGE	Booklet	1991	
	Learning by Doing Service Work in Local Governments: Achievable Goals and First- and Second-order Change in Local Government	Booklet	1990	
	Interlocal Cooperation	Booklet	1990	
	An Educational Model to Empower Adult Leaders to Build Capacity for Second-Order Change in Local Government	Paper		
	PLGE Intervention Protocol	Booklet	1991	
	Monitoring on Site Interventions: Keeping Yourself and the Client on Track	Booklet	1992	
	Various brochures			
	Program for Local Government Education	Booklet	1990	
	Planning for Cooperation: Local Government Choices	Booklet		
Wisconsin Community Leadership Development Cooperative Extension	Developing Curriculum for New Audiences: the WLD in an Urban Outreach Program	Booklet		**Curtis Gear** University of Wisconsin 535 Lowell Hall Madison, WI 53717

Institution and Host	Title	Product Type	Year Produced	Contact
Wisconsin Community Leadership Development Cooperative Extension (*continued*)	National Public Policy Seminar Cycle II Seminar 7	Wisconsin Community Development Program seminar curriculum	1992	
Berea College, KY Brushy Forks Institute for Leadership	Brushy Fork Leadership Development Program		1992	**Carol Lamm** Berea College CPO 35 Berea, KY 40404

Note: Many of these materials may now be out-of-stock

Appendix 3:
Colorado Rural Revitalization Project Training Manual, 1991

I. WHAT IS THE FUTURE OF RURAL COMMUNITIES IN AMERICA?

What I see as the future: What the group sees:

☐   ☐

☐   ☐

☐   ☐

II. COMMUNITY VISIONS

TO BE MORE THAN DREAMS, COMMUNITY VISIONS ARE:

- leader initiated

- shared and supported

- comprehensive and detailed

- positive and inspiring

Taken from "The Power of Vision" (videotape), Joel A. Barker, Charthouse Learning Corporation, Burnsville, MN 55337, 1990.

THE VISION I HAVE OF WHAT I WANT MY COMMUNITY TO BE IS:

The VISION we have for our community is:

III. COMMUNITY IMAGES

What are the important images of my/our community?

A) The images I have:

☐

☐

☐

B) The images my neighbors have:

☐

☐

☐

C) The images outsiders/visitors have:

☐

☐

☐

IV. TEAM BUILDING

A) THE MYERS BRIGGS TYPE INDICATOR

People are different. If you can learn to predict and understand these differences, you can increase your effectiveness.

The Myers Briggs Type Indicator does *not* measure:

- Mental Health
- Intelligence
- Maturity
- Excellence.

It *does* measure "preferences".

Things to Remember About Type

- Information about your type has been provided to help you understand yourself and your interactions with others. The proper use of this information is to help people recognize their own and others' gifts.
- Your "type" is the combination of preferences that you chose when you answered the MBTI.
- It is up to you to decide what type you truly are, since only you know your true preferences.
- There are no "good" or "bad" individual types and there are no better or worse combinations of types in relationships.
- All of us use all of the functions and attitudes at different times. Our type is made up of those that we prefer the most.
- The scores from the MBTI merely indicate how consistently you hold any of the preferences.
- Type is not an excuse for doing or not doing anything.

Additional Resources for the study of type (books and journals):

Gifts Differing by Isabel Briggs Myers with Peter B. Myers. Palo Alto, CA: Consulting Psychologists Press, Inc., 1980.

Journal of Psychological Type. The research journal of Association for Psychological Type. Center for Applications of Psychological Type, 2720 NW 6th Street, Gainesville, FL 32609.

Please Understand Me by David Keirsey and Marilyn Bates. Del Mar, CA: Promethean Books, 1978.

People Types and Tiger Stripes by Gordon Lawrence. Gainesville, FL: Center for Applications of Psychological Type, 1979.

MY PREFERENCES ARE:

Extroverts (E) get their energy from the outside world. They get energy from being around other people. They tend to talk while they are thinking and may change quickly from topic to topic.

Introverts (I) get their energy from within themselves. They like to be around other people but find they have to be alone to rekindle their energy. They tend to be quiet until they know someone and take time to think through ideas.

    I am an E_____|_____I.

Sensing (S) describes people whose thoughts are based on the five senses. They operate with sight, sound, feel, taste, and smell. They enjoy living in the present and prefer practical things.

Intuitive (N) people operate according to hunches and gut feelings. They may not be able to explain how they arrived at their conclusions. They think about the future and like to imagine different possibilities.

    I am a S_____|_____N.

Thinking (T) people go by logic, are concerned about truth and justice and decide with their heads.

Feeling (F) people want people to get along and then get things done. They are concerned about personal relationships and harmony.

    I am a T_____|_____F.

Judging (J) describes people who like to make decisions fast and feel better after a decision has been made.

Perceiving (P) people want to keep their options open. They know that something is going to happen any minute that will make their decision better so they want to wait until the very last minute to make a decision. P's often feel uncomfortable after a decision has been made because they can no longer keep their options open.

    I am a J_____|_____P.

My four letters are_____.

THE MYERS BRIGGS INVENTORY

The dominant characteristics of my type are:
(Refer to *Introduction to Type* book.)

☐

☐

☐

☐

☐

☐

Looking at our "Community Committee" what are the

Strengths	Weaknesses	Implications

IV. TEAM BUILDING

B)   ELEMENTS OF A GOOD TEAM

TEAMS I HAVE KNOWN:

MY DEFINITION OF TEAM IS:

AS A TEAM BRAINSTORMS WHAT ARE THE ELEMENTS OF A GOOD TEAM?

IV. TEAM BUILDING

C) COMMUNICATION

> Effective teams require effective communication

Since we learn to communicate at a very early age (even before we learn to talk), we tend to forget that communication is a complex process. All modern communications involve four main factors: a source or sender, a message, a channel, and receiver (SMCR).

Learning how to express our own feelings honestly and learning how to translate another's feelings when they are communicating with us are skills often overlooked. Too often the *content* to be communicated takes precedence over the *feeling* that people are communicating.

Recent research done by Bandler/Grainder (1987) concludes that individuals generally prefer to think and communicate in one of three major ways: vision, hearing, and physical sensation. Recognizing these communication preferences can help us tailor our communication skills.

CHECK FOR *THEIR* INFORMATION

CHECKING TIPS
- Watch the receiver's non-verbal messages for attentiveness and signs of confusion or misunderstanding.
- Ask that the receiver paraphrase your message so you can be sure you have given it clearly.
- Request that the sender summarize the main points of a discussion.
- Pause in delivery and ask the receiver if clarification would be helpful.
- Put agreements in writing and have both parties sign off on them.
- Ask for and expect questions to further elaborate on points.
- Give the receiver time to sort.

Listening is the most important communication tool.

- 98% of our learning is through our eyes and ears.

- 70% of the day of a white collar worker is spent in communication. This percentage is higher for students.

- Time breakdown for "average" communication includes:
  - 9% writing
  - 16% reading
  - 30% speaking
  - 45% listening

TIPS FOR LISTENING WITH RESPECT

- *Face the other* person squarely.

- Maintain an *open posture.*

- *Incline your body* toward the person.

- *Tune into both content and feelings* (be aware of both verbal and non-verbal cues including body posture, gestures, energy level, voice tone, rhythm, tempo, and emphasis).

- *Resist distractions.*

- Capitalize on the fact that you can *think faster than the other person can talk* by reviewing or summarizing what has been said.

"I know that you believe that you understand what you think I said but . . . I am not sure you realize that what you heard is not what I meant . . . "

MESSAGES

"I" messages are a feedback behavior that can be learned quickly. An "I" message allows us to tell people what impact their behavior has on us. At the same time, it lets them decide whether or not to change that behavior. Since we describe our responses and do not evaluate behavior or suggest changes, we are not forcing them to accept our ideas.

A "You" message in contrast often makes others feel badly, and as if they have to defend themselves. Then they resist making any change at all. "You" messages can be orders, commands, blaming or namecalling statements. They can provide unwanted solutions. Or, worst of all, they can be threats.

Which kinds of "you" messages are these?

> "Stop doing that! get into the car!"
> "You are driving me crazy!"
> "You should forget that idea."
> "If you don't . . . then I will . . . !"

An "I" message consists of three parts: (i) the specific behavior, (ii) the feeling we experience because of the behavior, and (iii) the tangible effect of the feeling.

Example:

> When you tap on your desk with your pencil, I feel upset because I get distracted.

or

> When I try to help you and you don't say anything, I am confused because I don't know how you feel about my help.

IV. TEAM BUILDING

D) CONFLICT MANAGEMENT

Effective teams use effective conflict management techniques

- Conflict on a team is inevitable.

- The way conflict is managed determines whether it is good or bad.

RESPONSES TO CONFLICT

When do these behaviors fit on the above scale?

- AVOID
- ACCOMMODATE
- COMPROMISE
- COMPETE
- COLLABORATE

From *Conflict and Conflict in Management*, Handbook of Industrial and Organizational Psychology. Kenneth Thomas.

STRATEGIES

- *A POSITION* is a predetermined solution that may or may not meet the needs or concerns of all who are involved.

- *AN INTEREST* is a specific need or concern that must be addressed in an agreement for the agreement to be satisfactory.

POSITIONAL APPROACH (Negative results)	INTEREST-BASED APPROACH (Positive results)
• Look out for one's own goals only • Maintain secrecy • Mask one's own goals, needs and interests and discount others' needs and interests • Use the element of surprise whenever possible • "Fake-out" or threaten	• Look for goals held in common • Promote openness • Clearly state one's own goals, needs and interests while validating others' needs and interests • Keep the other side informed of your process • Be candid and supportive

From Fisher and Ury,
Getting to Yes.
Penguin Books, 1983.

To work for collaboration clarify the underlying interests of all those involved.

MY INTERESTS	THEIR INTERESTS

Transitions from Positions to Interests

Check off two transitions you could use immediately.

- Don't ask for specific solutions early in the negotiation.

- Avoid responding to a position with a counterposition.

- Get the party to explain why their position is important, then identify underlying issues.

- State that you are looking for solutions that will benefit both sides.

- Reframe the party's position in interests and acknowledge their validity.

- Emphasize common interests.

- Separate the people from the problem.

- State *your* interests and concerns clearly.

What are the most significant community conflicts in our community?

☐

☐

☐

☐

Are there ways we might contribute to resolution of that/these conflict(s)? (If yes, List . . .)

☐

☐

☐

☐

IV. TEAM BUILDING

E)   LEADERSHIP FOR THE TEAM

Effective teams have effective leaders

The team leadership role requires:	(+ , −)
1.	
2.	
3.	
4.	
5.	
6.	
7.	
8.	

LEADERSHIP SKILLS

The following items describe certain leadership activities in a group. As a group leader, which of these would be easier for you to do? Which would be harder for you?

	Easier to do	Harder to do
1. Serve as a spokesperson for the group.	——	——
2. Settle conflict within the group.	——	——
3. Allow members complete freedom of action.	——	——
4. Accept blame for group failures.	——	——
5. Assign members to particular tasks.	——	——
6. Let members do their work in their own way.	——	——
7. Keep the group working at a rapid pace.	——	——
8. Schedule work to be done.	——	——
9. Share leadership with other members.	——	——
10. Help individual members with their problems.	——	——
11. Represent the group in front of other people and organizations.	——	——
12. Establish the agenda for group meetings.	——	——
13. Recruit new members for the group.	——	——
14. Conduct group meetings.	——	——
15. Build a team spirit among the group.	——	——

IV. TEAM BUILDING

F)   HOLDING EFFECTIVE TEAM MEETINGS

Effective teams have effective meetings

The elements of a good meeting are:

(+ , −)

☐

☐

☐

☐

☐

☐

☐

☐

☐

☐

PLANNING FOR TEAM MEETINGS

PURPOSE:	
DATE:	LOCATION:
PARTICIPANTS:	
CHAIR OR FACILITATORS:	
PREPARATION REQUIRED:	
AGENDA TOPICS	TIME FRAMES
RECORDING METHOD:	
EVALUATION METHOD:	

V. REFINING OUR COMMUNITY TEAM'S VISION STATEMENTS

Our vision is:

(Brainstorming:)
Some ways to make vision reality:

VI. NEXT STEPS: SHORT-RANGE ACTION PLAN

A)   OUR MINI-PROJECT IS: ___[DESCRIBE]___

1)   WE HAVE MADE THE FOLLOWING PROGRESS ON THE MINI-PROJECT:

2)   THE WORK REMAINING IS:

3)   THOSE RESPONSIBLE TO COMPLETE THE PROJECT ARE:

4)   THE TARGET DATE FOR MINI-PROJECT COMPLETION IS:

5)   WE NEED SOME CRRP ASSISTANCE WITH THE PROJECT [describe your request]:

VI. NEXT STEPS: SHORT-RANGE ACTION PLAN

B) OUR BROADER COMMUNITY ASSESSMENTS:

1) WHAT MORE WE NEED TO KNOW/DO BEFORE DETERMINING WHAT OTHER PROJECT(S) TO PURSUE THIS YEAR:

2) WHO IS RESPONSIBLE FOR GATHERING NEEDED INFORMATION? WHEN, AND HOW? [if Project assistance is needed, describe your request]:

3) TARGET DATE TO COMPLETE ASSESSMENTS AND MAKE LONGER-RANGE PROJECT PLANS [if possible, include date/time for staff-assisted long-range goal-setting/action planning session]:

VII.   TEAM PROGRESS AND PLANS

REPORT ON THE FOLLOWING:

1.   Your community team's refined vision statement, and ways to accomplish:

2.   Your team's mini-project [describe and tell of progress, plans, and your requests for Project assistance, if any]:

3.   Your wider community assessment plans and progress, including any requests for Project assistance:

4.   A critique of your team work: how well did you communicate? . . . how did the team handle differences of opinion? . . . solicit views of all? . . . define/assign team leadership and working roles? What objective does your team have to keep/make it both congenial and productive?

VIII.   EVALUATION FORM: TEAM PROCESS

Should your group wish to analyze its process, have each member anonymously
rate each variable on the scale from 1 to 5.

   5 = Operating Ideally
   1 = Missing Completely

1. LISTENING
Members don't really listen to
one another – they interrupt
and don't try to understand
others.

1 2 3 4 5

All members really listen and
try hard to understand.

2. OPEN COMMUNICATION
Members are guarded or
cautious in discussions.

1 2 3 4 5

Members express both
thoughts and feelings openly.

3. MUTUAL TRUST AND
CONFIDENCE
Members evidence suspicion
of one another's motives.

1 2 3 4 5

Members trust one another
and do not fear ridicule or
reprisal.

4. ATTITUDES TOWARD
DIFFERENCES WITHIN GROUP
Members avoid arguments,
smooth over differences,
suppress or avoid conflicts.

1 2 3 4 5

Members search for, respect,
and accept differences and
work through them openly –
they are not pressured to
conform.

5. MUTUAL SUPPORT
Members are defensive about
themselves and their functions.

1 2 3 4 5

Members are able to give
and receive help.

6. INVOLVEMENT–
PARTICIPATION
Discussion is dominated by
a few members.

1 2 3 4 5

All members are Involved,
free to participate in any way
they choose.

7. CONTROL METHODS
Subject matter and decisions
are controlled by the chairperson.

1 2 3 4 5

All members accept
responsibility for productive
discussion and for decisions.

8. FLEXIBILITY
The group is locked in on
established rules and members
find it hard to change procedures.

1 2 3 4 5

Members readily change
procedures in response to
new situations.

9. USE OF MEMBER
RESOURCES
Individuals' knowledge, abilities,
and experience not utilized.

1 2 3 4 5

Each member's knowledge,
abilities, and experience is
fully utilized.

10. OBJECTIVES OR
PURPOSES
Objectives are not clear or not
understood and there is no
commitment to them.

1 2 3 4 5

Objectives are clear, are
understood, and there is full
commitment to them.

Adapted from Northwest Regional Educational Laboratory – Partnership for Rural
Improvement, Portland, Oregon, 1978.

Author index

Subject index